Nest boxes for the Birds of Britain and Europe

by
Lennart Bolund

edited by Hugh Insley
with a foreword by Bill Oddie

Sainsbury Publishing Ltd
Nottinghamshire
England

Nest boxes for the Birds of Britain and Europe
originally published as 'Holkarnas Fåglar'
by Rabén & Sjögren, Stockholm

translated by John Kennedy

illustrations by Dag Peterson

copyright © 1987, Sainsbury Publishing Ltd.

British Library Cataloguing in Publication Data
Bolund, Lennart
  Nest boxes for the birds of Britain and Europe
  1. Birdhouses—Design and construction
  i. Title ii. Insley, Hugh iii. Holkarnas Fåglar, *English*
  745.593   QL676.5
    ISBN 1-870655 00-1

Typeset by Method, Epping.
Printed by Ebenezer Baylis & Son Ltd, Worcester.

This book is respectfully dedicated to the memory of Tom Woolston from whom I learnt so much.

George Sainsbury

Foreword by Bill Oddie

I was once asked to test a selection of 'bird-feeders'. Not to actually try them myself, you understand, but to put them up all over my garden and to watch which ones the birds preferred.

After only a day or two it was clear that several of them were pretty useless. The one with a little suction pad meant to stick to the window was on the floor. Two more had been torn apart by squirrels and a fourth still had all the seed uneaten because the birds could devise no way of getting at it without pulling a muscle or bending a beak. Of course some of the feeders worked just fine. Anyway, at the end of an appropriate period I had to write up the whole experiment for a national newspaper, saying which feeders I – or rather the birds – preferred and which they rejected. This I did. The result was I received several poison pen letters! These came from the manufacturers of feeders I'd dared to criticise or rather the birds had dared to ignore. The general gist of the correspondence was how dare I attack something that was clearly meant to give pleasure and sustenance to our feathered friends? My reply was, and still is: firstly, it's not my fault if the birds don't like the feeders; but secondly, and more important, 'good intentions' are not enough when it comes to keeping wildlife. Bird-hospitals that lack proper equipment and expertise sadly sometimes do more harm than good, even though I have no doubt the people who run them 'mean well'. Similarly, a badly designed feeder can, at worst, damage a bird, whilst, at best, it is merely useless. The same goes for nest-boxes, which is why I welcome this book, and I'm sure the birds will too.

Editor's Preface

The very first nest box I put up, as a schoolboy, in a Norfolk wood 20 years ago, was used by a pair of marsh tits which successfully reared seven young. The serial numbers of the rings I put on them before they flew, HJ 56955–61, form a permanent record of that happy event in my ringing log, and somewhere in the archives of the British Trust for Ornithology at Tring lies the nest record card, charting the progress of that particular nest.

The whole process would have met with the thorough approval of Lennart Bolund whose book this is. My own early efforts at making nest boxes were hardly Chippendale quality, but they were successful in as much as they passed the critical examination of that pair of marsh tits, which decided to use the box for the most important event in their short lives, the reproduction of their species.

Only a tiny proportion of the small birds ringed as nestlings are ever found again, but those that are provide valuable information on longevity, movement, cause of death and so on. None of those young marsh tits were ever recovered, but the nest record card data, combined with those recorded by many other birdwatchers, have already been used in at least one subsequent analysis and paper, thus making a small contribution towards our knowledge of these birds.

Lennart Bolund, like most of us, is a keen amateur birdwatcher. This book, which has already been published in Sweden and Denmark, is written not for scientists, but for all bird lovers and conservationists who want to get out and do something practical to contribute towards the continued existence of these beautiful animals.

Our two translators have dealt very competently with the tongue twisting complexities presented by the Scandinavian languages; John Kennedy with the main part of the text, which is taken from the Swedish edition, while Penelope Holten-Andersen kindly unravelled the text on the white stork, dipper, little owl and hoopoe from the Danish edition.

At an early stage George Sainsbury and I decided that it would be much more interesting and exciting to keep the Swedish flavour in this

English edition. Goldeneye do now nest in Scotland, and large organisations like the Royal Society for the Protection of Birds and the Forestry Commission have been co-operating in a joint venture to encourage these and other exciting northern species to nest in our state forests; so their inclusion in this book has a practical relevance. In contrast, the chances of three-toed woodpeckers or pygmy owls nesting in Britain are remote; but in spite of this it is fascinating to read a first hand account of these gems of the sub-arctic forests, and what better way to whet the appetite for a birdwatching holiday in Lapland?

Lennart Bolund's guide explains how to provide for almost all the nest box using species and gives practical advice on how to help several more besides. For one of the most rewarding and satisfying experiences you can have with nature take his advice. Get out the hammer, saw and nails and have a go. Your own imagination and enthusiasm are the only limiting factors and the results are almost guaranteed.

Hugh Insley
Balerno, Midlothian
August 1987

CONTENTS

1   Introduction

Why should we set up nest boxes?

Social development throughout Europe is proving a threat to bird life. In Scandinavia the rationalization of the forest industry has restricted populations of hole-nesting birds and elsewhere in Europe urbanisation and the intensification of agriculture have destroyed many natural habitats. By putting up nest boxes in suitable areas we can do something to help conserve birds which are otherwise under pressure from the habitat changes wrought by man. Woodpeckers for example are highly dependent on dead trees, broken tree trunks, stumps, etc., for their food and living quarters. Modern forms of land use, as well as the application of various herbicides and insecticides, have worsened conditions for the majority of species. In Sweden the number of woodpeckers has fallen, in some cases drastically, and the situation is very serious for both the grey-headed woodpecker in the mixed forests of southern and central Norrland and the white-backed woodpecker in the ancient untouched coniferous forests of Dalalven, while the middle spotted woodpecker has been eradicated. Reduced access to suitable nesting sites in trees has meant that in exceptional circumstances the black woodpecker, great spotted woodpecker, and three-toed woodpecker have taken to breeding in nest boxes. Other woodpeckers can also be helped by the construction of suitable nest boxes.

Some birds, which nest in cavities but are unable to construct their own holes, are heavily dependent for their existence on access to old woodpecker holes. Wherever possible one should certainly try to spare the habitat of birds by leaving old trees containing holes, but in recent years large numbers of trees have been cleared especially from farm hedgerows because they impede the use of the large machines now employed. On top of this loss of trees caused by the tidying up of farmscapes the arrival of the virulent form of Dutch elm disease removed millions more elms – often in areas where elm was not only the most abundant tree, but also the most fruitful in terms of holes and cavities. Destruction of the ancient coniferous forests in Northern Europe is endangering two species in particular, namely the three-toed woodpecker

1

and the pygmy owl. The three-toed woodpecker likes to make its home and breed in conifers in the dark inner depths of forests, and its nest holes are almost always used in the following year by pygmy owls. Both these birds thrive in coniferous forests, the woodpecker's nesting hole suiting the owl perfectly. Even if the remaining ancient forests are saved, they should be supplemented with suitable nest boxes put up in areas of younger forest as soon as possible.

Another species which depends on mature forest in the breeding season is the goshawk, and it can be helped by artificial nests being set up in forest areas. So far in Sweden, the goshawk is not as threatened as the three-toed woodpecker and pygmy owl, but there is some concern for the species with the spread of intensive forest management. In other areas of Europe such as in Britain the development of commercial forestry has assisted the spread of this species.

Elsewhere in Europe the intensification of agriculture and depletion of broadleaved woodland have put pressure on bird populations including those requiring old woodland and trees containing plenty of cavities suitable for nesting sites.

Research has told us that many species of birds are of great benefit to forestry, agriculture, and horticulture because their diet consists largely of the eggs, larvae, and adult forms of insect species which are for the most part harmful to vegetation. If we still want to hear bird song in the future, we must protect them. One way to help them is to construct and set up nest boxes. In Sweden forestry companies have in the past set up thousands of nest boxes, but with present-day pressures, and tight work schedules, this has unfortunately become increasingly difficult. These companies ought to realize that birds are unsurpassed as insect controllers; for example, study of a single marsh tit has shown that, besides other food, it will take 1500 eggs per day of the harmful nun moth, which it then feeds to its young. The Swedish Forestry Association however, has recently distributed 5000 nest boxes free of charge to any owners willing to put them up. because of the effect of small birds on forest insect pests. In West Germany the Bavarian Ministry for Food, Forestry and Agriculture provides grants of DM 20 (£6.75) to private woodland owners for each nest box put up in their woods.

In Great Britain the Forestry Commission and the Royal Society for the Protection of Birds combined forces in 1985 in a project to provide nest sites for goldeneye, black throated divers, merlins, ospreys and small birds such as pied flycatchers. Under this scheme 800 goldeneye boxes, nearly 100 artificial crow nests for merlins, and 26 osprey platforms together with over 1000 nest boxes for small birds were put up in Scotland and the north of England. Two of the osprey platforms were occupied during the first breeding season although because of the poor weather neither pair reared young successfully. However, in 1987 one of these artificial nest platforms has been used again and the ospreys successfully raised 3 young. Work has also started on providing artificial nesting rafts in an attempt to improve the breeding success of Scotland's 60 or so pairs of black throated divers, which suffer from disturbance especially when they are forced to nest by the shoreline of hill lochans because of a lack of natural islets.

These examples show that for both individuals and large organisations a wide range of opportunities exist to help birds, from providing tit type boxes for the smallest birds in urban gardens to platforms for the largest birds of prey in large forest areas.

Which birds breed in nest boxes?

It is mainly the birds which nest in holes and cavities which breed in nest boxes. This also happens to be one of the groups of birds under heaviest pressure from the removal of natural nest sites through habitat alteration by man. One normally thinks of nest-box dwellers as being small birds, but there is a range of larger birds which can manage to breed in boxes, such as the goosander, goldeneye, mallard, mandarin duck, tawny owl, barn owl, Tengmalm's owl, little owl, pygmy owl, kestrel, jackdaw, stock dove, great spotted woodpecker, black woodpecker, and wryneck.

The small birds which most commonly breed in nest boxes are: the pied flycatcher, starling, great tit, blue tit, marsh tit, coal tit, nuthatch, house and tree sparrows, all of which use conventional tit type boxes with round entrance holes in the front; while spotted flycatcher, redstart, robin, and pied wagtail (white wagtail on the Continent) will use open fronted boxes. Further south on the Continent the black redstart which frequents buildings (in Germany it is called the house redstart) also uses these open fronted nest boxes.

At Bankbote, 20 km south of Valdermarsvik in Sweden, a study was made of hole-nesting birds breeding in nest boxes from 1956 to 1984. The number of boxes was gradually increased, reaching 130 in the last 10 years. The total number of nesting attempts over 29 years amongst the commonest species was as follows: 628 matings of pied flycatchers, producing around 2800 young which left the nest; 150 matings of starlings, producing around 450 young which left the nest; 142 matings of great tits, producing about 580 young. In addition, redstart,

3

goosander and other tit species each nested around 30 times, while occasional nesting by other species was also observed. Almost 4000 young birds of assorted species grew up in these nest boxes during the 29 years, which is by no means an insignificant contribution to the survival of these families, which would scarcely have been possible without all these nest boxes.

Choose the birds that will sing outside your house

By setting up different types of nest boxes you will be able to influence which birds you will have living in your neighbourhood. In almost any area it is possible to chose and erect nest boxes which will attract nesting birds. In my part of Sweden pied flycatchers include new nest boxes in their selection of desired residences. They also like to feast on midges, flies, and earwigs, so you should be less troubled by these insects. In other parts of Europe especially in urban areas members of the tit family such as blue, coal or great tits will be the easiest birds to attract to new nest boxes. Most other bird species are uncertain about new nest boxes. They like to have them tested against the wind and weather for at least a year, so you can encourage them by 'weathering' the boxes.

Where do you live?

Do you live in the vicinity of meadow land, forests or a lake? The area in which you live will determine which birds you can attract to your nest boxes. Near a lake or the sea, wild ducks may come to the boxes while if near a wood, owls may come to breed. In the vicinity of enclosed pasture with groves of deciduous trees, the beautiful blue stock dove or jackdaws may use your owl nest boxes.

In Scandinavia if you are plagued with ants in your garden you should entice a wryneck, which is a species of woodpecker, to use your nest box. The wryneck is extremely fond of ant eggs and has a special knack for finding them.

Are you afraid that the birds may eat up your cherries or other fruit? Starlings eat few cherries. The young starlings will have already left the nest before midsummer, at which time they will accompany their parents for a while. The starlings from your nest boxes will not eat many of your berries, but wandering starlings will. Thrushes are the main consumers of berries but since they are attractive birds and such fine songsters in the breeding season this is well worth tolerating. Neither flycatchers nor tits eat berries, feasting instead on the harmful insects on berry bushes and fruit trees, thus giving you healthier fruit and berries.

4

It is often thought, that to be successful, nest boxes must be set up in large wooded areas. Yet these boxes can be set up effectively in a garden area of only 500–1000 sq-m. An area of 500 sq-m will accommodate a nest box in each corner plus one in the centre, while an area of 1000 sq-m will additionally house one nest box on each side, giving a total of 9 nests. Nest boxes for tits and flycatchers must be properly spaced as these birds behave territorially in the immediate vicinity of their homes. However, in Scandinavia one needs to take into consideration the fact that tits often have a second brood, for which they almost always set up home in a new nest site, so a selection of reserve nest boxes should be placed nearby. In Britain where the nesting season is almost completely synchronised with the appearance of caterpillars which feed on oak trees most tits are single brooded so this problem does not exist. Starling nest boxes can be placed closer together but not, in my experience, in the same tree.

One can also set up nest boxes in the small gardens of terraced houses. For several years now I have had tits breeding in a nest box set up on the end of a wooden fence separating gardens.

In gardens nest boxes should be separated by 10–15 m, in deciduous woods by 25 m, and in coniferous forests by 40–50 m.

Remember also that in Scandinavia and other Northern European countries birds fare best in nest boxes with south or east facing entrances. Further south such as in France or Britain southern aspects should be avoided because of the danger of over-heating in direct sun.

If despite all your efforts you get no birds in your nests, it will be for one of three reasons:
1. The nest box is situated in a place where there is too much disturbance. (If food is made available in the vicinity during the winter, tits will often stay overnight, and then when spring comes, will breed in the nest box. By this time they will have become accustomed to the nearby presence of humans. As long as normal care is taken the breeding will be very successful, even in small terraced gardens).
2. A shortage of water.
3. A shortage of food, because the nest area has insufficient bushes, trees, etc. The solution to problems 2 and 3 may be found on pages 188 and 187 which deal respectively with bird baths and supportive planting.

Owls also need nest boxes

Most people think only in terms of small birds when they set up nest boxes. Certainly, small birds have accommodation problems, but by far the greatest problems are experienced by owls, whose very existence is threatened. Their natural ecological niches are disappearing more and more, their environment is being poisoned by the use of chemicals in the countryside and the old decayed trees in which they breed are becoming increasingly scarce as hedgerows have been removed and deciduous woodlands cleared. People should therefore set up large owl nest boxes on a much greater scale than at present. It is easy enough for organisations and large land owners, but individuals can also make significant contributions if enough people put up the odd box on trees in their gardens.

In their 1977 wetlands campaign, the Swedish Hunting Association discovered that the nest situation was bad for goldeneyes and mergansers, but worse still for owls. In response to this the Association set up a concerted campaign to put up 10,000 large nest boxes suitable for all of these large hole nesting species. Such campaigns do not concentrate on any particular group of nesting birds, but do take into consideration that all hole nesting birds in particular are experiencing an acute shortage of accommodation.

Help birds of prey with artificial nests

Not all birds of prey nest in hollow trees or will use nest boxes; in fact most build their own nests from twigs. However, one can help to repair nests which have blown over or even create the necessary conditions for new nests to be established. By sawing off branches, it is possible to make a platform from planks, lay down some dry branches, and try to create an artificial nest base. In this way forest and woodland owners can promote breeding in many species of birds of prey which are currently under great pressure. In Sweden this has been done for the white tailed eagle, golden eagle, great grey owl, and also the goshawk, steppe buzzard and buzzard, all of which can experience difficulties in finding trees capable of carrying their nests in modern forestry plantations. As mentioned above the same technique is being employed in Scotland by the Forestry Commission and the Royal Society for the Protection of Birds to provide nest sites for ospreys.

Set up nest boxes in the autumn

Most people seem to think nest boxes should be set up in the spring. Hardware shops and garden centres first display their nest boxes in February or March. By this time it is too late because many of our nesting birds are non-migratory. They use the nest boxes throughout the whole of autumn and winter as a protection against bad weather and as a place to spend the night. So it is wrong to think only in terms of setting up nest boxes in the spring. Many of our nesting birds are already choosing their breeding territories in February and March; some, such as the treecreeper, even do this in late autumn. Admittedly the last few years have been unusually mild and without too much snow, but who wants to be carrying ladders and heavy nest boxes around in cold and snow? Nest boxes should be up by January at the latest, but it is still far better to have them up in autumn so that one can then look forward in peace and quiet to the bird songs of spring.

Nest boxes are occupied during autumn and winter

The nest boxes you set up should be made of thick wood and placed in shaded sites so that they provide good insulation against both heat and cold and protection for the birds. Many non-migratory birds also use nest boxes to shelter against unpleasant weather and for roosting during autumn and winter. The nest boxes should not be too small or the entrances too narrow, but should be well suited for the birds for which they are intended.

Before setting up nest boxes one should obtain the permission of the landowner. Aluminium or copper nails should be used to secure the nest box as normal nails create a high risk of eye injuries from splinters or damaged chain saws if the trees are cut by some unwitting person in the future. This is as real a danger in urban areas where tree surgeons may eventually have to remove old trees for safety reasons as it is in a forest where the trees will be harvested for timber.

Clean nest boxes

The nest boxes should be constructed so that they can be cleaned properly. They should be cleaned immediately after breeding or at the latest in September or October, and rubber gloves should be worn as some bird-parasitizing insects will bite humans, causing red marks and itching. Burning the old nests taken out of the boxes will get rid of these ever-present vermin and their eggs.

To winter-proof the nest boxes one can line them with cotton, dry straw, or wood shavings several weeks after washing, when the boxes are fully aired. This lining should be removed at the beginning of March and will probably contain a smaller amount of vermin, together with excrement from birds which have used the nest box during autumn and winter. Winter accommodation is not necessary, but it certainly has distinct advantages during severe winters. The chill of winter reaps many victims in spite of extensive winter feeding. Therefore you should combine winter feeding of protein-rich foods with the provision of warm nest boxes in the immediate vicinity. The nearer the food the less energy is expended in reaching it and the more there is left over for warming the small bird's body.

In the middle of February nest boxes should be 'serviced', repairing any damage and clearing out any squirrel dreys or owl pellets which may have appeared. Squirrel dreys should be removed early when the squirrels are still in hibernation, otherwise they will disturb the birds' nest building. In any other circumstances the removal of squirrel dreys could be considered morally unjustifiable. Remember that the red squirrel is a protected species in many countries, although this does not apply to the introduced grey squirrel in Britain. The grey squirrel is a voracious predator of birds' eggs and young and discouraging this animal may help your birds. In areas where kestrels are found, old squirrel nests should be left in the nesting box as this will increase the chances of the kestrels breeding.

Leave nest boxes undisturbed during breeding

Most birds are very shy during the breeding season, especially during incubation and when the young are newly hatched. Remember that tits, especially the great tit, which during the winter may even be so bold as to eat from one's hand, are very sensitive to disturbance during the breeding season. Disturbance may shock the young into leaving the nest a little too soon, resulting in them falling easy victim to predators. Therefore you must never look into nest boxes during the breeding season.

Keep a register of your nest box birds

If you have many nest boxes, it can be good fun to keep a record of visitors, in which case it helps to number the boxes. I have used black plastic numbers from old car registration plates. Fasten the numbers to the boxes using copper or aluminium tacks which will not rust. The box numbers can thus be seen from a long distance — a great advantage.

I have also successfully placed numbers on small pieces of thin waste wood which were sawn up into 10 cm long pieces and painted with wood preservative oil to inhibit rotting. Holes were drilled in the wood, and the plaques were fastened to trees using aluminium nails. These pieces of wood can thus all be placed at the same height and facing in the same direction so that observers can read them from a particular vantage point.

8

Numbering of nest boxes is absolutely essential, if one wishes to carry out studies of birds using the boxes; the risk of confusion is then minimized. It is also an idea to make a map of the area with the nest box positions marked by their numbers.

However, a pair of binoculars should be used if you wish to make a reasonably intensive study of your bird guests. Some bird books claim that the breeding process can be observed by looking into the nest box, but I think this entirely wrong as it encourages people who are not sufficiently acquainted with the ways of birds to open up nests and look inside, which may result in the nest being abandoned. Young which are ready to fly may be panicked when the nest box is opened and fly off, being scattered like bait in the wind, and falling easy victim to crows, magpies, and roving cats.

Instead you can observe, for example, the following:
1. The arrival dates of the various species of migratory birds in the area and which sex arrives first (males usually come first).
2. At what time of day and for how long during the breeding season the male bird sings.
3. When nest building begins (when the bird is seen carrying nest material in its beak).
4. If the male bird feeds the brooding female and, if so, with what.
5. When the parents begin to feed and when the young have clearly hatched.
6. When the young leave the nest.

All of these points can be observed with the eye or with binoculars without looking into the nest box. When you clean the nest box in the autumn you will also be able to see what the nest has been made from, and what old food, if any, remains in it. Once you do become experienced it is possible to check on progress without too much risk of disturbing the occupants. By avoiding the most sensitive times mentioned above and by being quick, careful, and never attempting stupid actions like touching the brooding adult it is possible to collect breeding information without causing any harm. You can fill out a card for each nest box and keep a record from year to year. Information may be entered on year or species based files such as that illustrated on the next page.

This sequence of data provides information on egg laying date, clutch size in relation to date, hatching and fledgling success rate, all of which taken with data from other nests, enables reseachers to build up a picture of the breeding biology and population recruitment for the species.

In Britain it is possible to contribute to the British Trust for

Species	Great Tit	Locality	Denny Lodge, New Forest	Year	1987

Observer	F. A. Courtier	Position	On pine trunk	Box type	Tit box
Box Data		Dimensions	25 × 16 × 16 cm	Hole diameter	3.5 cm
		Height from ground	1.5 m		

Date	Nest Contents	Notes
23 April	Being built	Female only building
5 May	1 egg	
15 May	6 eggs	Female sitting
1 June	5 young, 1 egg	Newly hatched
20 June	5 young, 1 egg	Well feathered, ready to fly
7 July	Nest empty	Young flown

Ornithology's nest recording scheme, thus contributing to research into bird conservation being carried out by amateur bird watchers on a countrywide scale. Details and nest record cards may be obtained by writing to the B.T.O., Beech Grove, Tring, Hertfordshire HP23 5NR.

The nest box has just celebrated its 200-year jubilee in Sweden. It was introduced into Europe and Sweden at the end of the 18th century. Starling nest boxes were then set up on a large scale on the islands of Oland and Gotland, but it was not until the 1850s that nest boxes became common throughout Sweden. Such boxes first appeared in India; European travellers were surprised to find a type of round bird-house made from bark and set up in long lines around villages. They brought back this pleasant new custom to Europe and Sweden. The results I have recorded in this book represent 29 years of field experience from my own private research using my own nest boxes of various types which have gradually grown in number to 130 in the last 10 years.

One of the longest running nest box schemes in Britain is that first set up by the Forestry Commission at Nagshead in the Forest of Dean in 1942. This scheme was kept going by the students at the forestry school there under Bruce Campbell's supervision for some 30 years and later by individual Forestry Commission staff until the area was included within a larger area leased as a reserve to the Royal Society for the Protection of Birds in 1973.

This book will attempt to give some tips on nest boxes for different species which you can either build yourself or buy, as well as to give some insight into the family life of birds which use these boxes. Good luck with your future bird visitors.

2 Making your own nest boxes

A good nest box should be warm and compact and should protect the bird during poor weather conditions. It should be made to the right dimensions, which are given on pages 206–9. Planks are one of the best and commonest materials. In spite of all the commercially available products, home made nest boxes are the best, provided the dimensions are appropriate for the intended species.

All descriptions of nest boxes say that the wood for the side panels must be sawn obliquely so that the roofs are sloping and water runs off rather than collecting and either rotting the wood or worse still wetting the nest inside. This of course is entirely true, but constructing such boxes is not so easy as one might imagine, and I think that instead the wood should be sawn straight and the nest box placed on a trunk which is leaning slightly forwards. This produces the same results and makes the construction of nest boxes easier for those who are not so handy.

One should always work towards making cheap, simple, and good-quality boxes which can easily be produced in large quantities. It is quantity which matters, no matter how fine and intricate the nest boxes may be, and such elaboration may be unnecessarily expensive and sometimes even result in structures which are entirely unsuitable for birds. Remember that a very refined nest box may be aesthetically pleasing to humans, but inappropriate for birds. Unfortunately a certain amount of 'status' has become associated with nest boxes. People who own attractive summer cottages naturally also want to have very picturesque nest boxes which will impress neighbours and visiting friends. I generally like to shock my acquaintances with my 'atrocious' boxes; they are altogether excellent for the birds, but hardly likely to win any certificates in carpentry. Using the simple sketches in this book you will be able to produce a great many nest boxes, remembering that quantity is important. Building one nest box may be sufficient for your purposes, but the shortage of living quarters for hole nesting birds which use nest boxes is unprecedentedly large and by setting up lots of nest boxes you will make a significant contribution to the conservation of wild life. Birds are territorial, so do not place the boxes too close together, otherwise the birds will only squabble and no breeding will occur.

Do not place perches near your nest boxes. These will only help predators to reach the eggs and young.

Nest boxes made from planks

If you can get hold of old wooden planks of 2 or 2.5 cm thickness, then you can start to produce nest boxes. A 2.5 cm thickness is preferable because squirrels will find it that little bit more difficult to gnaw their way through and plunder the nest.

During winter, the great spotted woodpecker may even go so far as to peck at the entrance of a nest box so that it can get inside for shelter. To overcome this you may wish to surround the entrance hole with sheet

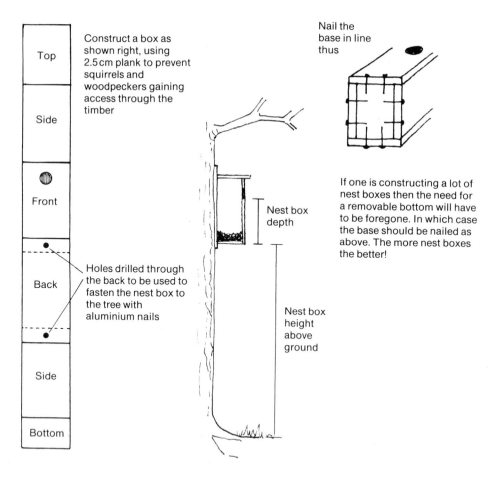

Top

Side

Front

Back

Side

Bottom

Construct a box as shown right, using 2.5 cm plank to prevent squirrels and woodpeckers gaining access through the timber

Holes drilled through the back to be used to fasten the nest box to the tree with aluminium nails

Nail the base in line thus

Nest box depth

If one is constructing a lot of nest boxes then the need for a removable bottom will have to be foregone. In which case the base should be nailed as above. The more nest boxes the better!

Nest box height above ground

metal, making sure that the metal fits closely to the wood to prevent the birds' toes and feathers becoming caught. The hole in the metal plate should be exactly the same diameter as the entrance. Alternatively, you could use the top of an old formica kitchen work surface, which is also resistant to squirrels and woodpeckers.

The roof should be made from hardwood so that it can withstand changeable weather. It should slightly overhang the sides and entrance to provide protection against poor weather conditions when the birds are flying in and out. The roof can also be made from timber covered with roofing felt. Wooden nest boxes should be externally coated with Cuprinol or creosote to give better resistance to rain and wind. If creosote is used the box should be put up early to allow plenty of time for weathering before the birds need to use it.

Cleaning nest boxes

The cleaning of nest boxes is something which unfortunately is very often neglected. About 90% of all boxes set up cannot be cleaned and after a few years are full of nesting material and unfit for habitation. Eventually a colony of bumble bees may come and set up home in the box, making great use of the nesting material.

If you wish, you can construct your box so that it can be cleaned from the ground using a pole; this should be carried out in both autumn and spring. An ingenious solution to this problem designed by Arvid Wallin is shown on page 15. The bottom folds downwards and is kept firmly in place by a piece of bent fencing wire. The nest can be cleaned using a pole fitted with a bent nail. Even the setting up is clever. A nail about 3 cm in length is hammered into the tree at an angle of 45 degrees and the nest box is hung from this nail by a hole drilled into its back surface. Another nail is then hammered in below the nest, and a tight-fitting plate is included which causes the nail to move outwards as the tree grows (a very important factor). Another alternative is to fit a sliding floor made, for example, from boards, to allow nest cleaning. The board floor can either run in a groove sawn into the lower edge of the nest box or in a track between the box and a metal plate which should be fastened outside the lower edge of the box and folded around underneath to form a supporting lip.

Block nest boxes made from old woodpecker nest cavities

Nest boxes made from hollowed out sections of tree trunks are particular favourites of marsh and blue tits, but are preferred by all birds because of

13

Methods of opening boxes for cleaning

'All-Year' Nest Box with removable front

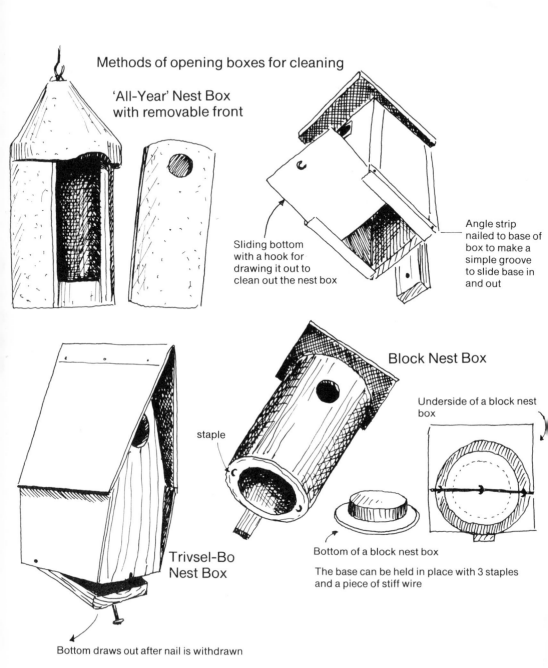

Sliding bottom with a hook for drawing it out to clean out the nest box

Angle strip nailed to base of box to make a simple groove to slide base in and out

Block Nest Box

staple

Underside of a block nest box

Trivsel-Bo Nest Box

Bottom of a block nest box

Bottom draws out after nail is withdrawn

The base can be held in place with 3 staples and a piece of stiff wire

14

Nest Box with an automatic catch for releasing the bottom for cleaning

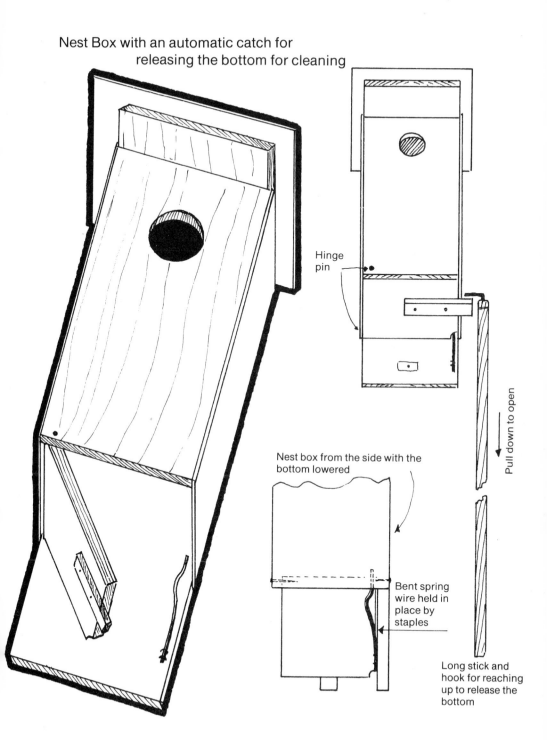

Hinge pin

Pull down to open

Nest box from the side with the bottom lowered

Bent spring wire held in place by staples

Long stick and hook for reaching up to release the bottom

15

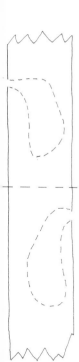

their superior insulating properties. Homes well insulated against cold during winter nights are especially valuable for small birds like tits which can otherwise become frozen. Nest boxes of this type can be made from birch, aspen, alder, pine, spruce, etc. Woodpeckers often drill their nest holes in birch or aspen, and when these trees fall over or are cut down, you can use these hollowed out sections of the trunks as nest boxes after sawing them into suitable lengths.

It should be emphasised however, that trees or branches should never be cut down simply to obtain these old woodpecker nest holes in order to make a natural looking nest box for your own garden. There is no merit in removing such a natural nest site because in so doing you will simply be adding to the destruction and removal of naturally available nest sites badly needed by hole nesting species.

Nest boxes can also be made from solid trunk sections using the same tree species, such as birch and aspen. As an experiment I once set up ten birch block nest boxes for small birds in pine trees, and all ten were taken up by pied flycatchers during the first season.

Block nest boxes from fresh trunks

A tree which has been used by woodpeckers in the past can come in very handy. With the help of a power saw you can make a lot of nest boxes in a short time.

You can also use fresh tree trunks, dividing them into four sections longitudinally (see diagram), though this is much more laborious than using ready made woodpecker homes. Older broadleaved trees with rotted interiors are easier to hollow out, saw up, and make good nest boxes from.

A strip of wood, which should be longer than the eventual nest box, is fastened onto one of the four sections; 3–4 holes are drilled through the section and nails hammered through the holes into the lath. Using a strong pair of pincers, the nails are bent on the outside. An entrance hole is then drilled as follows: 3.1 cm for pied flycatcher, marsh tit, blue tit, crested tit, and coal tit; 3.5 cm for great tit, house sparrow, and tree sparrow; 5 cm for starling, nuthatch, wryneck, and swift.

If you want your box to have a moveable floor which will facilitate cleaning, use a piece of hardwood sawn to the right size. Attach it with a nail in such a way that the bottom can swing outwards. The bottom is held in place with a nail which can be swung to the side when the box is to be cleaned.

The roof should be of hardwood. The various parts of the nest box are fastened together with small nails at both ends of the hollowed out block. You can also fix steel wire around the nest box by means of staples above and below the entrance hole. The wire is then drawn tight using heavy pincers, so that the nest box is securely held.

16

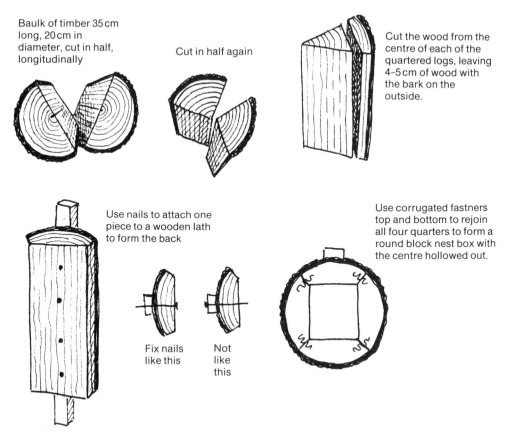

Baulk of timber 35 cm long, 20 cm in diameter, cut in half, longitudinally

Cut in half again

Cut the wood from the centre of each of the quartered logs, leaving 4–5 cm of wood with the bark on the outside.

Use nails to attach one piece to a wooden lath to form the back

Use corrugated fastners top and bottom to rejoin all four quarters to form a round block nest box with the centre hollowed out.

Fix nails like this

Not like this

Nest boxes for wild ducks, mergansers, and owls

In recent winters, a large number of dead tawny owls have been found firmly jammed into stove piping in summer cottages in Sweden. The shortage of accommodation has forced them to seek shelter in such places, where they have suffered a painful death. Other owls are equally desperate for somewhere to live.

Setting up nest boxes will help owls. The occasions when you are most likely to hear an owl hooting will be on starlit evenings or nights in February–March. If you go out with a map you can mark out the places where you hear any hooting, then you can ask the landowner for permission to set up nest boxes near these areas. Be willing to point out the actual tree on which you intend to place the nest box, in order to prevent any misunderstanding. Use aluminium or copper nails which

17

will present no hazards in any future felling and sawing operations. Normal nails create risks of splinters and injury to operators and damage to machinery should the tree require felling at some time in the future.

The best nest boxes are those made from solid blocks, but you may also make a larger nest box from wooden boxes . Four to five holes should be drilled in the bottom of the box in a straight line. From the inside of the box hammer some large 8 to 10 cm long nails through these holes and into a board which is longer than the box. A hole should be drilled into each end of this board so that it can be nailed easily onto the tree, or alternatively a large hole can be drilled into the board whereby the nest box can be hung up on a sawn-off branch. In the Swedish Hunting Association's game management school at Ostermalma, an excellent device for hanging up heavy nest boxes has been invented which is well worth a mention. The box is hung from a sawn off branch by, for example, a pair of slabs of timber cut from the outside of spruce logs or some equally durable timber (these offcuts are available from sawmills very cheaply) being nailed onto the back of the nest box and connected with a cross piece. A front side, made from boards or wood fibre tiles, is then nailed onto the box, and a square entrance hole is sawn or a round hole is then drilled into it. It is important to use rough sawn and not planed timber for this or else to provide some form of 'step ladder' fitted to the inside of the nest box, below the entrance hole. Young owls leave the nest box before they are completely ready to fly, while wild duck and goosander young do so only two days after hatching. Without a rough surface to grip with their claws these young find it difficult to get out. A year or so ago, tragedy occurred in a large number of goldeneye nest boxes newly erected in Bergslagen. Some of these boxes were too deep (for goldeneye the entrance should be no more than 25–30 cm above the base of the box) and some had no steps, so that when the nest boxes were cleaned in the autumn, they were found to be full of dead young which had been unable to get out.

Sawdust, wood-wool, wood shavings, or last year's grass should always be placed in the bottom of the box, since neither owls, wild ducks, nor goosanders build their own nests. Crushed decayed straw stubble is the best material for goldeneye nest boxes; this is very much like the material found in birds' natural nests and so is more likely to stimulate the breeding instinct. Wild ducks and mergansers will line the nest cups using down plucked from their own bodies.

The area below the entrance hole should be strengthened with a board because ducks and mergansers will fly into the hole at full speed and use this part of the structure for braking, thus imposing a lot of strain on it.

The nest box must also be held in place very firmly. The roof should be of hardwood covered with roofing felt and should project slightly over the front to prevent rain coming through the entrance hole (box measurements for the various species are on pages 208–9).

If a nest box is set up near a water course, or better still on a promontory where the ice will break up early in spring, there is a good chance that wild ducks will come to breed in it. In Northern Europe these may include goldeneye, goosanders, red-breasted mergansers and mallard. In Britain you may only be lucky enough to attract goldeneye in the north of Scotland, but goosanders may occupy riverside nest boxes as far south as the River Tyne. Further south, in areas where they have become naturalised, another tree nesting duck the mandarin may use boxes of this type.

The female duck or merganser will sit below the nest box and eagerly call to her young, which throw themselves fearlessly out of the nest, trying to break the fall with their tiny wing stumps. The ground below the nest box should therefore be even and free from sharp stones.

3   Buying nest boxes

ho do not have the time, inclination, or ability to make a nest buy one in a shop. They can be found in department stores, ntres and seed merchants. But one should be careful because there are many poor quality nest boxes on the market, and one should check up on all the relevant materials and measurements before buying one.

Below you will find several nest box types which I have field tested over some years and can recommend. But there are many many different kinds and if some do not appear here it does not necessarily mean that they are unsuitable. However, it should be kept in mind that wood and wood-cement board are the best materials, and that one of a nest box's most important characteristics is its insulating ability, since although birds may be breeding for only one month in the year, some species such as tits and wrens may spend six months sheltering overnight in such boxes in the autumn and winter. People who talk about nest boxes and recommend different products often pay far too little attention to this point.

It is also an untrue generalization to say that plastic nest boxes are unsuitable, but they are susceptible to problems which do not occur with wooden boxes. In direct sunlight they quickly heat up inside and great care should be taken to position plastic boxes so that they are always in the shade.

The box should be designed to allow for easy cleaning after the breeding season and this is often a feature which is forgotten by the manufacturers of plastic boxes. Failure to clean boxes after nesting can lead to a build up of harmful parasites, which may affect the next brood to be reared in the box. Finally plastic may become brittle in sunlight and holding a nest box in the wrong way (eg by an edge) may result in it cracking; the area under the entrance hole is particularly susceptible.

Trivsel-Bo nest boxes

Seven different varieties of this nest box are sold: for tits and pied flycatchers; starlings; tree creepers; spotted flycatchers and wagtails;

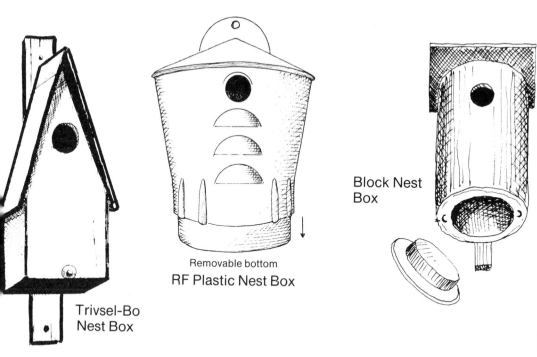

Trivsel-Bo
Nest Box

Removable bottom
RF Plastic Nest Box

**Block Nest
Box**

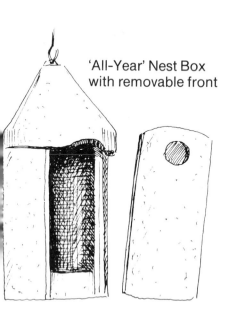

'All-Year' Nest Box
with removable front

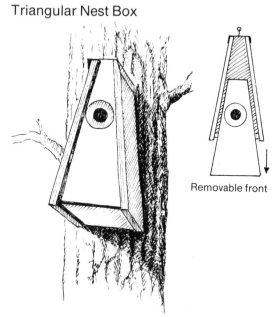

Triangular Nest Box

Removable front

21

Tengmalm's owls, stock doves and jackdaws; tawny owls, goldeneye and goosanders. They are made by the partially disabled in Gavle and may be ordered by post from: Mekotex AB, Snickeriavdelningen, Utmarksvagen 6, 802 26 Gavle, Sweden.

The nest box's front side, rear side and floor are made from soft wood, and the two sides and roof from hardwood. It should be possible to let the floor down so that the box can be cleaned easily.

The roof of this nest box is superbly constructed. It juts out sufficiently on either side of the entrance hole to prevent magpies and jays from inserting their beaks and plundering the nest. The floor is held in place with a large galvanized nail. Dampness normally causes the floor to expand and become jammed, but the use of this nail instead will make it easy to let down the floor and clean the nest box after the young have flown.

The pied flycatcher model or 'tit nest box' measures 26 × 12.5 cm with an entrance hole 3.5 cm in diameter which not only makes it large enough for great tits but also for sparrows which might sometimes be regarded as a nuisance. Pied flycatchers have nested around 100 times in this type of box in my research areas, and all have been successful.

The starling nest box has a total height of 31.5 cm, internal floor measurements of 15.5 × 12 cm, and an entrance hole diameter of 5 cm. This is a popular box with starlings.

The treecreeper model has a height of 46.5 cm, a 12 × 9.5 cm floor, a half moon-shaped entrance hole, measuring 10 × 3.5 cm, on either side. starlings and great tits have bred very successfully in this type of box, but no treecreepers as yet.

The spotted flycatcher model is open at the front and has internal floor measurements of 12.5 × 12 cm and a total height of 15.5 cm. The front, back, roof and floor are made from board and the sides from hardwood. This box is also suitable for wagtails and redstarts. As yet no breeding has taken place in this type of nest box in my area.

The model for Tengmalm's owl, stock dove, and jackdaw measures 62 × 20 × 20 cm, with an 8.5 cm diameter entrance hole, and has rungs inside to enable the young birds to reach the entrance hole.

The design intended for tawny owls and goldeneye is readily used especially by the tawny owl. Its total height is 62 cm, internal floor measurements 22 × 20 cm, with an entrance hole diameter of 11.5 cm, and rungs inside.

The largest model, for goosanders, has a total height of 90 cm, internal floor measurements of 29.5 × 25 cm, and an entrance hole diameter of 15 cm.

Nesting material, such as sawdust, must be placed in the bottom of nest boxes for owls and mergansers. These boxes are just as easy to clean as the smaller ones, and this need only be carried out every third year, remembering only to add a little fresh nesting material each year. Wild ducks, mergansers, and owls do not build nests and must be given this sort of help, otherwise they will not breed. As owls often sleep in the nest box for the remainder of the year, two boxes should be set up so that one can always be cleaned and aired without disturbing the owl. Nest boxes often become damp on the floor and along the sides after a few years and this will lead to rotting if it is not properly dried out. Once dry, the box should be closed and filled with dry nesting material.

RF (plastic) nest boxes

This box for tits is made from high-density polyethylene by RF products, Karlagatan 32C, 510 55, Lidkoping, Sweden. Its resistance to predators, wind and weather make this a very superior tree nest box. It has channels which provide ventilation thus reducing condensation. I have tested this box for two breeding seasons, with good results.

The floor sits firmly on a bayonet socket and is easy to remove for cleaning. The nest box is 12 cm deep, the diameter of the floor is 13 cm, and the entrance hole has a diameter of 3.5 cm. The floor contains a hole.

There has always been a good deal of criticism of nest boxes made from high density plastic and this may have been justified for the early models. But expanded plastic has subsequently been produced containing gas bubbles which imparts good insulating ability. Very high internal temperatures inside plastic nest boxes may kill the young. A further problem is that the rapid heating and cooling leads to condensation which collects in the ball of nesting material especially in the green moss used by tits, causing dampness which also leads to the death of a large number of young birds, although so far I have never observed this in RF plastic nest boxes. However to be safe one should always ensure, especially with plastic, that the nest boxes are put up in sites where they will always be shaded and never become exposed to full sun.

The research which revealed a high fatality rate amongst tits was carried out with a plastic box made from conventional high-density polyethylene, which provides very poor insulation and allows heavy condensation.

Unfortunately the press in Sweden followed up the publication of this research with photographs of expanded polyethylene nest boxes and stated that they were dangerous for birds. However, it was not the plastic nest box in general which was dangerous, but rather the high density plastic nest box, manufacture of which ceased ten years ago. But regrettably this gave all plastic nest boxes a poor reputation, which is a great nuisance, because when manufactured from the correct material these boxes are good, cheap, and last forever.

Research into fatality amongst young tits has only been undertaken from the point of view of nest box material, and has not so far touched upon the factor of cold spring times, which can increase the death rate because of the resulting food shortage. In addition, environmental toxins can sometimes cause sudden death in tits. Research has revealed high levels of DDT, polychlorinated biphenyls, and lindane in the eggs of flycatchers and tits.

'All-year' nest boxes

These boxes come in four models: for tits and flycatchers, for starlings, for treecreepers, and for owls.

They are made in West Germany from sawdust and cement and have excellent insulating properties. They are also extremely hard-wearing and can be used almost indefinitely. The mixture of materials is referred to as wood-cement board, and it goes to make a nest box which can be used throughout the whole year.

The 'All-year' box takes the form of a vertical cylinder with a pointed roof. The starling and owl models are larger and have more gently sloping roofs. The model for tits and flycatchers has an internal depth of 19 cm, a floor diameter of 15 cm, and an entrance hole diameter of 3.5 cm. The starling model has an internal depth of 22 cm, a floor diameter of 17 cm, and an entrance hole diameter of 5 cm. The treecreeper model has an internal depth of 18 cm, a floor diameter of 14 cm, and entrance hole length and breadth of 10 and 2 cm respectively. The owl model has equivalent inner depth, floor, and entrance hole dimensions of 18, 21, and 11.5 cm, respectively, with a total height of 40 cm.

These boxes may be ordered from the Swedish exporters who are Hillerstrom & Co., Box 262, Malmo 1, Sweden.

They are much dearer than boxes made from planks, but they do last for many years. I have had mine for about 20 years, and in Skane there are some which have been up for around 30 years and are still completely intact.

It is a first rate nest box which in the long run is cheaper than any other because the material from which it is built virtually lasts for ever. It neither cracks nor warps and is very easy to clean as the front can be lifted and removed. Care should be taken when removing the front to examine the nest during winter, as the area around the entrance hole can be broken off. If this does happen, the box front should be taken indoors where it can easily be glued on the outside and allowed to dry before replacing.

Aledal's nest boxes

This box is made from a hollowed out section of alder trunk, and is produced by Harald Stockheden, Aledals Nyckefabrik, Bankeryd, Sweden.

The roof is fitted with roofing felt. A 5 cm thick piece of wood is taken from the core left over from the hollowing out process; this is nailed to the bottom of the nest box to give extra insulation. The outside of the floor is provided with two staples. A very thick, angled steel filament is threaded through a hole in the floor and bent so that it sits tightly against the floor. This removable floor makes the nest box easy to clean. The back of the box has a strong, coated metal fixture from which it can be hung on a corresponding iron fixture fastened onto the tree. The metal in the tree is quite thick, which ensures that it moves outwards as the tree grows. A thinner piece of metal could easily become encapsulated within the trunk with the possibility of it causing serious damage during subsequent felling and cutting operations.

This nest box comes in models for small birds, starlings, and owls/wild ducks. The nuthatch is particularly keen on the starling model, which has an internal depth of 23 cm and a cavity diameter of 11.5 cm. The roof is 2.5 cm thick, the floor 5 cm thick, the total length 40 cm, and the entrance hole diameter 4.6 cm. The corresponding measurements for the small bird or tit model are 15, 9, 2.5, 5, 30.7, and 3.5 cm, respectively, while those for the owl/duck model are 35, 19, 2.5, 5, 60, and 11 cm, respectively. According to the manufacturer, goldeneye, tawny owl, and Tengmalm's owl have all bred in this latter model, and on a few occasions even goosanders.

Beware poor quality nest boxes

Shops unfortunately sell a whole range of boxes which are entirely unsuited as living places for birds or which could have potentially fatal consequences. Most nest boxes are factory produced, which means that as many as possible must be produced in the shortest time, to make them as cheap as possible. It is also unfortunate that a lot of people who know next to nothing about nest boxes are starting to make such boxes from waste timber which would otherwise have been thrown away.

The best nest boxes are those made from hollowed out sections of tree trunks, the so-called block nest boxes, the most common of which are made from birch. Such boxes are often fixed to trees via a lath which is nailed onto the box. It is important not to have nails projecting into the interior of the nest box.

Also, nest boxes may sometimes be too narrow or the entrance hole too small, so be sure to carefully check these dimensions on any nest box you buy. The internal depth should be 18–19 cm, the inner floor diameter at least 11–12 cm, and the entrance hole at least 2.8 cm in diameter for blue tits.

Some people recommend making nest boxes from old Tetra-Pak and other unusual materials. Do not buy a nest box because it looks unusual or pretty, but you should consider instead whether it will provide suitable accommodation for small birds both during summer and winter.

Sheet metal nest boxes

There are unfortunately many nest box models sold in shops which are made entirely from sheet metal. These become genuine ice boxes in winter and saunas in summer. It goes without saying that their insulating capacity is virtually zero. With a change in the weather condensation will form inside often with fatal consequences for any young birds unfortunate enough to be in such a nest box.

Sheet metal nest boxes are of course strong and durable, but they have the enormous drawback in that they become burning hot in the summer sun and fail to insulate against cold in the winter when boxes are often used every night as sleeping quarters by tits and other birds.

Because of this, sheet metal nest boxes are entirely unsuitable and should never be used no matter how sturdy they are.

Triangular nest boxes

At one time shops in Sweden used to sell a triangular nest box with 18 cm sides, 16 cm internal depth, and an inner floor with 6 cm sides. On the one hand it was so small and cramped that no birds could manage to stay in it, and on the other hand the entrance hole was so high up that it was too narrow. There was an imminent risk of birds becoming stuck in it. These nest boxes are still set up in many recreational areas. Some books recommend making one's own triangular boxes and sawing away the the top triangular portion of the front side instead of drilling an entrance hole. In such a case one has to be careful to saw off sufficient for the hole not to be too narrow. Considering some of the extraordinary nest sites chosen by birds each year there is no good reason why the boxes should not be whatever shape you chose so long as they are large enough, weatherproof, and have a suitable entrance hole and are placed in a secure position. I have field tested triangular nest boxes for around 15 years and provided that the round hole bored into the front is large enough for the birds' use the results have not differed from conventional boxes.

4 Pied Flycatcher (*Ficedula hypoleuca*)

Pied flycatchers will readily use nest boxes. They will even breed in new nest boxes provided these are up when the birds return in the spring. In areas within its breeding range the pied flycatcher is a species which can be encouraged almost more than any other by the provision of nest boxes. It is a nest box user of the first degree. Because of the reduction in the area of natural woodland containing old trees with plenty of holes and cavities, the pied flycatcher now breeds almost exclusively in nest boxes in Sweden.

One can easily identify the male from his black and white plumage, while the female is grey-brown; both have very energetic wing movements. They have no objection whatever to nest boxes in areas inhabited by people and are one of the most rewarding species for which one can set up nest boxes. The ideal box dimensions for pied flycatchers are 19 × 12 × 12 cm, with 3.2 cm diameter entrance hole. The distance from the lower edge of the entrance hole to the floor should be 12.5–19 cm. The nest box should be set at a height of 2.3 m with the entrance hole facing south or east. Those less handy at joinery can buy the highly popular Trivsel-Bo model for tits. This is a Swedish box which may be unavailable in other European countries but any wooden box of similar dimensions will be suitable. Of 468 nesting attempts by pied flycatchers which I have observed, 72 occurred in boxes with a 12.5 cm distance between entrance hole and floor, 148 in a box with a 13 cm distance, 168 where it was 16 cm, and 80 where it was 19 cm. No breeding has taken place when this distance has been longer or shorter than this range. So it is clear that this particular measurement is significant in determining whether or not a box will be used for breeding.

This species is very tolerant and will live in any type of nest box provided its dimensions are as given above; they will even settle in somewhat larger boxes. Tits have a very strong preference for old nest boxes, whereas the pied flycatcher is very partial to breeding in brand new ones.

Time of arrival I have made detailed observations and notes of the arrival time of the pied flycatcher over an 11-year period. As a rule, the

Plank Nest Box

Dimensions

26 cm

3,2 cm

9.5 cm

28 cm 2,8 cm 14 cm

10 cm

Plank Nest Box

Block
Nest
Box

Dimensions

27 cm 3,2 cm 15 cm

12×12 cm

Block Nest Box

Female

Male

Pied Flycatcher

29

time of the first arrival has been noted, but in some years the times when most of the males have arrived has also been recorded. Occasional males can be seen as early as the end of April, but in general the first arrivals in the Valdermarsvik region of Sweden occur in the first few days of May. The females normally arrive 3–4 days later, but some individuals have appeared at the same time as the majority of males.

The arrival dates for male pied flycatchers 1955–65

	1955	1956	1957	1958	1959	1960	1961	1962	1963	1964	1965
First arrivals	3.5	5.5	30.4	1.5	30.4	7.5	–	–	13.5	3.5	4.5
Main population arrives	5.5	7.5	4.5	–	–	9.5	–	–	–	7.5	8.5

Territory

When the male arrives in the spring he is ready for breeding and begins immediately, or shortly after his arrival, to search for a suitable territory, an area surrounding an acceptable nest. The time of breeding is regulated entirely by the amount of light the bird is exposed to at that particular time of the year.

The male normally guards 2–3 nests in the area and sings from them. His song performs the very important function of declaring the territory by marking out where it is and chasing away rivals. He will often sing during or after a battle. Sunrise is the most active time for singing, morning-to-midday is quieter, and sunset sees something of an upsurge again. The pied flycatcher is a very diligent singer, and according to research carried out by a Finnish ornithologist, this bird goes through its repertoire over 3620 times per day, which on average is once every 18 seconds during day light hours.

Any strange bird, pied flycatcher or otherwise, which enters the territory is driven away. Fights between the males can sometimes be very fierce, and on two occasions I have found dead males in breeding areas. In one case in 1964, a male pied flycatcher came and drove away a blue tit which was already occupying a nest box in which it had laid an egg. The flycatcher in its turn energetically defended his new nest box, which was evidently a very sought-after residence. During one of his battles with another pied flycatcher, he was driven back into the box seriously wounded and died there.

If a female pied flycatcher occupies a nest which already contains eggs or dead young she will quite simply build her nest on top of them. The great tit in particular seems to fly from its nest whenever a pied flycatcher appears, although those with full clutches put up more resistance.

The following notes were made about birds driven from their nest boxes by pied flycatchers between 1956 and 1977: In 1957 a crested tit was driven away after it had been sitting on its five eggs for a week. A female pied flycatcher built its nest on top of these eggs, laid its own eggs, and reared its brood of young. In 1963 and 1964, one pied flycatcher was driven away by another when it had just begun to build its nest. A blue tit was also driven away in 1964 when it was beginning its building. In 1974 a flycatcher built its nest in a tit type box and laid two eggs. This box had split during the winter and because I was working in another area I had not been able to repair it. On a blustery day it fell to the ground. A great tit was sitting on five eggs in a neighbouring box but was soon driven out by the homeless flycatcher which built its own nest on top of the tit eggs and laid six eggs which eventually produced six fledged young. The dispossessed great tit moved to yet another nearby box and built a new nest. The same thing happened in 1975, although this time the great tit had built her nest and laid her eggs but had not yet started incubation. On a further ten occasions great tits were ousted from their boxes by pied flycatchers just as they were starting to build nests or had only half completed them.

Each species of bird searches instinctively for the particular type of habitat which best suits it. One might imagine that this would lead to overpopulation in the most favoured area, but in actual fact a balanced distribution occurs. If a population of birds is expanding, the best niches are colonized first and only afterwards, as the number of individuals in the area increases, are the somewhat less favoured places occupied. So instead of the best places becoming overcrowded, the population is squeezed out into less popular outposts.

Both the male and female take part in defending territory, with the male dealing most vigorously with males of the same species or male tits. Both will issue warnings against crows, woodpeckers, squirrels, humans, etc., and will protect their nest against them.

In my research area, pied flycatcher territories measure on average 1500 sq-m (50 × 30 m). When the young start to fly, the boundaries of the territory melt away and the family moves into the surrounding area to find food.

Pair-formation

When the female arrives in spring she starts to build in some of the nest boxes which the male has guarded. She is enticed by his song and by the white band on his forehead. Nest building begins very soon after, provided a period of cold or rainy weather does not set in because this may suppress the initial burst of building.

At the start of the breeding period, the male is influenced by three tendencies: to pair, to fight, and to escape. The pairing tendency is directed towards females and the other two towards males. Sometimes his attacking tendency is directed at the female and he will show his aggression with a gaping beak and splayed wings. This is subsequently replaced by a less aggressive attitude, the male presumably becoming accustomed to the female. Finally, he will begin to court her and they will mate.

Polygamy occurs frequently amongst pied flycatchers. I observed this in 1964 and within the area studied there was an excess of females and polygamy occurred in three nest boxes (in recent years there has been a deficit of females). At one nest box, for example, a male sat and sang, eventually enticing a female to the territory. When the female began to build a nest, the male flew about 8–10 m away, sang from another nest box and thus attracted a new female. When the second female was building her nest and laying eggs, the first was hatching out her eggs, at which time the male returned and helped out with feeding the young. The female in the second box had to feed her young alone, but she did so successfully, producing five young, compared with the six of the first female.

Loss of a partner

If the male dies the female will feed the young herself. In 1964 a male was killed by another pied flycatcher, and the female sat on her six eggs and brought up her young despite the dead male remaining in the nest. Four young left the nest and two eggs remained unhatched, presumably because the dead bird prevented effective brooding of these eggs. She clearly did not react to the foul-smelling corpse. Like most other birds, pied flycatchers have a very poorly developed sense of smell.

However, if the female dies, the male abandons the eggs or young and begins searching for a new female.

Nest building

The pied flycatcher builds its nest between the first mating and egg laying. She builds the nest alone and usually begins to do so within two days of arrival. The female stays overnight in the nest box, the male in a box or nest hole in the vicinity. From two to three days before all the eggs are laid until incubation begins, the female also spends the nights outside the nest box.

The construction of the nest has an important influence on the temperature of the eggs during brooding. A cool summer climate naturally makes more demands on a nest's heat-insulating capacity than does a warmer situation.

The table below gives the dates when nest building was begun and when it was completed in the years 1956–65.

Nest building – date begun and finished 1956–65

	1956	1957	1958	1959	1960	1961	1962	1963	1964	1965
Nest begun	19.5	25.5	23.5	14.5	22.5	22.5	–	17.5	18.5	23.5
Nest finished	27.5	2.6	31.5	22.5	30.5	30.5	–	25.5	26.5	30.5

It therefore takes an average of nine days to build the nest.

In 1968 a small bat was found in an 'All-year' nest box for pied flycatchers. It left the box at 9pm one evening, and at 3am the next morning a flycatcher frantically started to build a nest, which it had completed by 10 pm the following evening. The bat did not return for 30 hours. The female flycatcher had been trying to build her nest for a long time before this, but presumably had been put off by the bat's presence or its copious excrement. These droppings have a strong smell of musk, but I do not think this was particularly significant because of the bird's poor sense of smell. The bat, in the meantime, stayed in the very uppermost part of the box. The flycatcher finished her nest and even laid one egg, but she subsequently abandoned everything. Good neighbourliness was clearly not in evidence here. The flycatcher pair moved to another nest box in the vicinity and bred normally.

In many cases these unlikely neighbours have lived together in harmony, in one instance the pied flycatchers producing eight young in the bottom of the box while four bats and their young occupied the top.

In my study area pied flycatchers build two types of nests. Some build their nest mainly from flakes of pine bark and the previous year's birch leaves, while some combine the latter with dead grasses. This suggests an inherited, unchangeable pattern of nest building. Flycatchers which begin by building normal nests continue to do so all their lives, and vice-versa.

The 'normal' nest consists primarily of heavy flakes broken by the flycatcher from trunks of pine trees, combined with a large amount of the previous year's leaves, a tiny quantity of birch bark, and some dead grass. The nest also contains flakes of juniper bark, dried fern, old pine needles, root fibres, lichen, small feathers, and down. The grass, down, and small feathers form the inner lining of the nest cup, which is warm and smooth for the eggs. The grass nest consists almost entirely of the previous year's grass, but also a significant amount of dead birch leaves and smaller amounts of juniper bark (twice as much as in the 'normal' nest), last year's oak leaves, birch bark, flakes of pine bark (only a quarter the amount found in the 'normal' nest), and lichen. Small feathers and down may form the inner lining or may be absent.

Egg laying

As soon as the nest is completed the female begins to lay her eggs. This usually happens around about the end of May. The number of eggs varies between two and eight, with six being the most common number, and 5.5 eggs being the average clutch.

Egg laying behaviour begins five days before the first egg appears. The female's egg-regulating mechanism is fully ready from this moment, after which point external factors such as wind and weather come into play. If the average diurnal temperature falls below 10°C egg laying stops and only restarts when it becomes warmer. The female spends her nights outside the nest box during the egg laying period, and returns to overnight in the box when the full complement of eggs has been laid and incubation has begun.

She lays one egg each day, except in cold weather, in the few hours between sunrise and 8am.

Clutch size

The number of eggs laid varies between individuals within the species and with the time of year, with later broods generally containing fewer eggs:

Number of broods with	3	4	5	6	7	8	eggs
1970	–	1	10	15	7	–	
1971	–	1	12	8	2	–	
1972	1	6	15	7	1	–	
1973	3	8	12	5	2	–	
1974	–	5	10	6	2	–	
1975	1	–	4	7	11	1	
1976	–	1	6	16	1	–	
1977	–	1	11	8	1	–	
1983	–	1	8	17	4	–	
Percentage of total	2.1	10.1	37.0	37.4	13.0	0.4	

The percentages of unhatched eggs and dead young in pied flycatcher nests during the 1970s were as follows:

	Number of broods	% unhatched eggs	% dead young
1970	33	8.4	7.4
1971	23	9.6	0.8
1972	30	7.4	8.7
1973	30	16.0	6.5
1974	23	19.6	5.8
1975	24	8.9	17.8
1976	24	10.2	5.8
1977	21	7.9	19.5
1983	30	7.9	1.2
Average	26	10.7	8.2

After a peak in 1973–74, the proportion of unhatched eggs fell significantly. This probably reflected the banning of chlorinated hydrocarbons in countries used by the pied flycatchers en route to their winter quarters, namely Portugal in 1972 and Spain in 1974. The high number of fatalities amongst young in 1975 and 1977 was due to the very low average temperatures (13–17°C) during the period when the young birds were growing which meant a poor supply of insects. Parents were unable to find enough food for their young. By contrast, the average temperature in the same period in 1974 was 18–25°C.

Incubation

Incubation begins as soon as the full complement of eggs is laid. The brooding instinct is not as strong in young females who have only just reached sexual maturity as it is in older females. Sometimes a person merely passing by the nest box is enough to cause the female to abandon the nest. Even the warning sounds made by other birds when one passes near their nests in woodland can often cause a young female in an area quite a distance away to leave her nest. Brooding is normally a solitary and intensive occupation for the female, which is reluctant to leave the eggs. With most females, one needs to be very careful when taking down the boxes to make observations (including lifting up the bird to ring it, which in Britain may only be done by ringers licensed by the Nature Conservancy Council), otherwise the eggs will be abandoned.

The brooding tendency is initially weak, and birds of all species are sensitive to disturbance at this stage, so ringing of the females should only be performed 6–8 days after the start of incubation.

Temperature also influences brooding behaviour. On a warm, sunny day when the nest box is warm the female may leave the eggs for long periods, but brooding will be more intensive when it is cold.

The male feeds the female very meagrely at this time, usually only at hatching and when the chicks are still very young.

The eggs hatch after an incubation period of 13–15 days and this often coincides with a day when the sun has warmed up the nest box a little. When hatching is completed, the female removes the egg shells from the nest box. Unlike birds in open nests, which are very careful to keep their nests hidden and take the egg shells far away, the pied flycatcher drops the shells in the immediate vicinity of the nest box. This difference in behaviour is also reflected in the egg colour. Hole nesting birds often have white or pale coloured eggs (pale blue in the case of the pied flycatcher) because within the darkness of the nest hole hiding the eggs from would be predators is not a problem. Birds which build nests in the open or lay their eggs on the ground however, usually have highly coloured eggs which are often elaborately patterned as part of their camouflage. Unhatched eggs and dead young are left in the nest for the remainder of the breeding period.

Growth of the young

At hatching, the young flycatchers are very helpless, with large heads, shapeless bodies, poorly developed legs and wings, and closed eyes. Their bodies are reddish and entirely naked and there are only a few tufts of down on the head. The only sound they can manage is a feeble chirping. Without the warmth of the nest they would quickly die, and for the first few days all they can do is raise their heads, open their beaks, and chirp hungrily. In the darkness of the nest box's interior, the parents are guided by the yellow edging on the young birds' beaks, and the reddish yellow spots inside the mouths of the young trigger off the parents' feeding instinct. The young also normally swing their heads back and forth, and if any of them are in a poor condition and cannot manage this action, they will receive no food and will die rapidly.

For the first eight days, the young birds are completely blind and lie at the bottom of the nest. After ten days they can stand on their legs and thus raise their bodies. The wings, legs, and eventually the coat of feathers develop. The sheaths of the developing feathers grow up out of the skin on the head and wings after five days, and after nine days the feathers themselves grow out and slowly lengthen. However, even when the plumage is almost fully formed, some of the original down can still be seen. After eighteen days the young birds are a grey-brown colour, but they do not acquire the colouration of the adult bird until they are in their winter quarters.

The female's weight is normal during egg laying and incubation, but with hatching and feeding the young it falls rapidly. She will lose around 3 grams up until the time when the young leave the nest. The male also loses weight, though only about 1 gram.

The young in the nest do nothing but eat and sleep. They are quiet while their parents are away, but upon their return they chirp and gape vigorously. The young themselves cannot take the food which their parents have brought and must have it stuffed down into their gaping mouths. It is a busy time for the parents. Once the young are several days old feeding starts at dawn, which in Sweden will be around 2am and continues until 9.30pm. In a nest which I studied, there were five young which had 590 meal times each day, which means that each bird received about 118 meals per day. The male averaged three insects at each feed and the female 1.5. On this basis the male, which fed the young 240 times each day, on average provided about 720 insects per day, while the female, provided about 525 insects in her 350 feeding sessions. This gave a total of 1245 insects per day, and as the young stayed in the nest for 19 days, they consumed altogether about 23,655 insects. In one year, there were 33 breeding pairs, so a grand total of 781,000 insects, midges, flies, etc, must have been used to feed the young during their time in the nest box alone.

When a young bird is fed by its parents it lifts up its rear end moments later and excretes its waste. The waste is enclosed in a soft membrane (the faecal sac) which does not break, making it possible for the parents to remove the excreta without soiling the nest bowl. Both parents remove waste, the male 65 times per day and the female 35. These sacs are carried at least 10 metres from the nest.

As the young get older the waste has to be removed more frequently, so that with 7-day-old young waste is removed after every 10–15 meals, and with young which are almost ready to fly it is removed after every 6–7 meals.

This particular task is important for both hole-nesting birds and those which build nests in the open. For hole nesters it is a matter of hygiene, but for open nesting birds it is also important because the presence of white droppings around the nest advertises its presence to predators.

Food

The pied flycatcher is a highly energetic hunter of insects. Like other flycatchers, he sits motionless and watches until he spots an insect before flying from his perch to pounce, eat his prey, and return to his immobile state at an appropriate vantage point from where he can spy out more victims. In 1965, to establish what the pied flycatcher diet consisted of, I pulled apart ten nests from the previous year and found the following insect remains:

Mayfly	*Ephemeroptera*
Click Beetles	*Agriotes lineatus, Ampedus balteatus*
Oak Leaf Roller Moth	*Tortrix viridana*
Wood Ant	*Formica rufa*
Wood Louse	*Isopoda*
House Fly	*Musca domestica*
Seven Spot Ladybird	*Coccinella septempunctata*
Springtail	*Collembola*
Female Glow Worm	*Lampyris noctiluca*
Pine Shoot Moth	*Rhyacionia buoliana*
Dragon Fly	*Odonata*
Caddis Flies	*Trichoptera*
Earwig	*Dermaptera*
Ichneumon Fly	*Rhyssa persuasoria*
Weevil larvae	*Curculionidae*

From this little investigation it was clear that the flycatcher consumes a random assortment of insects including some which are both garden and forest pests.

The end of the breeding period

The young start to leave the nest box on average after 19 days, and then the forest becomes a very lively place. The young birds fly rather badly and flutter about from tree to tree enthusiastically making a 'sirp-sirp-sirp' like call. The parents produce a similar sort of call and this serves to keep the young in contact with the parents. For the first few days the young are relatively immobile and cannot follow their parents. Their anxious cries reveal their whereabouts not only to the parents, but also to enterprising predators such as crows, which often take young during this short but vulnerable time. Once the young have left the nest they do not return.

Autumn observations

Towards the end of July the pied flycatchers join company with birds of other species, such as chaffinches, tits, and warblers, and large flocks are formed. At this time, the residue of spring and summer's territorial aggressiveness comes to an end and singing has already ended by the time the young are half grown. It is now that they make preparations for the long journey to warmer lands for the winter.

The pied flycatcher migrates to tropical West Africa. Few ringing recoveries have come from their wintering areas but those for birds on passage reveal that some of the flycatchers which sing outside our nest boxes have passed through Spain and Portugal. Of the 116 cases which I have looked into, 53 involved Portugal, 25 Spain, 19 France, 6 West Germany, 4 Italy, 3 Morocco, 2 Belgium, and 1 each Denmark, the Netherlands, Switzerland, and Tunisia.

Migration from the breeding areas takes place in the final weeks of August.

The pied flycatcher's faithfulness to his home territory

Some of the literature on birds maintains that pied flycatcher pairs return year after year to the same nest box, but I think one should view such statements with a good deal of scepticism. Research shows that around 40% of all migrating pied flycatchers survive and return. Of these, adult males show the strongest urge to return to their home territory, but only half as many adult females return to the previous year's territory. Only a few one year olds return to the territory in which they were reared.

From the few birds which I have ringed, 16 adult females in 1974, 11 in 1975, and 16 in 1976, the return rates were as follows: 3 (19%) from 1974 returned in 1975, 3 (27%) from 1975 returned in 1976, and 2 (12%) from 1976 returned in 1977. None of these birds bred in the same nest box as in previous years.

Research has shown that females which do not come sufficiently near to last year's breeding place do not attempt to return to their old territory and settle themselves anywhere within the 'breeding area'. During migration, birds follow specific routes. Many are of the opinion that this involves reading the landscape in precisely the same way that an orienteer reads a map. If the bird misses its destination because of a slight deviation from the route, it will not remember its old nesting area, but will breed instead in an area which may be many kilometres from the starting point.

German or Swedish pied flycatchers?

Since the end of the 1950s, 20–30 pairs of pied flycatchers have bred within my area. During 1976 I found one pair occupying a nest box with the identical colour of grey-brown and white. Normally in Scandinavia and Western Europe the male is black and white and the female grey-brown and white. During all those years, I had only encountered black and white males. In central Europe including West Germany, a high proportion of males are grey-brown and white, and in Skane (southern Sweden) there are approximately equal numbers of each colour-type of male, so clearly this bird was an incomer well away from its normal breeding area.

A cold period had occurred in the last week of May that year interrupting the egg laying of the pied flycatchers. As soon as the average temperature rose above 10°C again, egg laying resumed. But the odd couple had by this time already hatched out their young, six in all, all of which successfully left the nest. This pair must have come from a more southerly area to have commenced breeding so early. The female was ringed, and on a subsequent visit to the area immediately after midsummer, I found the same pair with a second clutch of eggs in a starling model of the 'All-year' nest box with a 5 cm entrance hole, compared with the 3.5 cm entrance hole of their previous nest box. This time there were five eggs, but four of the young died when newly born, and the fifth succumbed one week after hatching. Why this happened is not known. This was the only time that pied flycatchers are known to have double brooded in this area.

When the couple was studied from a hide, it was noticed that they were much more cautious than 'normal' pied flycatchers and were very quiet in the nest. They did not feed as often, though whether or not this was due to a shortage of food is unclear. This pair did not return in 1977, nor have any similar birds been seen since.

5　Tits

Awakening of the breeding instinct

As the days become longer and lighter during late winter, the bird's eyes detect the growing brightness and through the nervous system the pituitary gland in the brain is induced to release hormones which in turn stimulate the sex glands to release sex hormones. Many of the bird's activities, including singing, depend upon an increase in the sex hormone level.

Tits will begin to sing in January if the weather is mild. At the end of February, the flocks of tits break up. Many males and females, when their breeding instinct is reawakened, return to the same areas where they bred in the previous year, so the same two birds often pair up again. Once the young are able to fend for themselves the partnership dissolves and the male and female go their separate ways during autumn.

Territory

The male sings from within his defended territory, usually an area including several nest boxes if you have put up sufficient. In this way he gives notice to females that an unattached male with territory and suitable nesting places is available. The female then chooses which of the nest boxes is to become the living quarters, and the male defends it vigorously.

Origins of the nest

In most cases, only the female constructs the nest, which takes about a week to complete. Rough material, such as dead grass, is placed on the outside followed by a thick layer of green moss and more dried grass. The nest cup is then lined with a layer of soft, warm material such as down, hair, small feathers, cotton and woollen fibres, and horsehair.

Eggs

The number of eggs varies amongst tits. Great tits lay 5–13 eggs and smaller tits as many as 12–15. In Northern and Eastern Europe where tits are frequently double brooded, the first clutch always contains more eggs than the second. Eggs are laid at a rate of one per day, and brooding begins once the clutch is complete. During the laying and incubation periods, the eggs are covered over whenever the incubating bird leaves the nest. Amongst some tits the male shares in the brooding of the eggs. Hatching occurs after about 14 days. During incubation the female is fed fairly frequently by the male, although on warm days she may leave the eggs for several hours in the middle of the day to feed herself.

Small birds generally return very quickly to the nest when they have been disturbed during incubation, but if a brooding tit is lifted from the nest, ringed, and replaced, she will more often than not fly from the nest and perhaps never return. In other cases she will be extremely wary and only make her way back into the nest box when there are no humans in sight. The only exceptions to this are certain blue tits. All other tits are nervous and easily disturbed during nest building and egg laying. One should keep this in mind and avoid visiting their nests during these periods.

Young

The development of young tits almost exactly matches that of young pied flycatchers, except that if they do not obtain warmth from the mother's body, they will die. This intensive care is absolutely essential for young aged less than 8–10 days. Their mouths have clear distinct colours with which they signal to their parents, arousing their feeding instinct. The young are initially blind, and only open their eyes after 8–9 days and stand up on their legs after 11 days. Altogether, the parents provide around 400–500 meals per day, with at least two insects or larvae at each visit. They take a total of about ten 15–20 minute breaks during the day.

To start with, the nest is kept clean and tidy. All excreta are removed, some parents swallowing the faecal sac although most carry it off in their beaks (some do this from the beginning, others after a few days). It is taken a long way from the nest box to avoid revealing the nest's whereabouts to predators. As the young grow bigger the task of removing excreta becomes too much for the parents to manage, so the young birds get a little dirty. They try to deposit their excreta outside the nest box by turning their rear ends towards the entrance hole and spraying. Unfortunately it is usually so cramped in the box that most of the waste ends up on the walls and runs down into the nest. Nevertheless the nest does stay reasonably clean.

The young tits leave the nest after about three weeks. As soon as they have gone the nest must be cleared and cleaned. The nest bowl contains a lot of waste as well as parasitic insects such as fleas and mites. Immediate cleaning makes it possible for some tits to eventually lay a second batch of eggs in the nest box though this happens only rarely. The tits know from experience that the nest will be soiled and full of vermin a long time after breeding and so will not be fit to live in. Normally they will seek out an empty nest box in the neighbourhood where they will breed and lay a second clutch of eggs. Therefore it is a good idea to have some nest boxes close to each other to serve as reserve homes for the tits. As noted earlier this does not happen in Britain where tits are usually single brooded.

Fledgling period

After leaving the nest, the young stay with their parents for about four weeks, though this may be reduced to two if a second clutch of eggs is on the way. Thereafter they join up with flocks of tits, warblers, and pied flycatchers.

Winter losses amongst tits

The death rate amongst tits is very high in cold weather. As many as 80–90% of tits normally die in their first year of life, even in mild winter climates. The loss rate for mature birds is only 20–30%. It is important that loss of warmth during cold winter nights is minimised. More and more people are feeding protein-rich food to winter birds, which is an excellent thing to do. However, tits often like to spend winter nights in nest boxes, so boxes with good insulating properties should be set up in the vicinity of the feeding places. This helps the birds to use the short winter days more effectively, and avoids them having to squander energy on long flights or to waste precious food searching time.

The temperature in nest boxes can fluctuate a great deal, but good protection is afforded against wind, snow, and rain. A cotton wad can be laid inside the nest box, but this should be removed and thrown away in good time for the breeding season as the tits will also use the nest box as a toilet during the winter nights.

Tits sleep very deeply when it is dark and so do not use up many calories. They lay up stocks of food in advance and each species searches in those places where birds of its own kind habitually create such stores.

Of the 130 nest boxes I have set up, approximately 30% have been used by tits as overnight shelters in the winter.

Close study has revealed that the positioning of the nest box was a major factor in the bird's choice. If it is situated in a place where there is a lee and sheltering woodland, then it will prove very popular as a night shelter.

Nest boxes for the small tit species, crested tit and coal tit, should be set up no more than 1–2 metres from the ground. The willow tit does not normally breed in nest boxes, but hacks out its own nest in decayed tree trunks. However, if a nest box is set up at a height of one metre and one-third filled every year with wood shavings, then even willow tits can be persuaded to breed in the box. This sort of nest filling is a good imitation of the rotten wood found in old tree trunks and will also attract crested tits and coal tits to breed in nest boxes to a much greater extent than usual.

Great Tit *(Parus major)*

Favourite nest boxes for the great tit In my research area, great tits have really taken to the flycatcher model of 'All-year' nest boxes, RF-nest boxes, as well as plank nest boxes which I have made myself.

Plank nest boxes 2 cm thick timber should be used. The internal depth should be 20 cm, the inner side measurements 15 cm, the entrance hole 3.5–4 cm, and the roof height 25 cm. The box should be set at a height 2.5–3 m, but the direction in which the box is facing is of no particular significance in this case, except that, as with other nest box-inhabiting birds, a north-facing entrance is unpopular. A movable floor facilitates cleaning after the tits have finished each year and should always be included in the design if possible.

The great tit is one of the most common of our tits. The male and female have a similar appearance, though the female's colours are somewhat paler. They are common in gardens, parks, and woodland, and during the winter they are the leaders of tit flocks, though tending to feed on the woodland floor while the smaller and more agile species remain more in the canopy.

Hormones influence the behaviour of the great tit and if it is sunny, fine, and relatively warm, he will start his hoarse little melody as early as January or February. I have even heard great tits singing on New Year's afternoon, as if they were ringing in the New Year. Being one of the first bird songs to be heard at this often dull time of year this hoarse but cheery little ditty acts a welcome harbinger of spring. You will hear their song as often in the town as in the country.

At the end of February, flocks of tits will break up and the male and

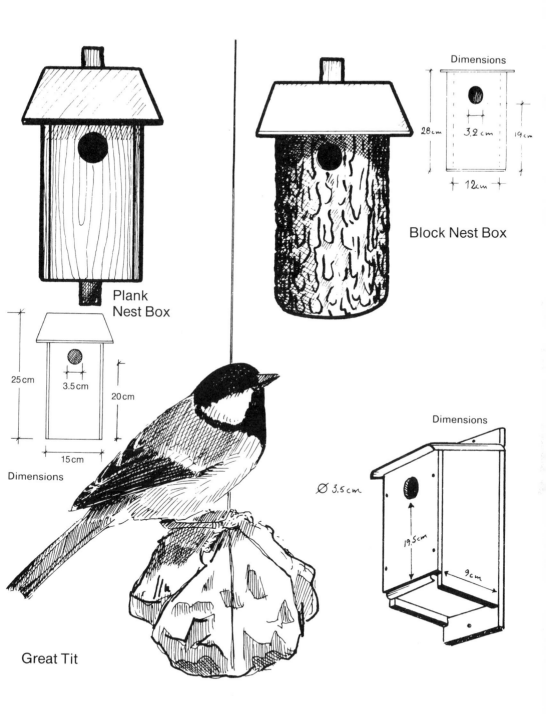

Plank
Nest Box

Block Nest Box

Dimensions

28 cm   3,2 cm   19 cm

12 cm

25 cm   3.5 cm   20 cm

15 cm

Dimensions

Great Tit

Dimensions

Ø 3.5 cm

19,5 cm

9 cm

45

female will seek out the area where they bred in the previous year. Therefore, the same pair will often breed year after year in the same nest box. If one of the couple dies, then its place is very quickly taken over by a new bird. Males which have only recently come to sexual maturity will look for left-over nest boxes and holes and will attempt to entice sexually mature females who are still unattached.

From the time that the young are ready to fly, up to the new breeding period in the following year, the male and female live entirely apart. Great tits very much prefer sheltered, out of the way places for breeding and are fussy when it comes to choosing a nest box. They appear to have trouble in making up their minds and the male often starts constructing nests with a little fern and moss in several boxes at the same time until the female finally decides on one particular box. Sometimes he will build in starling nest boxes, sometimes even in goldeneye boxes, in which case he fills up the entire bottom of the box with moss and ferns and builds the nest bowl in one corner. I once found a great tit nest in a letter box, which was large and rectangular and provided with a lid which did not shut properly, leaving a chink through which the great tit could pass. The bottom was completely filled with green golden maidenhair fern and in one corner lay a nest bowl with ten eggs.

At the beginning of April, the male starts to become aggressive towards males of his own and even of other species; he is now maintaining his territory. However, he draws a line when it comes to the rather fierce pied flycatcher and blue tit. His submission to these two species even occurs when his female has laid eggs, though not so often when there are young involved.

The nest is built by the female and takes six days to complete. It consists of mosses, ferns and dried grass. The interior is lined with a soft, warm material such as down, small hairs, horsehair, and wool.

The number of eggs varies from five to 12. When a full clutch has been laid, the female broods alone for 12 days, and during the egg laying and brooding periods, she will cover over the eggs whenever she leaves the nest. Though she is fed quite often by the male, she will leave the eggs for hours at a time in the middle of warm days, when she will seek out her own food.

Even though for most of the year great tits will live in the immediate vicinity of humans, and in winter will even feed from the hand, they are very cautious and sensitive to disturbance during the nest building and incubation periods and when the young are newly hatched. The female is strongly attached to her eggs, but if she becomes frightened, she will leave the nest and not return, and this should always be kept in mind.

For the most part, great tits feed on insects which are pests in gardens, parks, and woodland. Each day they eat 2.5 times their own body weight in the form of insect larvae. When it has young, a great tit can clear 80–90% of the moth larvae on an infested fruit tree, thus saving the tree's foliage.

In 1962 there was a plague of pine moths along the east coast of Sweden and many pine trees were killed off in spite of aerial spraying. No pine trees died in my nest-box area, even though there had been no spraying there. In that particular year, six pairs of great tits and 16 pairs of pied flycatchers bred in the area, and all of them had fed to some extent on the pine moths; the great tits did so almost exclusively.

A pair of great tits with 8 half grown young will consume around 1000 insect larvae per day. The two parents together provide food about 400–500 times per day, with an average of two larvae each time. So in the 19 days that the young were in the nest up to 19,000 larvae may have been eaten, giving a total of about 114,000 for six pairs.

During the first two days the young are fed every eight minutes, on the third day every five minutes, and from the fifth day every three minutes. This of course is assuming that there is access to a good supply of food, and the feeding schedule can vary from year to year and from pair to pair depending on the availability of food in the vicinity of the nesting place. If for any reason there is a dearth of insects, then the fatality rate will be very high among large broods of young.

The young of great tits need intensive care for the first 8–10 days of life, unlike young pied flycatchers which can manage without their mother's help by the second day. Without warmth from their mother's body, the small great tits will die, and during this period the male normally brings food to the female who then feeds the young.

If the pair are double brooded they will always raise their second brood in a different nest box. They know from past experience that the first batch in a nest box results in a nest bowl full of insects and mites and thoroughly soiled with the droppings of their young. Neverthless, as soon as possible after breeding is over, the nest box should be cleaned out and the used nest burned, otherwise the insect eggs laid there can survive the winter, and hatch out in the warmth of spring, thus re-infesting the nest box.

Once the young have left the nest, they stay with their parents for about a month, but this period is shortened to two weeks if the parents produce a second brood. Thereafter, the young join up with flocks containing tits, warblers, and flycatchers.

Of all the tits, the great tit is the one most likely to shelter overnight in nest boxes in autumn and winter. If the great tits are to survive the cold winter nights, the nest box must be well insulated, and the hollowed-out section of trunk (so-called block nest box) and wood-cement board are the two best materials. Research shows that even during mild winters, losses amongst great tits in their first year can be as high as 87%, and in adult tits around 25% (Kluijver, 1951).

Great tits are non-migratory birds and only move within a limited area during winter. However, ringing has shown that some great tits do make long journeys. Continental ringed great tits occasionally even turn up in Britain.

Besides warm living quarters, great tits also need calorie-rich food to survive the winter. Hemp seed, sunflower seed, and coconut fat are the best foods for this purpose (see page 192).

Blue Tit *(Parus caeruleus)*

Plank and block nest boxes are the favourites for blue tits. The internal depth should be 18 cm, the diameter of the floor 11 cm, and the entrance hole diameter 2.8 cm.

The blue tit is a colourful little bird, with a grey-green back and crown and blue wings and rump. The underside is yellow and a blue black band runs along the chest. The cheeks are white and bounded by a black and blue band which runs across the eyes, back to the neck, then under and foward to the chin.

The song is a pleasant trilling noise, which begins in spring as the blue tit hovers up and down, often in birch trees, looking for insects. The song and the mating call can sometimes even be heard above the din of city traffic.

In the nesting place, whether an old woodpecker nest or a nest box, he is rather a combative little beggar and almost always manages to secure some living quarters. Great tits often give way to pied flycatchers when they arrive in the spring, but only once in 29 years have I seen a blue tit do this. On the other hand, they cannot manage the wryneck, which will sometimes throw blue tits out of their nest box.

However, if the blue tit has a full clutch of eggs, it will almost always emerge victorious from any combat, the wryneck only rarely getting the upper hand. The tit's brooding behaviour is so strong that it will not leave the eggs. In such cases it will fight to the death if necessary. (Sadly this problem seldom if ever arises in Britain because there are now few breeding wrynecks left.) Even on bird tables it is stubborn and is often at

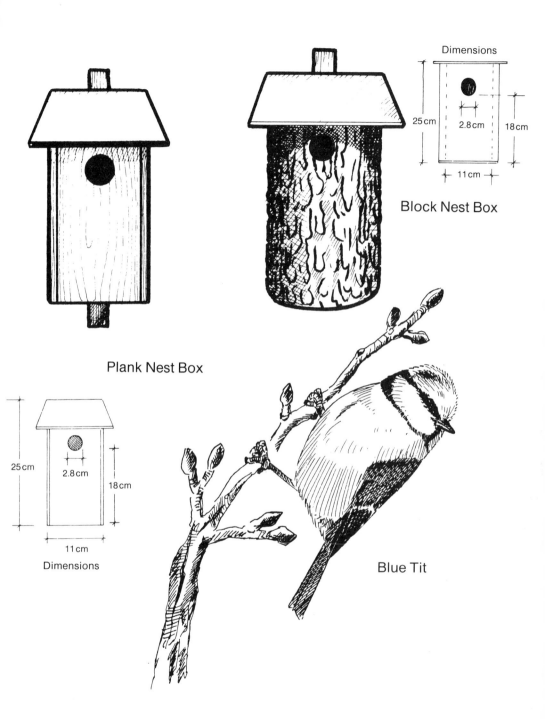

Block Nest Box

Dimensions

25 cm   2.8 cm   18 cm

11 cm

Plank Nest Box

25 cm   2.8 cm   18 cm

11 cm

Dimensions

Blue Tit

49

the front of the queue for pieces of fat or coconut. It can hang upside down for long periods while hacking away at its food.

Most blue tits are non-migratory, but some do fly abroad. They can often be seen in winter looking for pupae on the underneath of leaves. At the beginning of April, the blue tit starts looking for a suitable nesting place, and as soon as one is found, often a nest box if available, building commences. Only the female constructs the nest, which takes around seven days, and involves the fetching of about 4000 small loads of material.

The nest bowl consists mostly of moss and ferns on the outside, followed by horsehair, and finally small feathers and down which the female plucks from her own body to line the nest cup.

Immediately before and after nest building is completed one often sees the male court the female, who vibrates her wings and chirps submissively like a young bird. The female displays herself so as to show that she is not aggressive like another male and to assure him that she will submit herself. The male feeds the female, as if she was still a young bird. It is all part of the mating ritual, but serves a useful biological function in that it increases her protein intake prior to egg formation and laying.

Seven to 16 eggs are laid, with nine being the most normal number. The female lays one egg each morning, and when the clutch is complete the parents begin incubation. The female takes the major share of the brooding and is fed by the male either in the nest box or out in the trees around the nest box. She leaves the eggs unusually frequently during the day, and on some of these occasions the male takes over the brooding, though normally the nest is left empty. Sunshine, the insulation of the nest box, and the warmth of the nest all keep the eggs warm.

The eggs hatch after 12 days incubation. For the first four days the young are fed by the parents between 4am and 8pm on average every eight minutes. Like other tits the blue tits have about ten breaks during the day, of 15–20 minutes each, which means that the pair provide 190 meals per day, each consisting of at least two larvae. After the fifth day, the young receive feeds on average about every five minutes, the parents continuing to take breaks as before. For 14 out of the 18 days that the young spend in the nest, they thus consume at least 10,500 larvae, most of which are harmful to woodland or gardens.

In the final days, the young always sit and chirp at the entrance hole. Whenever the male or female returns with food, the young birds frantically clamber over each other to get at the meal. In 'All-year' nest boxes, where the entrance hole diameter is 3.5 cm, I have sometimes seen three small heads protruding at the same time. Therefore, to shut out

50

other birds and only allow access to blue tits, the entrance hole should only be 2.8 cm in diameter.

When the young leave the nest, their powers of flight are poor, but after only 1.5–2 hours they can fly excellently. They continue to be fed by the parents outside the nest box for a while longer, and keep in contact for a full month unless the parents produce a second brood. Thereafter they join up with flocks of tits.

Marsh Tit *(Parus palustris)*

Plank nest boxes The marsh tit will willingly breed in plank nest boxes made from 2–2.5 cm thick timber. The internal depth should be 19 cm, the diameter of the floor 12 cm, and the entrance hole diameter 3 cm. The floor should be removable to facilitate cleaning. The box should be set 2–3 m from the ground.

In Northern and Eastern Europe the marsh tit often lays two clutches of eggs, and if you have lots of free ground you should set up several nest boxes. The first batch is laid in one nest box and the second in another.

The marsh tit, or to give it its country name, the mouse tit, differs from the willow tit in the not very noticeable black marks on its chin and by the lustre on its black crown. The neck is also a glossy black, the cheeks dirty white, the back grey, and the underside whiteish with grey sides. The male and female are similar.

The marsh tit nests in tree holes or nest boxes. Nest building starts at the end of April, and is carried out by the female only. The materials consist of ferns and mosses, straw, wool, and tufts of hair and the lining is made up from feathers, hair, and down. Building normally takes nine days.

The number of eggs varies from five to nine, with only one batch being laid. The female sits alone on the eggs for 13 days without a break, and if she is frightened away at this time, she will not return.

Both the male and female feed the young, and some maintain that the male is content just to deliver the food which he has collected together to the female, who then distributes it to the young. In my experience, both the male and female feed the young directly.

In spring and summer, the diet mainly consists of insect larvae and spiders which are harmful to the maintenance of woodland, including the eggs and larvae of the pine beauty moth and nun moth, which are among the most feared insects in pine forests. A pair of marsh tits provides food about 500 times per day, and as the eggs of these insects are small, as many as four at a time can sometimes be carried. Study of a

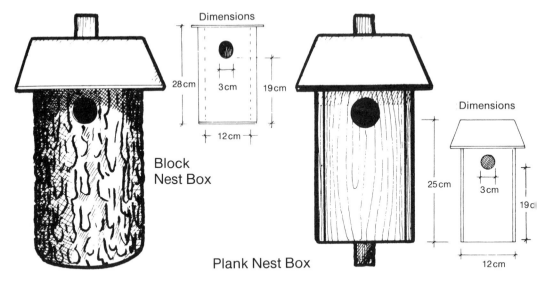

Dimensions

28 cm

3 cm

19 cm

12 cm

**Block
Nest Box**

Dimensions

25 cm

3 cm

19 c

12 cm

Plank Nest Box

Marsh Tit

single marsh tit showed that during one day it collected 1500 nun moth eggs, as well as other food, to feed its young.

The young are ready to fly after 19 days, and the parents continue to feed them for two weeks after they have left the nest. They stay with the parents for five weeks then join up in flocks with other tits, warblers, and flycatchers.

Most of them are non-migratory in the winter, living in flocks in woodland. Some individuals will venture into areas inhabited by humans to feed on sunflower and hemp seed from seed dispensers. They will take seed in their beaks, fly to a nearby tree and place them in the fork of a branch, where one by one they will squeeze the seeds between their toes, hack away the outer shells, and eat them.

Crested Tit *(Parus cristatus)*

Plank nest boxes The crested tit does not frequently breed in nest boxes. Like its relative the willow tit, it prefers to hack out its own nest hole in the rotten wood tree trunks. However, some individuals will breed in boxes, with a preference for those made from 2.5 cm thick timber or wooden blocks. The internal depth should be 19 cm, the side measurement of the floor at least 12 cm, and the entrance hole 3.2 cm in diameter. The nest box needs to have been hanging up in a natural setting for a least two years before the crested tit will use it. The roof and movable floor should be of hardwood.

The crested tit is smaller than the great tit and has a tuft on its head. The back is brown and the underside grey-white, and the two sexes have a similar appearance. The call is a magnificent trilling comprising strings of rolled 'rrr's'. In Britain crested tits are only found in a few areas in the Highlands of Scotland such as Speyside and Glen Affric.

The female starts to build the nest as early as 20th April in Central Sweden. She performs the job alone, producing a soft bed of moss, fern wool, and similar material which insulates well against cold in particular as she lays her eggs early, round about 25th April in Central Sweden, at which time snow can still be lying in drifts.

The nest is finished within five days, after which the female lays one egg per day, to give a total of 4–7 eggs. Brooding lasts for 13 days and is performed by the female only.

Feeding begins as soon as the eggs hatch. The male limits himself to the food he has collected for the female, who then distributes it to the young. The diet consists of pine beauty moth as well as sawfly larvae, leaf

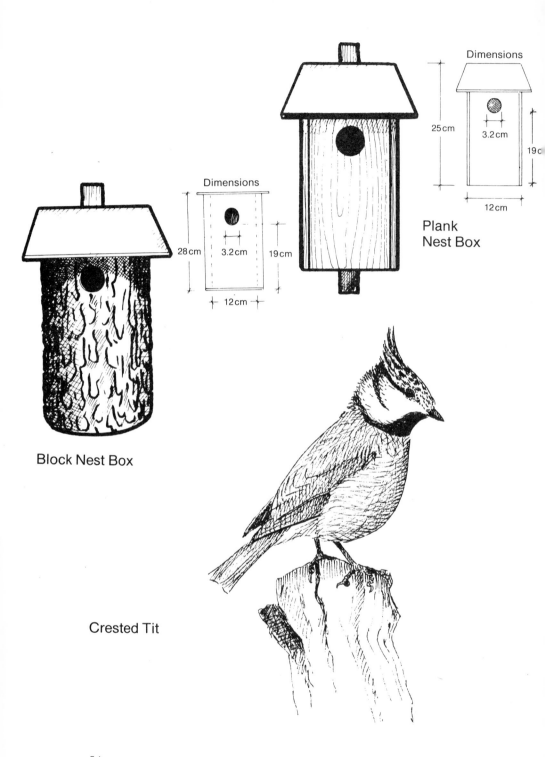

Dimensions

28 cm   3.2 cm   19 cm

12 cm

Block Nest Box

Plank
Nest Box

Dimensions

25 cm   3.2 cm   19 c

12 cm

Crested Tit

54

caterpillar, juniper berries and pine seeds. The latter two constitute the bulk of the winter diet, when the birds are living in flocks.

The young leave the nest after about 20 days and stay with the parents for two weeks, after which time they join up in flocks with other tits. Crested tits are non-migratory, although the first-year birds tend to disperse from the areas in which they were reared.

Coal tit *(Parus ater)*

Plank nest boxes The coal tit likes a nest box with an internal depth of 20 cm, a floor side measurement of at least 12 cm, and an entrance hole diameter of 3.5 cm. If there is enough space available set up several of these nest boxes, as the coal tit often lays a second clutch of eggs. Only once in the past 29 years have I seen the first and second clutch laid in the same nest box. Like other tits, they generally prefer another box in the neighbourhood for the second brood.

'All-year' nest boxes Coal tits have also shown a great liking for the treecreeper model of the 'All-year' nest box.

The coal tit is small and short-tailed, with a large white flash like a half-moon on the neck, white cheeks, and black crown and throat. It looks like a small great tit without the yellow colouring on the breast. The male and female are similar in appearance.

They breed under tree roots, stones, or old stumps and sometimes in nest boxes. Both sexes join in the nest building, which takes about one week to complete. The first egg is normally laid at the end of April or in the first days of May, and the final total will vary from five to ten. As with other small birds, one egg is laid each day. The female alone sits on the eggs, for 18 days, during which time the male feeds her with spruce cone seeds.

The young are fed by both parents, mainly on pine shoot moth and conifer seeds, about 400 times per day. Dr David Lack once made artificial bird mouths from pairs of tweezers and manipulated them from outside the nest to see what coal tit young were given to eat. Each youngster born in the first brood received on average 69 items of food per day, whereas those born in the second brood received only 59 items on average. Leaf eating larvae dominated the menu. However, this research was carried out in groves of woodland where deciduous trees were predominant (Lack, 1966).

The young leave the nest after 18 days and the female often lays a second clutch of eggs straight away, sometimes in the same nest box or

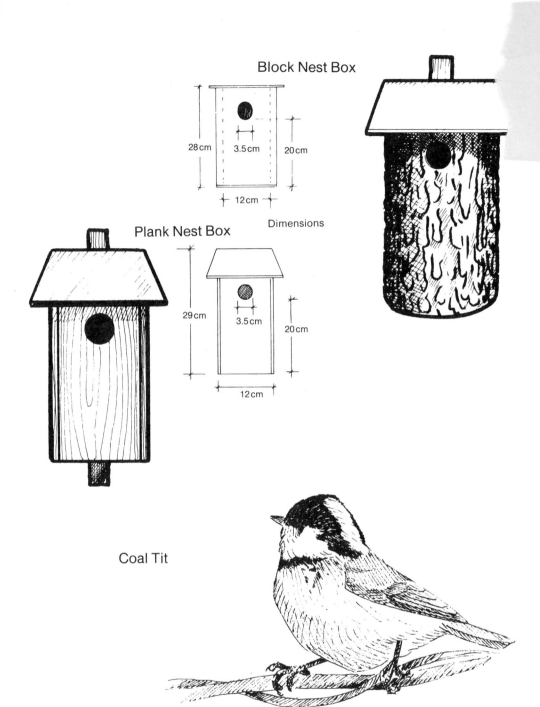

Block Nest Box

28 cm 3.5 cm 20 cm

12 cm

Dimensions

Plank Nest Box

29 cm 3.5 cm 20 cm

12 cm

Coal Tit

otherwise in a neighbouring box. The male then takes over the feeding and rearing of the young from the first brood. After 2–4 weeks in the field, the young join up with flocks of tits wandering around the forest. The coal tit is a non-migratory bird.

Winter studies (Lack, 1966) show that 9/10 of the day is spent searching for food, and on average a bird will spend 24 seconds per tree on this task. Hence, each bird will scour over 1000 trees during an 8-hour winter day. The winter diet consists mostly of moth larvae, which overwinter in the outer scales of pine cones into which they have burrowed. The bird therefore has to peck through the thin outer layer of the scales to get to the larvae.

Many coal tits fall victim to severe cold and snow. Winter is easier for them to cope with if you regularly provide them with fat as food in a specific area of the forest throughout the whole of winter and if you make available a well-insulated nest box in this vicinity. I have previously experimented with the string bags one normally fills with nuts and oranges at Christmas. Unfortunately they are easily ripped apart by crows and squirrels, and I have even known foxes to jump up and bite open the bags. Instead you can wrap some plastic-coated chicken wire around the tallow and tie it to the tree trunk with steel wire or very strong cord. The chicken wire must be plastic covered because small birds have exposed skin between the horny toe pads on their feet, and in very severe cold they might become frozen fast to naked wire.

6   Other small birds which use nest boxes

Nuthatch *(Sitta europea)*

Block nest boxes Nuthatches will readily breed in block nest boxes, measuring 23 × 11.5 cm, and with 5 cm diameter entrance hole.

Plank nest boxes Nuthatches will readily breed in plank nest boxes, preferably made from 2.5 cm thick timber. The internal depth should be 22 cm, the floor side at least 15 cm, and the entrance hole diameter 5 cm.

'All-year' nest boxes In recent years, nuthatches have frequently used the starling model of this nest box. In all cases, the nest boxes used have been facing south.

The nuthatch is a stocky, short-tailed bird, with a straight powerful beak and a black band across its eyes. The plumage is grey-blue on the upper side and white with reddish brown side feathers. The two sexes are almost identical, except that the colours are slightly less pronounced on the female. It is the only bird which can clamber either up or down a tree trunk with equal facility, its head pointing up or down, and with no support from its tail. It is sometimes mistaken for the treecreeper.

In the spring, the male sits in the top of a tree and whistles so loudly that it can be heard from up to 100 metres. The call is so noisy that it is difficult to miss the presence of this bird which breeds in broadleaved woods all over England and Wales, but not in Scotland or Ireland.

Nesting normally takes place in an old woodpecker hole or a nest box. If the entrance hole measures more than 5 cm, the nuthatches will fill it in with wet clay until it measure 4–4.5 cm, and in a few cases 3.5 cm. The clay dries to rock-hardness. Those pairs which I have observed breeding in nests with 3.5–4.6 cm entrance holes have not bothered to carry out any filling in.

In one case, a pair of nuthatches bred for many years in a hole in an old fruit tree. The entrance hole measured 4 cm so only a small amount of filling in was done. Eventually the branch above the hole broke off, resulting in an entrance hole which was far too big for the nuthatches. The house owner fixed a coffee can over the entrance and made a 4 cm

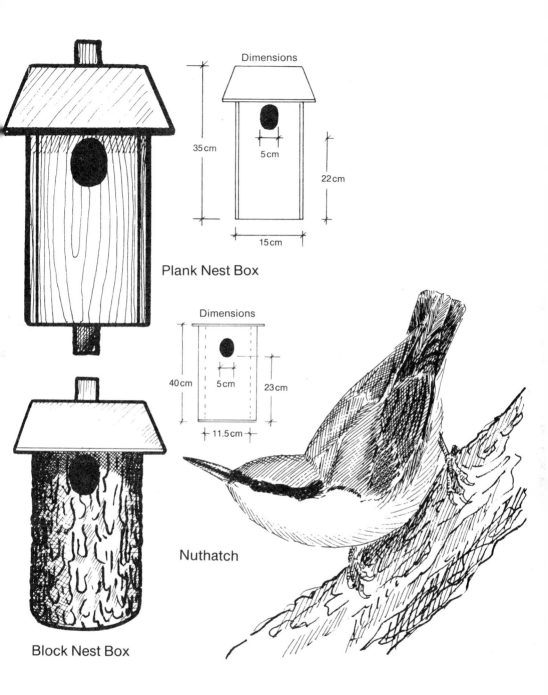

Plank Nest Box

Dimensions

35 cm

5 cm

22 cm

15 cm

Dimensions

40 cm 5 cm 23 cm

11.5 cm

Block Nest Box

Nuthatch

hole in the bottom. This new accommodation was gratefully accepted by the nuthatches which continued to use it year after year. Only a little filling in was needed in the cracks between the can and the tree trunk. Gradually the can rusted apart, and when a 5 cm hole developed in its underside, the nuthatches began filling it in as if possessed. The entire half-kilo coffee can was walled in with clay, as was the entrance hole until it measured 4 cm again. The nesting place was obviously popular, but since the pair were unringed it is impossible to say whether or not the same birds were using the site down the years. They may at some point have been replaced by their own direct descendants who considered that the home of their childhood was the place to be. Perhaps, therefore, we should think twice before we cut down a rotten nesting tree in the forest or a hollow fruit tree in the garden. Think of the shortage in bird accommodation. If one has no choice but to cut down a tree which has been providing such a nesting site, then it should be one's moral duty to replace it with nest boxes.

For nuthatches the entrance hole should be 5 cm in diameter. The male and female will then fill in any cracks and part of the entrance hole itself with wet clay. The male finishes off the latter while the female broods.

The female nuthatch begins nest building around 15th April, and completes her task within 14 days. The nest simply comprises an untidy heap of pine bark flakes. One autumn when I cleaned out a nest, I counted no less than about 600 2–3 cm square flakes of pine bark. The female will sometimes carry 2 flakes at once, but this still involves around 400 trips. Nest building takes place intermittently and sometime comes to a complete halt. Temperature appears to have some influence, and it is thought that in cold weather the hormone which promotes this behaviour is no longer secreted, so building ceases. Generally this activity is at its most intense at the end of April.

The first egg is laid in early May. Like all small birds, the nuthatch lays one egg each morning, after which she leaves the nest for the rest of the day. Brooding begins when the clutch is complete. The eggs often vanish amongst the flakes of pine bark, and a glance into the nest box is rather like looking into a box of cornflakes. Even the newly hatched young are difficult to spot.

Only the female sits on the 6–9 eggs; she does not leave them at any time and is fed by the male with insect larvae and flies. When the young hatch out, they are fed by both parents for 24 days with insect larvae, flies, spiders and beetles.

By the time the young are 8–15 days old each parent brings food (1–2 insects) every 5 to 7 minutes between 4am and 8pm. During a day's feeding the parents will take about 10 breaks, of 15–20 minutes each. Feeding therefore takes place about 20 times per hour, or 252 times per day. During their time in the nest, the young consume about 13,000 insects, many of which are amongst the greatest enemies of the forest industry, as well as a similar number of seeds.

After leaving the nest, the young stay with their parents for about 8–10 days. In August, they join up with flocks of tits. The female and male stay together for the whole year, often in their breeding territory. Few other birds show this degree of loyalty to their mates and their territory throughout the year. Their sharp 'sit-sit-sit' call can often be heard during the autumn and winter, as they maintain contact with each other.

In winter the nuthatch often visits garden bird tables and is especially fond of sunflower seeds. It flies to the nearest tree, wedges the seeds in cracks or forks, pecks them apart, and eats them. Like tits, they hoard lots of seeds in various hiding places in the tree for use when food supplies run short. Tits and nuthatches have their own special hiding places which they always seem able to find again. When a nuthatch arrives at a seed dispenser, it makes violent attacks in all directions causing small birds to scatter in terror. This is an out and out show of strength by the nuthatch, and no bird ever stops to argue the point.

Treecreeper *(Certhia familaris)*

Nest boxes for the treecreeper This bird builds its nests in crevices in bark, behind loosened bark, and in cracks made in trees by lightning or storms. Its nest box should resemble its natural habitat as much as possible, which means that it should sit close to the tree and have a long fissure-like entrance hole measuring 10 cm by 2 cm. The hole should be situated up against the trunk so that the bird can crawl directly in. The nest box should be set up in a glade, about 75–100 cm above the ground and early in the year, as the treecreeper is already starting to choose his territory for the next breeding season as early as September–October. To stimulate breeding, about 20 small dry spruce twigs (5–6 cm long) should be placed inside the box.

'All-year' nest boxes There is an 'All-year' nest box made from wood-cement board specifically for treecreepers. However, it has only one entrance hole (entrance slot) and treecreepers often choose natural sites which have two entrance slots, the second providing an alternative exit. Nevertheless, breeding will occur in this nest box as long as one provides dry spruce twigs.

Natural trunk Treecreepers breed successfully in nest boxes made from natural spruce trunk. The internal depth is 18 cm, the floor diameter 12 cm, the entrance hole dimensions 10 cm high by 3.7 cm wide and the box is placed 1.3 m above the ground.

Plank nest boxes You can build one of these yourself. Hammer together two 2 cm thick planks, 25 cm × 15 cm. Two entrance slots, measuring 10 cm × 2 cm, should be included; the third side, or back of the box, is the tree trunk itself. The roof should be of hardwood and the floor of timber. Some people maintain that breeding will automatically occur if a piece of roofing felt is nailed above the nest box as a shade, but this has never worked for me and I consider this idea extremely doubtful.

Of all our tree climbing birds, the treecreeper is the only one with a long, curved, narrow beak for picking out insects from cracks in the bark. It has small, black peppercorn eyes. The tail feathers are brown, stiff, and pointed to help support the bird as it clambers up the trunk to find food. The treecreeper always starts at the bottom of the tree and works his way up to the top in a spiral fashion, going round and round the trunk. When he reaches a height where the trunk starts to narrow, he drops obliquely down to the foot of the next tree and starts again.

The treecreeper is often confused in name with the nuthatch; the latter is grey-blue in colour, with a strong, sharp beak, and can climb both up and down tree trunks, but cannot support itself on the trunk with its tail.

The treecreeper is one of those few species which chooses its territory very early for next year's breeding season, as early in fact as September–October in the previous autumn. Its song is a very clear, delicate, high-pitched melody, extremely pure and lucid. The mating call is a very high single note.

The nest is built behind loose bark, in outhouses, in cracks produced in trees by lightning and storms, and similar places. The outer part of the nest consists of 400–500 small, dry twigs ; the length of these vary from 5–13 cm, with the most normal length being 5–6 cm. Inside this is a mixture of moss, fern leaves, horsehair, and flakes of bark. The inside is lined with small feathers and down. When built in a nest box, the nest contains only about 250 twigs.

The treecreeper lays 4–10 eggs at the end of April though seven is the most normal number. The female broods intensively, which is appropriate in view of the fact that it is generally cold at this time. The young hatch after 15 days and remain in the nest for 14 days. The female often lays a second clutch of 4–5 eggs. The treecreeper is a non-migratory, but wandering bird which feeds on insects and spiders.

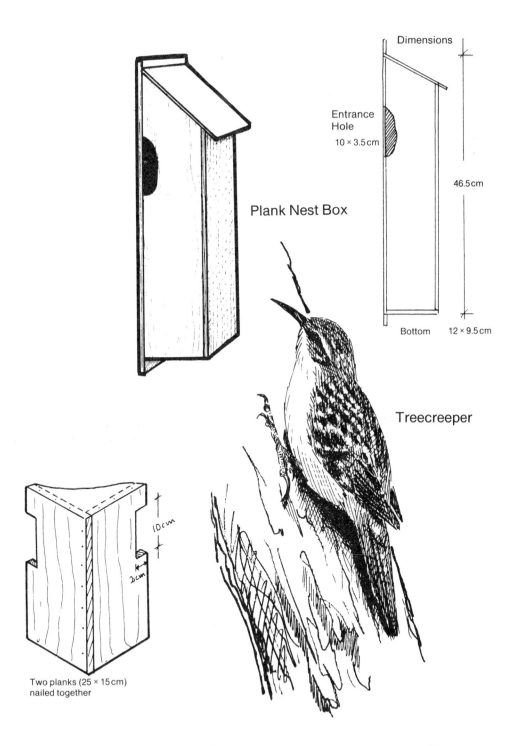

Plank Nest Box

Dimensions

Entrance
Hole
10 × 3.5 cm

46.5 cm

Bottom   12 × 9.5 cm

Treecreeper

10 cm

2 cm

Two planks (25 × 15 cm)
nailed together

If the temperature during winter remains under –20°C for a prolonged period, then the cold will penetrate the treecreeper's night shelter and most of them will die. Therefore it is vitally important that lots of insulated nest boxes are set up for this bird. They can be fed by laying down strips of fat at the base of trees in forest glades. These strips should be no more than 2 cm long and a couple of millimeters thick (see winter feeding,

In very severe winters, like those of the 1940s and 1962–63, treecreeper populations fall to a low level. However, as this bird lays up to ten eggs, and often produces a second brood, the population usually recovers very quickly.

Pied Wagtail *(Motacilla alba)* and Grey Wagtail *(Motacilla cinerea)*

Nest boxes for wagtails can be set up under bridges over rivers, on a pole on the shore of a lake or side of a pond, on a garden or house wall, etc. The box should be 25 cm high, with a 20 cm square floor, and an 8 cm square entrance hole. A little dry grass, reeds or small twigs should be laid inside the bottom of the box, though these are not necessary. The box should sit not more than one metre above the ground.

The pied wagtail is a slim bird with a long tail which bobs up and down. The belly is white, the back and wings grey, and the head white with a black crown and neck. From the throat down to the middle of the breast is a bib; the tail is black with white sides. In Britain and Ireland the males develop completely black backs and the females dark grey backs during the breeding season. On the Continent the pied wagtail is replaced by the white wagtail which is a slightly different race of the same species. White wagtails as their name implies are much paler in colour than pied wagtails and this is especially noticeable on the back which is pale grey even in breeding males.

Pied wagtails are found throughout the country particularly where there is water, but also in parks and gardens. White wagtails migrate to the Mediterranean in August–September, returning to their breeding areas in April and generally arriving at the same time, year after year. In Britain pied wagtails are partial migrants, the first year birds from the north moving furthest south in winter (some have reached Morocco) and adults in the south often not moving at all.

They build their nests in stone walls, wood piles between stones in rock gardens and piles of rocks, as well as in nest boxes. The nests consist of straw, twigs, roots, last year's leaves, and moss, and the nest bowl is lined with hair and feathers. One to two clutches of 5–7 eggs are laid.

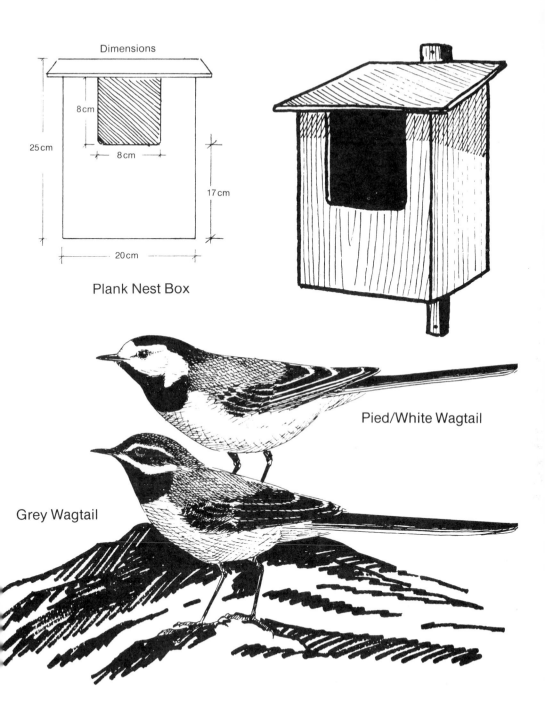

Dimensions

8 cm

8 cm

25 cm

17 cm

20 cm

Plank Nest Box

Pied/White Wagtail

Grey Wagtail

er small invertebrates.

he same design of nest box. This species is associated much more closely with running water than the pied wagtail, although it will nest in gardens within easy flying distance of streams and rivers. It has a pale grey crown and back, a yellow underside and the male has a black bib which is even more pronounced during the breeding season.

Rock Pipit *(Anthus spinoletta)*

The rock pipit nests on or near the ground, often under stones, in grass tussocks, and among the various sorts of debris found on shorelines. It is normally associated with rocky coastlines, and in Britain it is found breeding all around the coast except where the shoreline is low lying marshland or sand dunes, such as in East Anglia.

A suitable nest box can be constructed for this bird. It should be relatively small with a low roof, and quite deep from front to back, so that the bird can crawl inside properly. It should measure 50 cm in length, 17 cm in width, and 10 cm in height. Two 6 × 6 cm square entrance holes are required, one in a corner and the other in the opposite long side of the box. There should be no floor, so that the bird can make a hollow in the grass or gravel. Wagtails have also bred in this design of box.

A simpler form of box can also be used. For this lay a plank (at least 50 cm long) edge down on the ground with its top edge leaning against a block of stone, and steady it with smaller stones. The pipit will use the simple tunnel created between the plank and the slab as a nest site. This simple device works best on sites where there is a grass sward, so that the bird can hide its nest in the tunnel among the grass which as it grows up around the entrances at either end also helps to secrete the nest. This type of nest 'box' is also a favourite with wheatears.

The wooden fish boxes which often wash ashore on tidelines can be used as pipit nest boxes by making a 6 × 6 cm square hole in one corner as well as one in the opposite long side. A stone can be placed on these fish boxes or over the other types of pipit boxes described to secure them against being blown away by the wind.

The rock pipit is bigger and slimmer in build than the tree pipit and has darker legs than the other pipits. Three races are recognised in Western Europe. The water pipit *(Anthus spinoletta spinoletta)*, which breeds around Alpine meadows on the Continent, has a breeding plumage which consists of an unmarked slightly pinkish-white belly, a pale eyestripe and white outer tail feathers. The race which breeds around shorelines in Scandinavia, (*Anthus s. littoralis*), is darker, with brown and olive green shading and a strongly marked underside; and outer tail feathers which are greyish. In the Faroe Islands, the British Isles and north-western France, this race is replaced by a darker, greyer race, (*A. s. petrosus*).

The mating call is sharper and more distinct than that of the meadow pipit, while the alarm call is rather like that of the tree pipit. The song is an unpretentious, accelerating 'si-si-si', which converts to a further 'se-se-se', during the song flight. The rock pipit is very much a coastal bird, which breeds on islands and skerries. The nest is normally well hidden in a rocky crevice or under a large rock, but sometimes it can be found on more open ground, protected by grass, brushwood, or tidal debris.

There are generally two clutches of 4–6 eggs, which have a slate grey base colour overlaid with darker markings. The female incubates the eggs for two weeks and for this period is fed by the male. The young are fed by both parents for two weeks in the nest and remain dependent upon them for a further week after fledging. The diet consists of insects and insect larvae, as well as spiders and in the winter, molluscs, algae and seeds.

Dipper *(Cinclus cinclus)*

In Britain the dipper can be found breeding beside streams and rivers throughout Scotland, Wales and the north and west of England. In Ireland where there is a separate race, the dipper is widespread.

Because of the shortage of really good safe nest sites, especially now that mink have become so common, it can easily be pesuaded to nest in suitably placed boxes.

A square wooden box, 20 cm on all sides with an entrance hole 7 × 7 cm or bigger in the front, should suit the dipper. The box should be placed in as well hidden a place as is possible under a bridge, or by a dam wall or waterfall. In both of these situations if it is possible to place it in the gap behind the falling water then it will be ideal. Many modern bridges have nothing in the way of ledges underneath the span, so that even the provision of a simple shelf may be enough to encourage dippers to nest. A box or shelf high above the water on the smooth concrete wall of a bridge has the added advantage of being difficult for mink and small boys to reach.

The dipper is about the size of a starling, but it has a shorter, more compact body. The back, wings and tail are slatey grey brown, the head

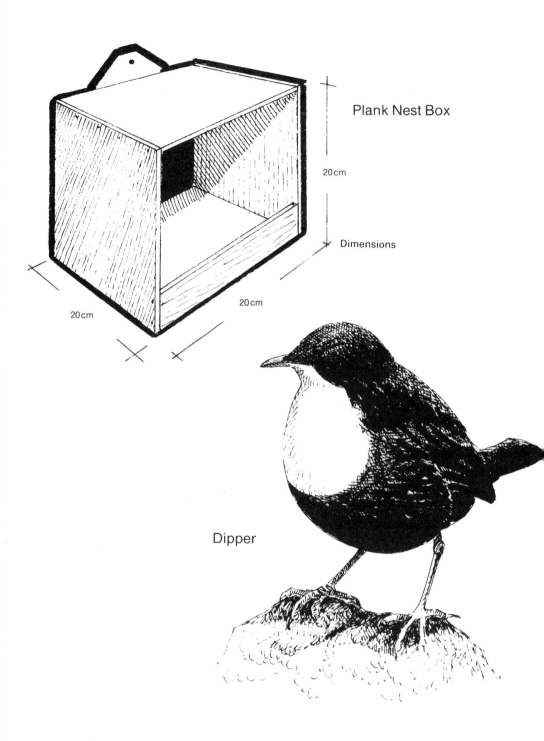

Plank Nest Box

20 cm

Dimensions

20 cm

20 cm

Dipper

brown, its belly chestnut merging to dark brown around the vent. Its most striking feature is the pure white throat and breast. The sexes are alike.

It is to be found near running water, especially by unregulated streams, but also on fish farms and occasionally by the banks of lakes. The food consists of insects, small crustaceans and worms, which it fetches from the bottom of the stream. It is an excellent swimmer and diver, and is remarkable in being able to walk on the river or stream bed, always upstream, while gripping the bottom with its feet.

The dipper always makes its nest near to running water, under bridges and between rocks, or in a hollow on a bank under a tuft of grass or suspended in roots, even behind waterfalls. The nest is a round ball built mainly with moss, with an entrance hole in the front. While the outside may often appear to be sopping wet, inside it is lined with dry leaves and grass. Dippers are early nesters and building often starts in February and almost always by early March. The female lays 4–6 white eggs, which she incubates for 16 days. The young remain in the nest for around 20 days and are fed by both parents. As soon as the young leave the nest they can both dive and swim and it is not long before the young become independent. Dippers usually produce two and often three broods.

In winter Norwegian and Swedish dippers move south into Denmark and Western Europe. A few remain to breed in Denmark though dippers are not common there. These continental black-bellied dippers are a slightly different race from those which nest in the northern and western parts of Britain. They occur as rare winter visitors in the eastern counties where dippers seldom breed and any dipper encountered, for example around a water mill in Norfolk during the winter, will invariably be a black-bellied dipper.

Wren *(Troglodytes troglodytes)*

During the winter wrens will roost in nest boxes which contain old used nests. This happens in tit type boxes as well as in dipper nest boxes. Wrens have also used dipper nest boxes for breeding, with the wrens building their own nests in the boxes.

The nest boxes for wrens do not need to be very big, 15 × 15 × 10 cm being large enough. Once again, the box should be completely open at the front apart from a small ridge 2–3 cm high, to prevent the nest from falling out.

Sometimes large numbers of wrens share the same nest box for roosting in during the winter, and this happens quite frequently in

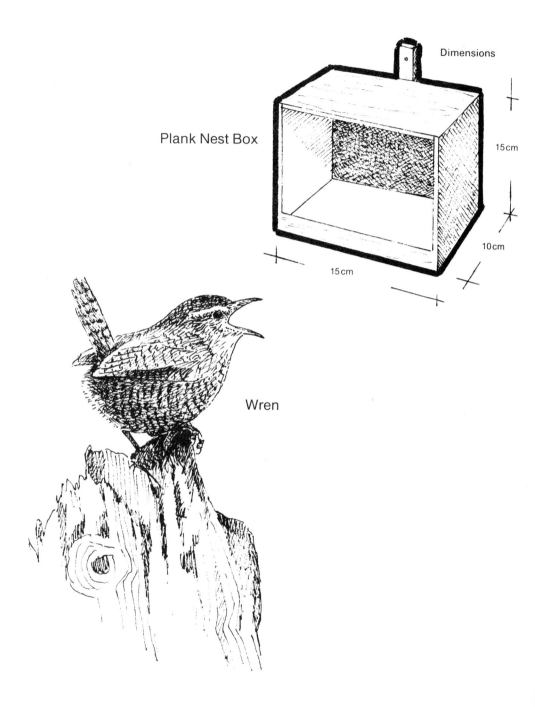

Plank Nest Box

Dimensions

15 cm

10 cm

15 cm

Wren

Britain. Presumably by huddling together these tiny birds are much more able to keep themselves warm during the long and cold winter nights. Where wrens use old dipper nests for this communal roosting the old dipper nest must form a very well insulated site with its vaulted, ball-shaped outer nest made from moss, while the nest proper is constructed from dried grass and thickly lined with dead leaves. It is easy to understand how the wrens can quickly warm up the air in such a nest to a comfortable temperature. In these circumstances one has the exception that proves the rule and it is clearly not always correct to clean out the old nests immediately after breeding if there is the chance that they may be used as a winter roosting site by wrens. Wrens are often common alongside water including dipper streams, a fact which underlines the close relationship between these two species.

After the goldcrest the wren is our smallest bird. It is a stocky round little bird with a short tail which is invariably held cocked up over its back. It is chestnut brown all over the top of the body, head and wings, with fine, dark cross barring, the underside is paler brown. It has a clear gold-brown eyestripe. The sexes are similar in appearance.

The wren can be found living on the ground among leaves and twigs or searching for insects among nettles and other low vegetation, like a small warbler. Its flight is straight and direct, its contact call a short 'zerr', and its alarm call a metallic 'zeck', while the song is unusually powerful, a rushed endless jingling and rapidly warbling stanza of clear high notes. What it lacks in size the wren more than makes up for in noise, and once its calls are learnt these are by far the easiest way to locate wrens which can be found in almost any habitat.

The woven ball-shaped nest is usually built in thick vegetation, among ivy on walls or on tree trunks, in the roots of wind blown stumps, or in holes in walls, or rather like robins in garden sheds, on shelves and in old boxes, kettles and other paraphernalia. The nest is a ball with a round hole in the side, and is normally made from moss, grass and fern leaves. The male wren builds several nests within his territory and only that chosen by the female is finally lined with feathers and hair before egg laying. The 6–7 eggs, which are white with fine dark red-brown spots on the larger end, are among the smallest laid by any European bird, with only the goldcrest and long-tailed tit producing smaller eggs. The female incubates these for two weeks, and in the meantime the male, which can be polygamous, may be busy attracting a different female to another of his nests. The young remain in the nest for two weeks and are sometimes, but not always, fed by the male as well as the female.

Wrens are single brooded.

Starling *(Sturnus vulgaris)*

Plank nest boxes Starlings breed in old woodpecker holes most often those left by great spotted or green woodpeckers in deciduous trees. Because woodpecker populations are decreasing and the trees in which they nest are being felled more rapidly than ever, Swedish starlings are tending to breed more and more in nest boxes. It is therefore just as important to set up nest boxes for starlings as for small birds.

They thrive in plank boxes made from 2.5 cm thick timber. The internal depth should be 30 cm, the inner floor side measurement 17 cm, and the entrance hole 5 cm in diameter.

Those less adept at carpentry can buy the starling models of the 'All-year' and Trivsel-Bo nest boxes.

The box should be set at a height of 3–5 metres and should be facing a field where the male and female can find food for the young. The starling is what can be called a social bird, so nest boxes can be set up near to each other, though not in the same tree. Normally birds need to have their own territory around the nest where they can find food, but starlings nest in one place and fly long distances together with other starlings to look for food in fields and similar places. There is therefore no necessity for guarding a large area around the nest box.

Many starlings from Scandinavia and Eastern Europe move south and westwards in winter, many coming to Britain and Ireland before returning around the end of February and beginning of March. In spring, the male's plumage takes on a rainbow hue, but towards summer he adopts the more brown-black colour of the female, and in late autumn (end of October), the winter plumage takes over.

In the first weeks of April, starlings start to guard their territory, which amounts to no more than the nest box itself and area immediately surrounding it.

The male sings enthusiastically from its tree hollow or nest box. If a female ventures into the vicinity, he goes into raptures, with his song reaching an elevated pitch and his wings flapping frantically. The starling is an imitative singer and often mimics other birds, telephones and even the cries of babies and the noisy whistles of youths.

The singing starling is a manifestation of the awakening of the breeding instinct. Starlings are very loyal to their territory, returning year after year to the same nest box. The male and female stay together only during the breeding season, but because they search out the previous year's breeding territory, it is usually the same female and male which share the same nest box each year.

Dimensions

30cm

5cm

17cm

Plank Nest Box

Block Nest Box

Starling

73

Unlike other small birds, the starling frenziedly clears away the old nest bowl. Many think that all small birds perform this task, both in tree hollows and nest boxes, but it would be impossible for many such small birds to throw out an old nest bowl which has been packed with a batch of noisy youngsters and completely impregnated with droppings. After one winter, such nest bowls often become rock hard. It is true that they sometimes return to the same hollow or nest box, but then they build a new nest over the old one. They will often build in a hole or box nearby. So nest boxes should always be cleaned out after the breeding season has ended, primarily because of parasites which would otherwise become a worse problem each year. When nests are built one on top of another breeding becomes impossible after a few years.

In the case of the starling, we should clear away most of the dirty, hardened nest bowl when the young have left. The male and female both help in building the new nest, which consists of dry grass, feathers, twigs and down.

Starlings for the most part like to be left in peace in their large nest boxes, but in some instances they can be driven away by pied flycatchers or great tits. In one instance a pair of starlings was starting to build a nest for their second brood immediately after the first brood had fledged, when their nest box was besieged by a redstart, which succeeded in driving them out.

Both parents sit on the 4–7 pale blue eggs during the 13-day incubation period, though only the female broods during the night. When the eggs hatch, the male stops his singing and helps the female to feed the young with, for example, earthworms, centipedes, wood lice, and cranefly larvae.

When the young are 14 days old, cleaning up becomes an overwhelming task for the parents. The young turn their rear ends towards the entrance hole and squirt out their excreta, which effectively whitewashes the hole, the nest box, tree trunk, and ground below, making it obvious which boxes are being used at the time.

When the young are around 17 days old, they spend all their time sitting beside the entrance hole screeching, and a mad bout of pushing, shoving and screaming accompanies every attempt to secure a morsel of food when one of the parents returns. On one occasion I observed three heads protruding from a 5 cm diameter hole. They were rather lucky not to find themselves permanently jammed there.

At this time, the parents constantly hover in front of the nest box dispensing food. When the young hear their parents arrive outside the nest, flapping around and calling the mealtime, a furious scrimmage ensues at the entrance hole. The youngster which stretches itself and its gaping mouth out furthest gets the food.

Feeding occurs every seven minutes, from dawn until late in the evening, amounting to about 125 meals per day provided by each parent. Around 15 rest periods of 20 minutes are interspersed throughout the day, giving a total of five hours rest per day.

The parents provide around 1000 items of food each day, and as the young stay in the nest for 21 days, this amounts to an approximate total of 21,000 items. A large portion of these are worms, but a considerable percentage consists of insects which are harmful to gardens and woodlands.

The young leave the nest after three weeks, and for a shorter period than this they stay in their parents' company and continue to be fed by them. This period is marked by a lot of boistrous shrieking throughout parks and gardens, and finishes at the end of June or beginning of July, when the young birds leave their parents and become members of flocks. If a second clutch of eggs is to be laid, breeding recommences after midsummer. The parents stay with their young if they do not produce a second brood.

At this time, starlings do consume some of the berries and fruit in gardens, but for the most part they eat those growing wild, such as rowan berries, sloes, rosehips, and crabapples. You should not begrudge these birds just a few berries from the garden, and it should not be imagined that your berries will escape the starlings if you avoid setting up nest boxes in the garden. Starlings leave the nest box immediately after midsummer and set off on excursions with their offspring. So it is never your own starlings which eat your berries.

Starlings are sometimes regarded as pests in Europe and the USA, where flocks can contain hundreds of thousands of birds. Damage to crops can become significant. Austria has problems with starlings in its vineyards; the birds appear in such large numbers at harvest time in the area around Neusiedler See that a serious loss of grapes can occur. The increasing mildness of winters has meant that more and more starlings have not migrated from the area during winter. Various methods have been employed to combat the problem, including conventional approaches such as bird scarers, and even using aeroplanes to chase away the innumerable flocks of starlings. Hunting by falcons has also been tried, and recently the legal protection which starlings have enjoyed during certain times of the year has been removed in the hope that hunters will be able to help in keeping the population down to an acceptable level.

Starlings also cause considerable damage to crops, for example in Tunisia, where a year or so ago 30 million starlings ate their way through about £1 million worth of olives. Some very unpleasant methods of control have been used in the USA, including spraying the birds with agents which cause them to freeze to death. We have very little sympathy for such methods, and equally little for those in certain European countries where starlings and other small birds are caught in nets and eaten. The bird catchers will often gouge out the eyes of these birds and use them as decoys to attract other birds. These practices come in for a great deal of criticism and attempts have often been made to impose boycotts in those countries where they occur.

By September–October, young starlings assume the appearance of adults with a grey-brown-black plumage, including some white on the breast. Some have already started to acquire the white flecks of the winter plumage. At this stage they look more like thrushes than starlings and people often mistake them for such. However, it is easy to distinguish between the starling's rapid wing beat, which alternates with a gliding flight, and the thrush's slightly undulating flight. The young birds migrate as soon as July–August, but the mild autumns of recent years have meant that more and more of these young starlings have stayed on until October before leaving with the older birds. The adult birds fly to the Netherlands, Belgium, Ireland, Scotland, and above all to England, while the juveniles go to Denmark, West Germany, and France.

In Sweden the number of starlings has decreased markedly in recent years. The real reason for this is not known, but rationalised agriculture and the use of pesticides have possibly both been involved.

Spotted Flycatcher *(Musicapa striata)*

Breeding box A small breeding box can be made for the spotted flycatcher from 2 cm thick planks. The box has 15 cm sides. Three of these sides are 10 cm high, while the back is 25 cm high and supports a protective roof of hardwood. The box should be set up about 2 metres from the ground, preferably in a corner in the angle between two outhouses, or on a wall in amongst a climbing plant such as ivy or Virginia creeper. Those who are less handy can buy a Trivsel-Bo nest box or any of the open fronted type of nest boxes sold for robins, wagtails and spotted flycatchers.

The spotted flycatcher is a grey-brown bird with a long tail and large eyes, both sexes having a similar appearance. Because it tends to be a

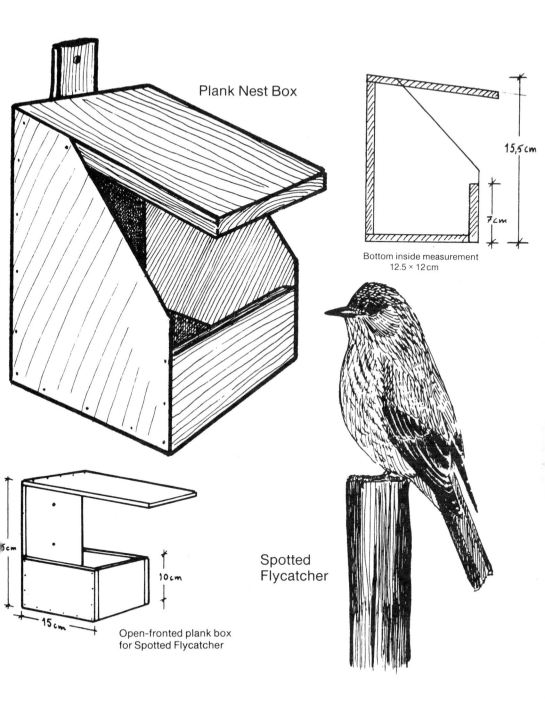

Plank Nest Box

15,5 cm

7 cm

Bottom inside measurement
12.5 × 12 cm

Spotted
Flycatcher

5 cm

10 cm

15 cm

Open-fronted plank box
for Spotted Flycatcher

77

garden bird in Britain it is much better known than the pied flycatcher which is primarily an oak woodland bird.

It is the most taciturn of all our small birds. It lives on flies and midges, and from its vantage point on a fencing post or branch will make sudden attacks on any passing insects before returning to its perch. The spotted flycatcher likes to live in the proximity of mankind, and will build its nest in the most bizarre locations, such as in outside porches, letterboxes, on trellises, inside neon light advertising hoardings, in woodpiles, and inside toolsheds.

Spotted flycatchers arrive back in Northern Europe towards the end of May, an earlier appearance carrying the risk of a shortage of insects, on which they are completely dependent. Its 'zit' like call almost immediately becomes evident around wooded gardens and tennis courts. Insect life in early summer only begins to stir just before midday, as the nights are often cold, so the spotted flycatcher is particularly active during the afternoon and evening. In fact summer evenings often echo with the calls of spotted flycatchers and swifts. The quiet and discreet lifestyle and the subdued colours of the spotted flycatcher make it a rather unobtrusive bird despite its preference for living near human habitation.

The nest is built by both sexes, though mainly by the female, and takes about eight days to complete.

The first clutches usually contain four to six eggs, with only 2–4 eggs in subsequent clutches. Both birds share in the incubation, which lasts for 12 days. During incubation the female sits very tightly and refuses to budge from the eggs, even in the presence of humans. The male is more nervy and makes an 'isst-isst-isst-yepp' warning noise if a human approaches too closely. With most small birds it is normally the female which is more timid.

Once the eggs hatch it is a busy time for the parents with the young holding open their mouths eagerly each time the parents arrive with flies and midges. After seven days, the young are being fed every three minutes, giving a total of 360 meals per day. As with other small birds , the parents take rest periods, in this case totalling three hours per day. At this stage the young are already starting to stand and exercise their wings.

When the weather is bad, the supply of insects is depleted, and as a last resort the spotted flycatcher will resort to eating berries. On migration in the autumn this is less unusual and many warblers and flycatchers gorge themselves on elder and blackberries until they are stained purple around the gape.

The young leave the nest after 14 days, staying with their parents until the end of August. The spotted flycatcher is a night migrant which overwinters in tropical Africa.

Robin *(Erithacus rubecula)*

The robin lives in coniferous and mixed woodland as well as in parks and gardens. It prefers a plank nest box 15 cm square or a block nest box 15 cm in diameter; in both cases the height should be 20 cm, and the square entrance hole should measure 8 × 6 cm.

The box should be set up between 0.5 and 1 metre from the ground, and should be hidden behind overhanging branches or placed inside a bush. Because it is placed so low down the nest box should be attached to a pole rather than a tree, to avoid the nest being plundered by cats and other predators.

The robin often appears in the garden. During spring or autumn digging, it will often be seen hopping around the gardener, carefully scrutinizing every spadeful for something edible.

It is an inconspicuous olive-grey bird, slightly smaller than a house sparrow, with throat and breast coloured a striking orange. The male and female are similar.

Its diet consists of insects, berries, and such like. On the Continent it is a migrant, moving south to Spain and Portugal in winter. As soon as it arrives back in Sweden in March–April, it eagerly attends bird tables. In Britain and Ireland the robins are sedentary and remain close to their breeding territories throughout the year.

If a nestbox is not available the nest is built under bushes or tree roots as well as under brushwood on the ground, but those which live around gardens will use a variety of man made sites such as old kettles, cans or boxes and shelves inside sheds and garages.

In Britain 5–8 eggs are laid from about the end of March to the beginning of June, and sometimes a second and occasionally even a third clutch of eggs will be produced.

Redstart *(Phoenicurus phoenicurus)*

Plank nest boxes The female redstart prefers a shallow nest box which will enable her to keep a watch for and escape from any approaching enemies. The internal depth should be 10 cm, the inner side measurement of the floor 15 cm, and the entrance hole 5 cm in diameter. The roof should be of hardwood.

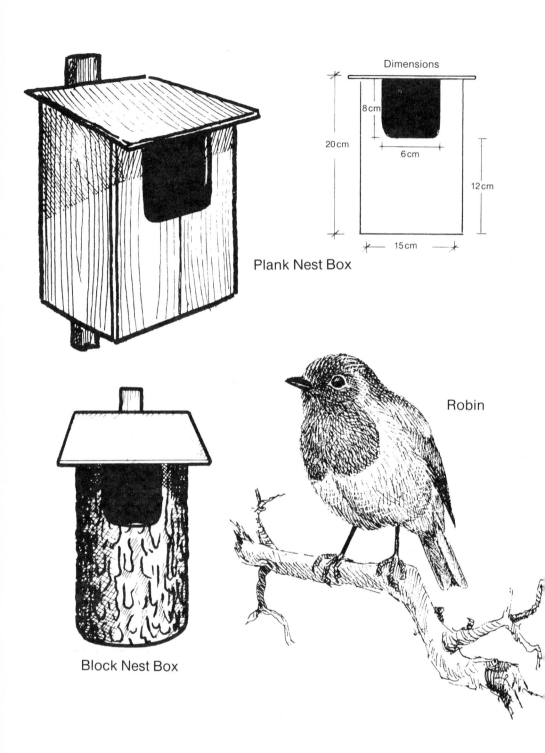

Plank Nest Box

Dimensions

8 cm

20 cm

6 cm

12 cm

15 cm

Robin

Block Nest Box

Plant Pot nest boxes You can also tie a medium-sized clay plant pot to a wood plank with steel wire, so that the bottom of the pot is outside. The small drainage hole in the bottom should be carefully widened to a diameter of 5 cm. This structure is then set up in a tree or on a house wall. It is a very popular form of habitation.

'All-year' nest box The starling version of this box has proved to be well liked by redstarts in my research area.

Trivsel-Bo nest box If you are not skilled enough to build your own nest boxes, you can buy a Trivsol-Bo starling model and set it up for redstarts.

The male redstart has a beautiful red colouration on its breast and tail, with a white blaze and coal black bib. The female is grey brown with a red tail. This exotic gaudy bird seems almost out of place in Europe.

The redstart is very vociferous and highly strung, which is perhaps why the female likes a nest box in which she can peep out through the entrance hole. If you approach near to this nest box, both birds start up a noisy and anxious cry, 'huitt-huitt-teck-teck-teck, huitt-huitt-teck-teck', a sound made by no other bird. And all this time there is a great deal of nervous flitting about and tail wagging.

The males normally arrive at the end of April or beginning of May, and the females follow a few days later. The male begins to defend its territory, and this usually involves violent confrontations with pied flycatchers. Sometimes the latter is victorious and takes over the nest-box, sometimes the redstart prevails.

The female builds the nest alone and takes around five days and 600 flights transporting nest material before it is complete. The nest consists of twigs and roots about 20 cm long, dried grass, moss and dried leaves (mostly birch). It is lined with feathers, horsehair, hair, and wool.

The redstart is very shy during nest building and egg laying, and on several occasions I have noticed that even the smallest of disturbances will cause it to desert its eggs. One should therefore exercise great caution in any dealings with this 'orchid' of nesting birds.

The first egg is laid in mid-May, the completed clutch numbering three to seven eggs. Redstarts are single brooded in Sweden but further south and in Britain two broods are usual. When all the eggs have been laid the female commences 14 days of solitary brooding, and remains with the young in the nest for the first days after hatching.

The diet consists of insects, such as the larvae of pine looper moth, pine beauty moth, and grasshoppers. The young are fed about 370 times

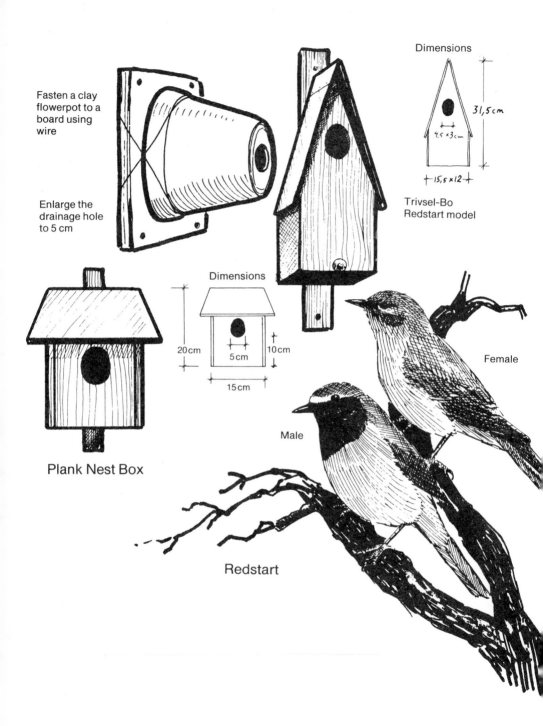

Fasten a clay flowerpot to a board using wire

Enlarge the drainage hole to 5 cm

Dimensions

31,5 cm

4,5 × 3 cm

15,5 × 12

Trivsel-Bo Redstart model

Dimensions

20 cm

5 cm

10 cm

15 cm

Plank Nest Box

Female

Male

Redstart

per day by both parents, who also spend around three hours per day in taking breaks during the feeding operations. The young open their eyes after 6–7 days, and by the time they are eight days old, their sight is fully developed and they stand up in the nest and beg for food whenever the parents appear. After 10–13 days they begin to flutter their wings, start their tails quivering and polish their beaks. They leave the nest after 20 days and stay with their parents, becoming completely independent after about one month.

Our redstarts are night migrant and overwinter in the Sahel scrub zone from Senegal to Ethiopia. Thousands have perished from the same dryness which in recent years has caused such large scale human problems in the same area. To compound the effect of the droughts the destruction of much of the scrub in this zone for fuelwood by the human population has still further reduced its capacity to support many of the species which visit us in summer. In Sweden, as in Britain, the numbers have fallen sharply. Two pairs bred in my research area in 1977, after several years' total absence.

Blackbird *(Turdus merula)*

Breeding box A breeding box can be constructed for the blackbird using 2 cm thick planks. The base should measure 25 × 30 cm, the back and sides should be 25 cm and the front 15 cm high. The roof, which should be made of hardwood, should overhang the front of the box to make it difficult for predators like jays and magpies to reach the nest. This box should be set up in a sheltered position on the wall of a house, garden wall or fence at a height of 1–2 m.

The blackbird is very common. The male is coal black with a yellow-orange beak and eye ring. The female is dark brown with a pale streaked throat and only a little yellow in her brown beak. Both have long broad tails. The song consists of a series of long series of high-pitched, rich melodic and melancholy tones, followed by mellow floating chords and chirping calls. It is slower, more solemn and continuous, and less repetitive than that of the song thrush. The blackbird is a truly beautiful singer. Its warning call is a vigorous 'shuck-shuck-shuck', which towards the end can change to a slightly hysterical scream; it also beats its tail up and down when alarmed.

The blackbird moves over the ground in short hops searching for earthworms, often stopping to flick piles of dead leaves aside in its search. It is an omnivorous bird, living off fruit, berries, insects and bird table scraps as well as earthworms. When the berries of cotoneaster,

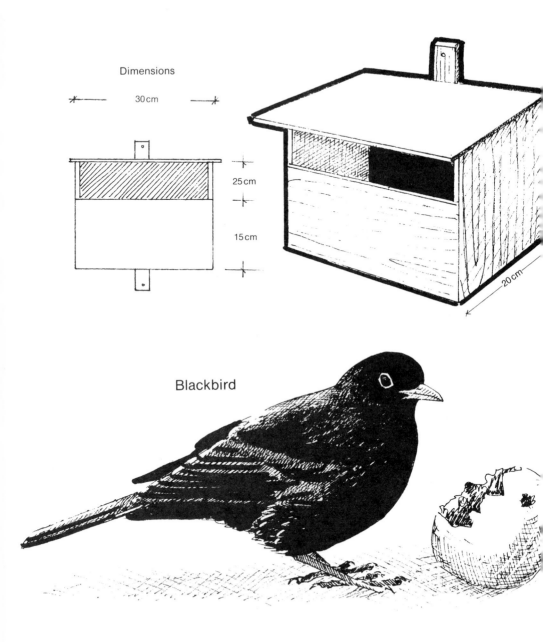

Dimensions

30 cm

25 cm

15 cm

20 cm

Blackbird

elder and rowan ripen in the autumn the blackbird is among the first birds to devour them.

British blackbirds are sedentary although the young tend to disperse from their natal areas. On the Continent blackbirds are migratory, those from the north and east moving south and westwards to winter. Large numbers are still slaughtered each autumn in France, Spain and Italy by so called sportsmen. In Britain the arrival of blackbirds coming in over the North Sea on October and November mornings is an exciting reminder of the reality of bird migration.

Tree Sparrow *(Passer montanus)*

Plank nest box The tree sparrow will breed in a plank nest box with an internal depth of 19 cm, an inner floor side measurement of 14 cm, and an entrance hole diameter of 3.5 cm.

'All-year' nest box Tree sparrows have frequently bred in the tit/pied flycatcher version of the 'All-year' nest-box, and they also have a predilection for overnight stays in the starling version of the box. Pairs of tree sparrows stay together throughout the year and also share overnight accommodation with each other, often with their young from the previous breeding season, so that there may be as many as 5 birds in a box.

Trivsel-Bo nest box Tree sparrows also fare very well in the tit version of this box.

The tree sparrow and house sparrow are often mistaken for each other. The tree sparrow is a more slender bird, and unlike the house sparrow does not differ much between the two sexes, which have a chocolate brown crown and a black spot on each white cheek. The house sparrow is shorter and stockier and has a 'sparrow-like' appearance compared with the more delicate 'finch-like' tree sparrow.

Research has shown that the tree sparrow population in Sweden has recently increased, while that of the house sparrow has decreased. This seems to be due to the tree sparrow being less dependent on man and his building structures than the house sparrow, although with the spread of building it has had to accustom itself to living within human settlements and has done so more successfully than anticipated.

The tree sparrow breeds in rather loose nests built in trees and bushes as well as under roofing tiles and in nest-boxes. Both the male and female build the nest, using materials such as dried grass, down, and feathers,

Dimensions

25 cm

3.5 cm

14 cm

Plank Nest Boxes

Dimensions

26 cm

3.5 cm

9.5 cm

Side: 12.5 cm

Tree Sparrow

Female

Male

House Sparrow

which often fill the entire nest box so that the nest bowl itself needs to have an entrance hole. The nest is reminiscent of those freely hanging nests which weaver birds construct in the tops of trees in Africa. These birds are in fact a close relative of the tree sparrow.

Three to six shiny eggs covered with dark brown and grey spots are laid. Often one egg has a very different colour from the rest, which also happens with the house sparrow. Why this happens is not known, but the odd egg is not, as many seem to think, a cuckoo egg. Both parents share the 14 days of brooding, and once hatched the young stay in the nest for 12–15 days, being fed by their parents, mostly with insects but also with seeds. Unlike the house sparrow, the tree sparrow takes insect larvae from the canopies of trees during summer.

As with the house sparrow, things are very lively as soon as the young leave the nest. They follow their parents around, begging excitedly for food, which they are given on the ground in the form of weed seeds. One can approach very close to them at this time because they are so totally engrossed in feeding.

At least two and often three broods are produced each season.

During autumn and spring they join up in flocks with house sparrows. Those flocks of grey-speckled birds which feed on weed seeds during late summer and autumn are generally dominated by tree sparrows, and one often sees flocks consisting totally of tree sparrows making pathways towards seeding weeds, with their tails sticking straight up. If they are approached at this time, they will immediately take off with a sharp rush of wings. The tree sparrow goes to roost later than the house sparrow and can still be heard chattering away in the twilight.

It is the only bird which actually builds a nest to overwinter in. It is almost as finely covered a nest as that in which breeding takes place, though it is never built in the same nest box. The male and female overwinter here together. The first year birds of the family usually stay together during the winter, often spending the nights in starling nest boxes, sometimes in gangs of four or five. Like their parents, these young birds also build winter nests in October.

When tree sparrows come to feed at the bird table during winter, the adult birds always attend in pairs. Their favourite food is hemp seed, the beak being used to remove the seed's outer husk. They often fall victim to salmonella poisoning which has become rife in recent years, most especially among those birds which visit bird tables or food dispensers during the winter.

So do keep feeding places clean and use food dispensers which are easy to clean and with which bird droppings fall onto the ground and not onto the food . This should prevent the spread of infection from one bird to another.

House Sparrow *(Passer domesticus)*

Plank Nest Box House sparrows will readily breed in plank nest boxes with an internal depth of 20 cm, an inner floor side measurement of 15 cm, and an entrance hole diameter of 3.5 cm.

'All-year' nest box The tit/flycatcher model is very suitable for house sparrows provided that the entrance hole diameter is at least 3.5 cm.

Trivsel-Bo nest box House sparrows fare well in the tit model of this box.

The house sparrow and tree sparrow are often mistaken for each other and the surest way of telling them apart is the house sparrow's lack of cheek spots. The male has a grey crown, is short and stocky, sparrow-like, and with a black bib. The female and immature birds are grey-brown. In rural areas the diet in spring and summer consists of grass seeds, and so the house sparrow tends to do especially well in arable areas where cereal fields provide a veritable feast.

The eager chirping of house sparrows in thick hedges as early as February and March, especially on sunny days, is one of the first signs of spring. It is a pleasant and cheerful sound and infects us city dwellers with its joy at a time when the depression of a long winter still hangs over us. House sparrows mostly nest under roof tiles, but also in nest boxes. The male tries to entice the female to his nesting place with a keen 'tship tship tship' call, and sometimes violent fights ensue between males over the favours of females; so absorbed may they become in these battles during the spring that they fall victim to cats or magpies. The nest is a rather slovenly affair, consisting of feathers and grass straw, but the inner chamber of the nest is very delicately constructed.

Four to five eggs are laid and incubated by both parents for 14 days, and after hatching the young remain in the nest for a further two weeks. At least two clutches of eggs are laid each year.

During autumn, adults and young all go out in search of food, living mainly on seed from agricultural fields on the outskirts of built-up areas. These excursions often take them far from the protecting bushes and hedges which they normally inhabit when not feeding. At any sign of danger the whole flock instinctively acts together, so that when one bird takes off the rest follow suit, forming a swarming cloud. When this happens on roadways, the motorist may be startled, but one can usually avoid running over any birds by easing off on the accelerator. Young house sparrows have rather poor powers of flight and no previous experience, and so are particularly at risk from fast-moving cars.

The male and female stay together throughout the year, and also share the company of other house sparrows in flocks outside of the breeding season. They will often come to feed at bird tables during the winter, though they do prefer a hedge to be nearby in which they can shelter in the event of a sparrowhawk appearing. Sparrowhawks often try to kill small birds at feeding tables, and once they have discovered such a site within their hunting territory their visits may become almost daily.

Like many other small birds, the house sparrow is susceptible to salmonella poisoning, particularly in mild winters. Predation by sparrowhawks is quite effective in removing many of the weaker, chronically diseased birds, thus helping to stem the spread of the disease.

When a sparrowhawk strikes, the house sparrows will dart as quickly as possible to the nearest hedge and scramble into the centre where they cannot be reached. There is always one bird in a feeding flock keeping watch, and as soon as he moves, the rest are off too, at great speed. Healthy sparrows generally do not fall victim to the sparrowhawk's attacks.

The house sparrow often roosts in nest boxes, outhouses, and under roofs during the winter. At the Wessels department store in Malmo, a male house sparrow lives above the bird seed department, which is quite a nice place in which to pass the winter. His eager chirpings can be heard echoing around the roof beams.

House sparrows, which are often referred to as 'rats of the air', are thought to have originated in the African savannahs. They have been so successful in association with man that they have now colonized almost the entire planet. They have learned to live as parasites on the human agricultural community. The birds have taken over those areas left empty by the withdrawl of man into towns and cities, and only in certain areas have they abandoned the countryside themselves. Through their unique form of group living and their ability to adapt, they have become one of the most common birds in the world.

House sparrows are just as successful as town birds. They can be a veritable nuisance in town cafeterias during the summer, giving plenty of justification for the 'rats of the air' label. Even in our gardens, they learn quickly when they are likely to receive crumbs or titbits from the coffee table . They sit up in the guttering and chatter away enthusiastically. If a piece of bread is dropped on the ground, they will swoop on it one by one, until it is covered in a carpet of house sparrows. They are entirely dependent upon each other and have learned to live and react collectively in order to survive.

House sparrows are thought to be infested with a certain number of insect parasites and to be spreaders of disease, but for the most part this is just a nasty rumour. Few birds are as clean as these. They will gladly take a dip whenever they come across a pool of water or a bird bath maintained by some thoughtful person. Even in the middle of winter, they will have a bath at the first opportunity.

To get rid of their insect parasites house sparrows make a small hollow in the soil of flower beds or in the sand in sand boxes, and throw up the soil or sand so that it falls between their feathers. At the same time they ruffle their feathers and turn round and round in the soil. This is certainly a very effective way of removing parasites, and one may sometimes find a children's sand box chock-a-block with house sparrows going through their toilet. The parasites die immediatley after leaving the warm body of the bird, so there is no need to worry about children picking up any of these pests.

House Martin *(Delichon urbica)*

Removing natural nests in the autumn House martin nests often fall down during winter. This does not matter and in the long run may be better for the birds. Where they remain 'in situ' until the following spring they are almost invariably occupied by the more aggressive house sparrow before the martins have returned. Secondly, after being subjected to the winter frosts they are loosened and more fragile than when freshly made, so that even if the martins do reoccupy them there is a risk of tragedy if the nest falls once the eggs have been laid or the young hatched. Finally, once used house martin nests are lousy with parasites, and by having to build a new nest each year they do at least get a clean start. For all these reasons, if the used nests are still complete at the start of winter it is a good idea to take a long pole and knock them off the wall.

Sawdust and cement nest boxes House martins can be attracted to breed on houses by setting up nests cast out of sawdust and cement. These are strong and provide good insulation. They also help the martins get off to an early start with breeding because of the time the birds save in not having to build a mud nest or even in waiting for rain to create muddy puddles, if they are in areas away from streams or ponds. These nests measure 17 × 16 cm with a hole 5 cm in diameter.

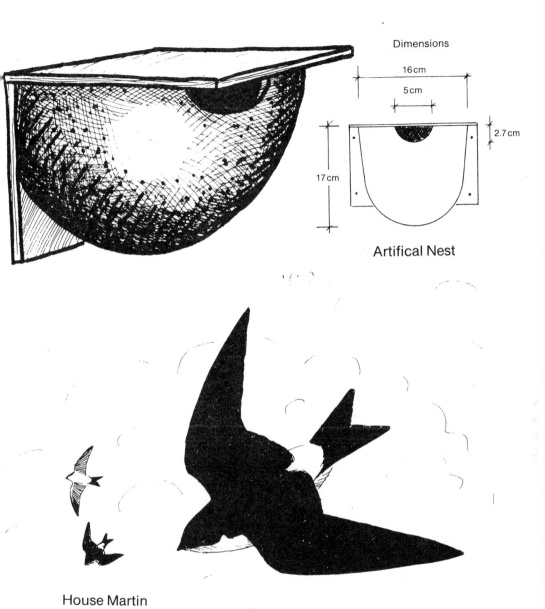

Dimensions

16 cm

5 cm

17 cm

2.7 cm

Artifical Nest

House Martin

The house martin has a blue-black upper side with a snow white breast, white upper rump, and a tail forked half way along its length. It has short small legs and the feet which end in claws are coated with snow white down, as with owls. It is the only small bird with this characteristic. Its call is a pleasant 'chattering'.

Both the male and female collect mud from the margins of puddles, pools, and stream sides, taking large amounts into their mouths. Most of their building occurs between 10am–12pm, 3pm–5pm, and 8pm–9pm, the morning shift appearing to be the busiest. This results in a fragile nest which is then reinforced with feathers and straw, to give a strong enough structure to support the weight of the whole family during breeding. After nine days they have built about 5 cm, and within 15 days the back and half the front are finished. The nest is completed in around three weeks, although this may depend upon the availability of mud. In dry summers the house martins can be greatly helped if you keep a muddy puddle supplied with water.

House martins lay 4–5 completely white eggs. They are double, or in good seasons, even treble brooded. Both sexes share the incubation which lasts for 14 days. The young are fed on midges and flies. After several days the young ones turn themselves round so that they can excrete through the nest opening. The availabilty of food varies greatly between warm, dry summers and cold, rainy ones; the pile of excreta under the nest can be quite considerable during warm, dry summers but very small during cold summers. After three weeks the young fly out of the nest, though they return regularly for a further week and are fed by their parents, sometimes inside the nest and sometimes hanging outside it. From the middle of September they begin to leave, although in Britain the last stragglers may still be around in the first few days of November. House martins spend the winter in South Africa, but in contrast to swallows there have been few recoveries of ringed birds, and much remains to be discovered about their whereabouts in winter.

Making sawdust and cement nest boxes Breeding in artificial nests proceeds in the same way as described above. To produce an artificial nest, first make a wooden mould the same shape as the interior of a natural nest, and remember to leave a small bulge at the front to form the entrance. The mould should be made so that the nest cup formed by it is about 14 cm wide, 6 to 8 cm deep, and the entrance is 7.5 cm wide and slightly over 2 cm deep. The mix used should be of well dried sawdust with sand and cement, using either lime or a commercial plasticiser (washing up liquid is just as good, and much cheaper) to make the mixture easy to mould. The 'boxes' can then either be air dried, or fired in an oven to give them strength. Firing is not essential, and with a little experimentation it is possible to make up a mixture which is just as strong after a few days' air drying. Normally it is easier to partially dry the 'boxes' on the moulds and remove them once they are strong enough to do so with out breaking them. They should then be left for several more days to dry and strengthen completely. Finally this cement cup should be glued to two strips of hardboard, one to form the back, the other the roof. The finished boxes can then be fixed up under the eaves of buildings using screws put through holes drilled in the outside corners of the hardboard backing strips. It is important for licensed ringers who will want to be able to get access to the nestlings, to leave a semicircular opening, 8 to 10 cm across, in the top strip of board just above the nest cup.

If you are not confident enough or do not have the time to try making these artificial house martin nests they can be bought in Britain from Nerine Nurseries, Welland, Near Malvern, Worcestershire WR13 6LN.

The mortality rate amongst all species of small birds is extremely high, and among house martins is probably 70–80% in the first year. As a result, new lodgers will turn up quite often in artificial nests, although, as with other summer visitors, it is always exciting to discover through ringing just what proportion of the previous year's birds do return to the same nest site after their globe trotting migrations.

Avoiding problems caused by nesting house martins Many people are irritated by young house martins 'shooting' excreta out of the nest. If the nest is situated over the entrance to a house, this can become a bit inconvenient. Many nests are deliberately torn down by people who don't want their paths, windows, or steps showered with fledgling excreta. This can be avoided by strategic placing of chicken wire under those parts of the eaves where a nest would be inconvenient. If despite everything, a nest is situated in an inappropriate place, then a board can be placed underneath it. This should be sufficient to intercept the bombardment. But it should be set up with great care, making sure not to block the house martin's entrance or exit. It is not necessary to tear down the nest if a little care is exercised in this way.

Swift *(Apus apus)*

'Starling' nest box Swifts need to be provided with nest boxes to breed in because as more and more old buildings are pulled down and replaced with tidily roofed new houses there are fewer sites available to them. At one of my friend's houses two pairs live under roof tiles as-well as another two living in nest boxes set up on walls. One of these boxes is situated 5 metres from the ground on a veranda wall, and the swifts fly expertly through fruit trees in order to reach the entrance. The other is set at a height of 4 metres, with free access across open fields. The internal depth of both boxes is 23 cm, the side measurement of the inner floor 20 cm, and the entrance hole diameter 5 cm. The front piece is made from 2.5 cm thick unplaned wood, which the birds are able to clamber up. The roughness of unplaned wood is essential for without it, swifts have been known to die in the box because they were unable to get out, and many maintain that the internal depth should be no more than 7 cm so that the birds are able to leave the box.

The nest boxes are cleaned out once the swifts and their young have left, and a handful of dried grass is placed inside. A plastic lid is then fastened over the entrance hole with a drawing pin to prevent starlings from breeding there, an event which would lead to fighting in the following spring. The lid is removed as soon as the first swift is spotted round about the middle of May.

Wooden nest box Swifts will also readily nest in oblong or square-sided wooden boxes. These can be fixed directly under a roof on the wall at the end of a house. They should have an internal depth of 30 cm and an internal floor side measurement of at least 15 cm. Dried grass should be placed in the bottom to stimulate breeding.

Square-sided boxes can also be set up in groups of four on the gables in barns. These boxes should be 30 cm deep, with a side measurement of 20 cm to 25 cm and an entrance hole diameter of 5 cm.

Block nest box Swifts will also nest in hollowed out sections of tree trunks. These so-called block nest boxes should be 30 cm deep, with an inner floor diameter of 20–25 cm, and an entrance hole diameter of exactly 5 cm. It is absolutely essential that a 12.5 cm layer of dry moss be placed at the bottom. Where moss is not available, wood shavings or rotten wood may be used instead. Swifts are highly evolved as efficient flying machines with sickle shaped wings and torpedo shaped bodies; even their eyes are set back in streamlined grooves. They are brown-black all over except for a pale whitish throat patch. Swifts spend their whole life in the air, even sleeping and mating there. They are the last of the summer visitors to return from their winter quarters, arriving back in early May.

Starling-type box for Swifts

Dimensions

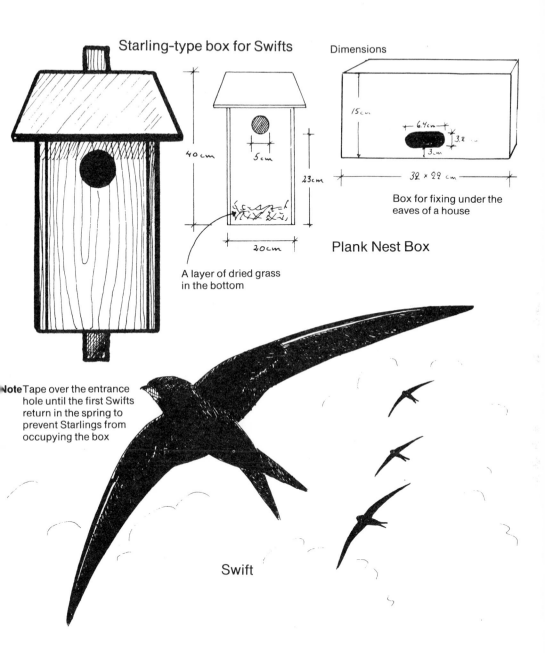

40 cm

5 cm

23 cm

20 cm

A layer of dried grass
in the bottom

15 cm

6.4 cm

3.8

3 cm

32 x 22 cm

Box for fixing under the
eaves of a house

Plank Nest Box

Note Tape over the entrance
hole until the first Swifts
return in the spring to
prevent Starlings from
occupying the box

Swift

The swift nests under roof tiles on barns and houses. To set out from the nest it needs to have sufficient height to launch itself into flight otherwise it will fall to the ground. The feet have only three forward-facing claws, which are barely enough to walk with. It uses these for clinging to walls for periods of a few seconds.

In Lapland, the swift breeds in woodpecker holes, and sometimes, in central and southern Sweden, in starling nest boxes. It is an excellent flyer, and it can be seen to flash by with great speed and precision in and under the roof tile or into its nest hole. The speed can be as high as 100 km/hour on the immediate approach to its nest, before it reduces its speed to zero almost at the last moment.

At a stretch it can reach around 140 km/hour, and in August, just before they leave to return to their winter quarters in Zaïre, they gather in small parties which rush in and out of the streets and around the houses at a dizzying pace, making a screeching call. During this behaviour they fly round over and over again as if taking part in some social game. It is amazing to see the superlative ease with which they avoid colliding with trees and houses in their crazy flight. This manner of flying normally involves a rapid beating of the wings followed by a gliding action in which the spool-shaped body comes into its own. Over water, the swift will glide over the surface with its wings held aloft and dip its beak to drink.

This bird does not make an actual nest, but rather scrapes together whatever it can find under the roof tiles and what it can snap up out of the air during flight, including pieces of grass, feathers and bits of down. A transparent, quick-drying and hardening spittle is used to glue things together. The swift is a close relative of the East Indian cave swiftlets which make the so-called edible birds' nest soup.

Two elongated eggs are laid, and occasionally three. The female broods for 18 days. The swift captures its food by flying around with an open beak, collecting small insects. Research in England has shown that a single pair can catch and carry to their young around 22 000 insects per day.

The young are fed only at certain times with cherry-sized balls of mucous and insects. In a good summer the young are ready to fly after one month, but in poorer summers this takes 6–8 weeks.

During bad weather the parents can fly hundreds of kilometres in search of food. At times when other young birds are dying of starvation, young swifts can survive by lowering their body temperature, but when the summer is very cold and rainy, even this technique cannot save them from starvation.

Once a swift has managed to reach the adult stage it can live to a ripe old age, with 17 years being the oldest known in Sweden. The average rate of reproduction is one youngster for every breeding pair each year, but this is clearly sufficient to maintain the population level.

Wheatear *(Oenanthe oenanthe)*

Pipe nesting tunnels Cement or iron piping measuring about 12–14 cm in diameter and about a metre in length can be laid in areas frequented by wheatears. The piping is then covered over with earth after digging a small nest chamber at its end.

Convex roof tile placed over a small crevice Wheatears build their nests in holes and crevices in walls or in scree. To stimulate breeding I have laid a convex roof tile over a small cleft and stuffed it with moss. This has not, however, so far found favour amongst the wheatears in the few years it has been here, though it is used with great enthusiasm by a field mouse as a winter store room. Bits of gnawed hazelnuts bear witness to this. Nevertheless this type of set up has in other instances been used by wheatears.

The wheatear has an ash grey back, orange and white breast, a black band across the eyes, as well as black-grey wings and tail tip. It is a nervous and shy bird which lives on open ground and nests in natural or in man-made stone piles and dry stone walls. It is often to be seen standing on a stone, looking round; then it many drop to the ground and bounce forwards with a lightning fast hop on its long black legs. Occasionally it will come to a dead stop and take some prey with a crouching dive. Should any human approach their territory, both the male and female let out a nervous 'huitt-huitt-huitt' cry and rapidly flit from place to place so that one seems to be surrounded by a whole flock calling out in warning. If the nest itself is approached, a vigorous 'sheck-sheck-sheck' warning is heard and the birds bob up and down a great deal.

The wheatear flies very low and fast over the ground and can be recognized with certainty by the bright white colour of its inner tail.

Six to seven eggs are laid and both parents take part in the 14 days of incubation; the hatched young remain in the nest for about 14 days and are fed by both parents with various insects.

They stay with their parents for about three weeks after leaving the nest. In September, the wheatears migrate down through France and Spain on their way to tropical Africa where they overwinter.

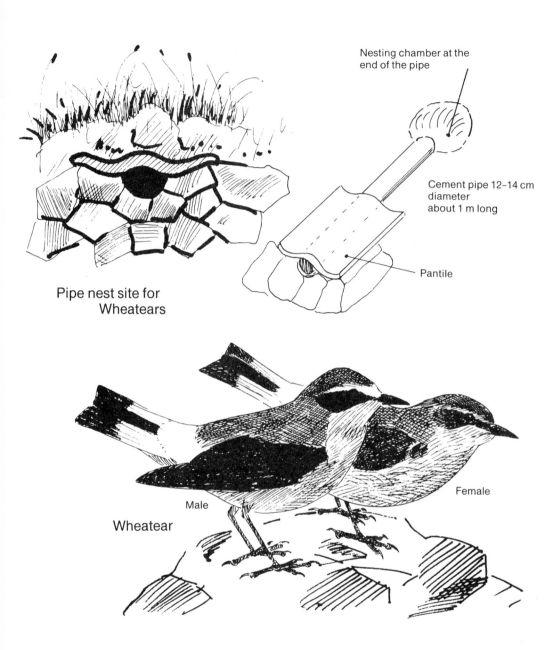

Nesting chamber at the end of the pipe

Cement pipe 12–14 cm diameter about 1 m long

Pantile

Pipe nest site for Wheatears

Wheatear

Male

Female

7   Woodpeckers

Because of modern forestry methods in Sweden, woodpeckers have lost many of the trees which provide them with both homes and food, and find themselves in a very vulnerable position, but can be helped with nest boxes. The situation is most serious for the grey-headed woodpecker in south and central Norrland and the white-backed woodpecker in Dalalven. The middle spotted woodpecker has disappeared completely from the oak woods of the Ostgota plain. Experiments with artificial nest boxes have shown them to be acceptable nesting places for woodpeckers, and the great spotted woodpecker and black woodpecker have been breeding in them for some time, while attempts have been made to encourage the three-toed woodpecker to use them. The wryneck, which is the only migratory woodpecker, has long been a well-known user of nest boxes in Sweden. In Britain there are only three species of woodpecker, excluding the wryneck which as a breeding bird is on the extreme fringe of its range, and is now only represented by a handful of pairs. While few people have tried to entice woodpeckers to breed in nest boxes, the species which seems most likely to do so is the great spotted woodpecker, which also is the most common and least threatened in population terms.

Woodpeckers as pests When old nesting holes are no longer fit for use or have disappeared through tree felling, woodpeckers take up new ones in winter or spring for nesting or roosting. Damage can be caused to timber houses, wooden poles, and even bird nest boxes. In each case the reason behind the behaviour is likely to be different. Cedar shingles on houses may attract attention if there are large numbers of bluebottles overwintering beneath them; telegraph poles are sometimes selected as drumming posts in spring; and nest boxes are most often chiselled open when they contain nestlings which the woodpecker will prey on occasionally. Damage of this kind is infrequent, but can be serious enough for those who encounter it. If one thinks there is a chance of the nest boxes being damaged, they can be made with a plastic front, for example from an old formica kitchen surface.

Wryneck *(Jynx torquilla)*

Plank nest-boxes The wryneck breeds in plank nest boxes, most often in the starling model, which has an internal depth of 25 cm, a floor measuring 17 × 17 cm, and an entrance hole 5 cm in diameter. It has bred in my research area in a tit nest box measuring 20 cm, 11.5 × 11.5 cm, and 5 cm, respectively; this, however, can be regarded as an exception.

'All-year' nest box for starlings This box is also very popular with wryneck, which during the last five years has bred in such boxes in my research area.

The wryneck belongs to the woodpecker family though it lacks the supporting tail other woodpeckers use to help climb up tree trunks. The wryneck sometimes slithers up, but most often sits, on the upper sides of branches which are inclined slightly upwards. Sometimes it will even sit across a branch, like a passerine (perching bird) and unlike other woodpeckers. However, the wryneck does have the characteristic long tongue of the woodpecker for reaching ants. The scansorial foot has two toes facing forward and two facing back, yet another indication of its relationship to woodpeckers. The toes are shorter and blunter than those of other woodpeckers, making it difficult for the wryneck to clamber up trunks.

In some respects the wryneck has a similar appearance to the nightjar, with a dark band running down its back, while the underside is lighter and crossed by wavy bands. The two sexes are similar. It is a difficult bird to spot, often sitting close up against a tree trunk and merging with its surroundings. However, it is clearly betrayed by its loud, repetitive 'ty-ty-ty-ty' call.

It returns from its winter quarters in April, and in May the male and female begin an eager exchange of calls. Because of the delicacy of its beak, the wryneck is unable to chisel out a nest cavity and needs to find an old nesting hole or a nest box. It lives on ants and their eggs, and because of this tends to be rather late in starting to breed so that generally all nest boxes and nesting holes have already been taken up by other birds by the time it starts to search out a nesting site. When the wryneck is ready for breeding it flies round on an inspection tour of all the available nesting places in the vicinity. This usually causes great disturbance amongst the tits and pied flycatchers, with wrynecks swarming around like hornets. This inspection can sometimes be so thorough that both nest and eggs or young of the other birds are thrown out.

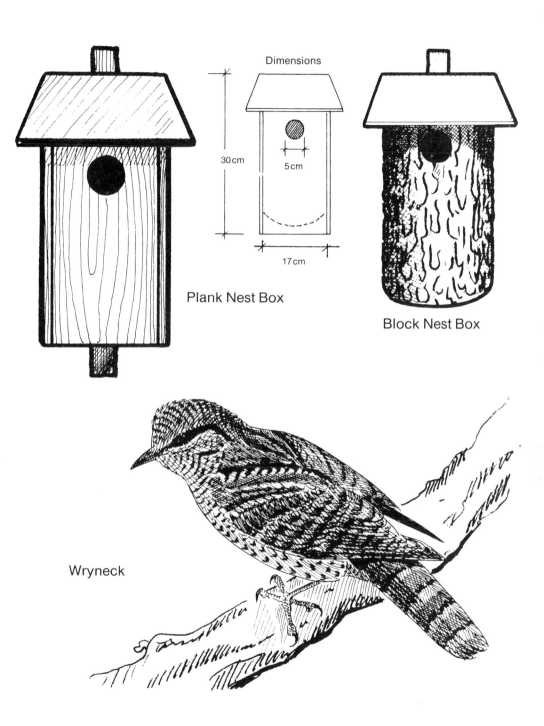

Dimensions

30 cm

5 cm

17 cm

Plank Nest Box

Block Nest Box

Wryneck

101

Eventually, a nest box is selected and peace returns to the area. The wryneck is very quiet and careful during breeding and so is not often seen at this time. If one approaches too near the nest, the bird will stretch out its neck and head, and twist them from side to side like a reptile, while the crown and tail feathers move up and down.

At the end of May, 7–10 shiny white eggs are laid although the colour is duller than that of other woodpecker eggs. Only one clutch is laid. The eggs are laid directly onto the bottom of the nest box, and are incubated by both parents for 14 days. Unlike other woodpeckers, the wryneck leaves the egg shells in the nest. The young are naked and blind when born and are very noisy, making a loud screeching noise even when their parents are away. By the time they are almost ready to fly this noise has acquired the quality of an unoiled machine. They intertwine their throats and warm and support each other. By the beginning of July there is almost always one youngster to be seen sat at the entrance hole begging. The young are fed with ants and their eggs, which the parents capture with their 6 cm long tongues. In feeding, the youngster will stuff half its head down into the parent's mouth to take the ants which will have taken up to one hour to collect.

The young fly from the nest after about three weeks, and accompany their parents for about two weeks, before separating. At the end of August they migrate to tropical Africa, being the only European woodpecker to migrate.

Green Woodpecker *(Picus viridis)*

The green woodpecker is not a true nest box bird, but nevertheless can breed in boxes and sleep in them during autumn and winter. Normally it will peck out its own nesting hole from the decayed interior of a broadleaved tree. A nest box for green woodpeckers should be about 60 cm high, with an internal diameter or side measurement of 15 cm and an entrance hole diameter of about 6 cm.

A small quantity of wood shavings should be placed in the box before it is hung up at a height of 3–4 metres.

The green woodpecker has a gaudy plumage, with a green upper side, grey-green underside, yellow on the upper side of the rump, and a vivid red on the top of the head. The female has a black moustachio stripe and the male a red one.

It flourishes in deciduous and mixed forests as well as in parks and gardens. In Britain it is only found as far north as the Highland

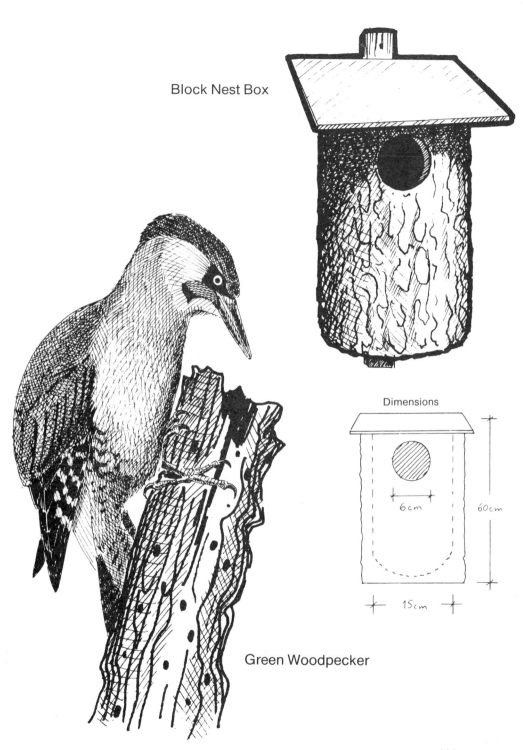

Block Nest Box

Dimensions

6cm

60cm

15cm

Green Woodpecker

103

Boundary Fault line. It does not occur in Ireland. In the north of Sweden its place is taken by the grey-headed woodpecker.

It is a noisy bird that for almost the whole year maintains its loud penetrating 'kly-kly-kly' call, which fades out towards the end. It also drums by drilling its bill against hard dry wood very rapidly to produce a loud resonating noise which carries across the forest, especially during the spring.

Five to eight shiny white eggs are laid in May and incubated by both parents. The young leave the nest when three weeks old but return at the first sign of danger or to sleep overnight.

The diet consists principally of ants and their larvae and pupae, and in winter the green woodpecker can be seen gouging large holes out of wood ant heaps to reach the inhabitants. Other insects and their larvae are also eaten, and on some occasions even berries. Whereas the adults are non-migratory, the young do wander.

Black Woodpecker *(Dryocopus martius)*

If a nest box is set up where a black woodpecker has pecked out a nesting hole or roosting hole in the wall of a wooden house or outhouse, it may be persuaded to accept this as a nesting place. The box should be made of planks, with an internal depth of 40 cm, an inner floor side measurement of 20 cm, and an entrance hole diameter of 10 cm. It should face south and be placed at the height where the damage has been found. Boxes can also be set up in areas where black woodpeckers have been seen.

The black woodpecker is our largest woodpecker and is coloured black all over apart from its red crown. Its loud, energetic call can be heard from a distance, and its flight is the undulating one typical of all woodpeckers. The wing action produces a clear and distinctive sound which can be heard from quite a long way off. Its drumming in spring is longer and louder than any of its relatives, and its springtime call of 'kty-kty-kty' is like that of the green woodpecker, though louder. Like other woodpeckers, it is a rather curious, nosey bird, and any intruders will be subjected to a very keen visual inspection. The scratching sound made by the powerful claws can be heard clearly as the bird clambers up tree trunks. It is especially fond of pine weevil larvae and will peck energetically at old tree stumps to get them.

The shortage of suitable nesting trees has caused the black woodpecker to resort to using the poles carrying power lines. Like the great spotted woodpecker, it can sometimes be seen drumming around a loose plate it may have found on a telegraph pole during the springtime,

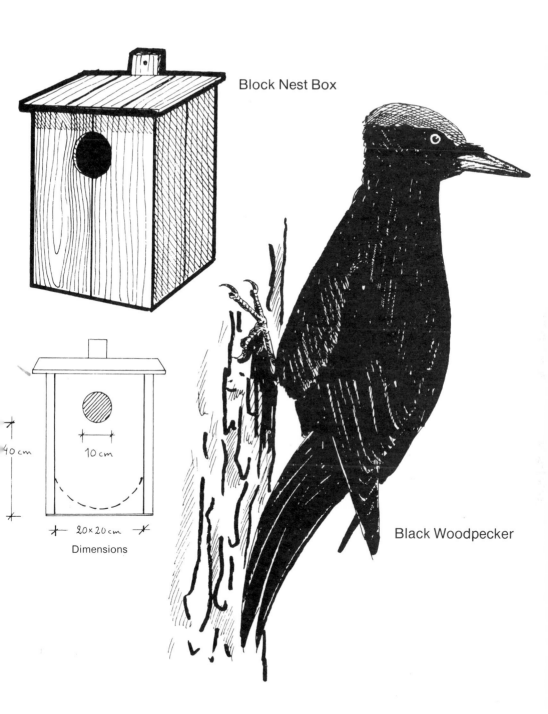

Block Nest Box

40 cm

10 cm

20 × 20 cm

Dimensions

Black Woodpecker

105

and this drumming can be heard over a distance of about one kilometre. The nest hole would normally be chiselled out in a healthy spruce or pine tree at a height of 5–10 metres. The entrance hole has a vertical oval shape, with a diameter of approximately 10 cm. The nesting cavity is somewhat pear-shaped, as with other woodpeckers, though much deeper (as deep as one metre), and will contain wood shavings at the bottom, where the eggs are laid. Both parents incubate the eggs for about 14 days. The young start to stand up at an early stage by working their feet against the cavity wall, and for this reason nest boxes should be made from thick wood and the inner walls should be grooved or roughened a little before the box is nailed together.

The black woodpecker is a non-migratory but wandering bird and sometimes during the winter large numbers of them can be seen around the golf course at Falsterbo Bird Observatory, looking for food. In some years they almost have the appearance of an invasion force.

Like the wood grouse and goshawk, it is a typical inhabitant of old coniferous forests, which is why its numbers have been severely depleted in Sweden where this forest type has been cut back as the forestry industry has extended and rationalised its operations; though as yet the species is not in danger of extinction.

Great Spotted Woodpecker *(Dendrocopus major)*

This is the woodpecker which most people recognize and which actually prefers to live in the vicinity of human habitation. It will often come to eat tallow at bird tables during the winter and is also very fond of the white flesh of hanging coconut halves. These birds can be helped by setting up plank nest boxes with an internal depth of 25 cm, an inner floor side measurement of 12 cm, and an entrance hole diameter of 6 cm.

It normally chisels out its nest in the decayed interior of aspen, giving it an entrance hole of about 6 cm in diameter. The young are fed with insect larvae; they jostle frantically and whistle hoarsely whenever their parents arrive with the food. This is somewhat reminiscent of the starling's hectic family life.

The great spotted woodpecker is a black and white bird, with large white shoulder flashes and a blood red ventral area; the male bird also has red on the back of the head and juveniles have a red crown. The flight is undulating, as with other woodpeckers and its loud drumming comes in short, fast bursts, like a drum roll. In summer it feeds on ants and pupae from the soil, larvae from trees, etc., while in winter it mainly eats the seeds from spruce and pine cones. It can be seen hopping around like

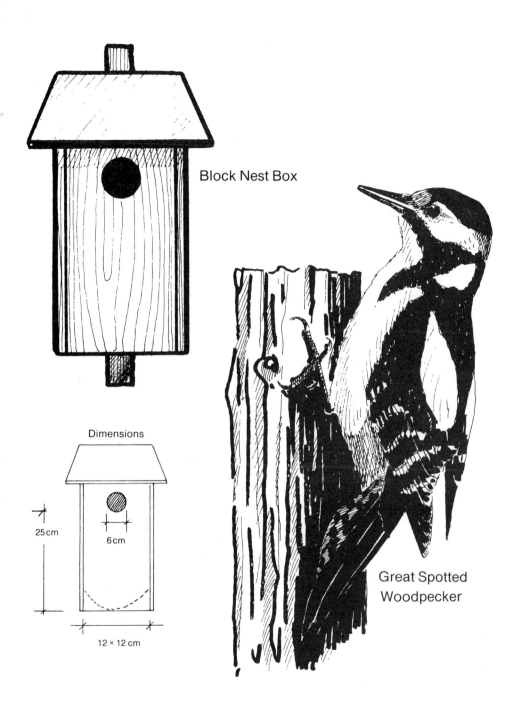

Block Nest Box

Dimensions

25 cm

6 cm

12 × 12 cm

Great Spotted
Woodpecker

a parrot far out on pine branches or amongst spruce cones. It will grab hold of a cone with its foot and, with a well directed stab, cut loose the cone and take it in its beak. It then flies with the cone to a so-called 'smithy' in the vicinity, where it wedges it in a crevice in the bark or a hole which it has created in a fork, tree trunk or a telegraph pole. The bird then hacks away at the cone to get at the seed. A large pile of used cones can often be seen under these 'smithies'.

The great spotted woodpecker is a non-migratory but wandering bird, which appears in large numbers in certain years.

Three-toed Woodpecker *(Picoides tridactylus)*

This woodpecker prefers a block nest box made from spruce, with the bark left on most especially spruce with a decayed interior. The internal depth should be 25 cm, the total height 35 cm, the inner floor side measurement 12–14 cm, and the entrance hole diameter 4.5 cm. The box should be placed 0.6–2.5 metres above the ground.

Virtually all the nest holes made by the three-toed woodpecker in nature are used the following year by pygmy owls, and like other woodpeckers this one pecks out a new nest hole each spring. The three-toed woodpecker and pygmy owl prosper in large forests, and as long as reasonable portions of these forests remain, it is helpful to set up nest boxes and encourage this woodpecker to breed in them. The pygmy owls also need these boxes as there is a shortage of the three-toed woodpecker nest holes on which they depend for breeding.

The yellow band on the male's crown is an excellent way of identifying this bird. It belongs to the coniferous forests of Norrland and needs lots of dead trees if it is to thrive. Totally debarked pine trunks are a fairly common sight in such forests. This bird specializes in eating bark beetles and chisels out its nest hole in the usual woodpecker manner in the decayed interiors of tree trunks, preferably pine. It is a non-migratory but wandering bird, which also makes an occasional appearance in central Sweden.

In the Arbyskogen nature reserve at Eskilstuna, a three-toed woodpecker chiselled out a series of holes in a spiral from the bottom to well up the trunk of a pine tree one winter. This spiral has holes at regular 1 to 1.5 cm intervals and will stand as a reminder of the species for decades to come.

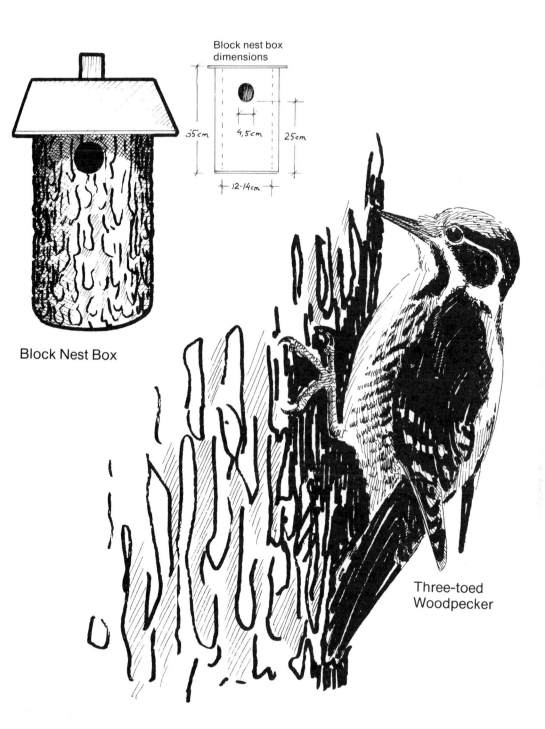

Block nest box
dimensions

35cm 4,5cm 25cm

12-14cm

Block Nest Box

**Three-toed
Woodpecker**

8 Large birds in nest boxes and helping burrow nesters

Hoopoe *(Upupa epops)*

The hoopoe occurs throughout Europe, though not regularly in Holland, Denmark, Scandinavia or Britain and Ireland. It is mainly a species of the drier southern European countries and there is little chance of getting it to breed in a nest box in Britain. However, in recent years the species has spread a little northwards, and as it seems quite willing to use nesting boxes, it is worth a try, though perhaps more so for ornithologists with holiday homes in the south of France or in Spain than anyone living further north.

A wooden box or hollowed out tree trunk 40 cm high, 15.5 cm square or in diameter, with an entrance hole diameter of 6.5 cm should be suitable. A little sawdust on the floor of the box is an advantage. The height at which the box is sited does not seem to be important, though to avoid predation by small mammals or snakes it is advisable to put it at least 1.5 m above the ground.

The hoopoe cannot be mistaken for any other bird. It is about the size of a mistle thrush, though more slender. Its body is a light rust-brown colour, its tail and wings black barred with white. The beak is long and curves down slightly. On its head the hoopoe has a crest of black tipped feathers which it can raise and lower like a fan.

Its cry is deep and very distinctive and can be heard from far away: 'upp-pupp-pupp', and once heard is never to be forgotten.

The hoopoe is to be found where permanent grass is criss-crossed by hedgerows or broken by lines of trees. The old common lands on the Continent used to be one of its favourite habitats.

It often breeds in natural holes in trees, holes in walls between stones and even in holes in banks, as well as nest boxes if available.

The 5–8 eggs are usually laid in May. No nest is built and the eggs are laid directly onto the cavity floor. Incubation is by the female alone and lasts for about 18 days. During incubation the male brings food to the sitting female. The male also brings food while the young are small and the brooding female distributes this to the chicks. Later both parents fetch food for the nestlings.

Block
Nest
Box

Dimensions

40 cm   6.5 cm   23 cm

15.5 cm

Plank Nest
Box

Hoopoe

111

The food consists of insects, for example mole crickets, beetles, caterpillars, and in the northern parts of its range especially, grasshoppers. Hoopoes can be seen seeking food on dry sunbaked grass fields, where it flicks over cowpats to find the insects hiding beneath.

The hoopoe is a summer visitor to Europe and in September or October leaves to overwinter in tropical Africa, returning at the end of April or in May.

Stock Dove *(Columba oenas)*

Plank nest box The stock dove prefers a plank nest box with an internal depth of 35 cm, an inner floor side measurement of 25 cm, and an entrance hole diameter of 12 cm. A little soil or leaf mould should be laid on the floor to a depth of 5 cm. Several nest boxes should be set up on broadleaved trees in groves. The boxes should be near to each other but not on the same tree, as the stock dove has a tendency to breed in colonies.

The stock dove is blue-grey in colour and is smaller than the wood pigeon, from which it also differs in not having any white on its throat and wings. Like the tawny owl, it lives in tree groves with a preponderance of broadleaved trees. As mentioned above it lives in small colonies, and occasionally as isolated pairs, and uses old nesting holes made by the green and black woodpeckers, as well as artificial nest boxes. The black woodpecker generally makes its nesting hole in a different place each year, whereas the green woodpecker often hacks out a new hole each year in the same tree. Small colonies of stock doves are often found in these empty nest holes.

In Sweden this bird has experienced an unprecedented drop in numbers, possible reasons for which are the continuing decrease in the woodpecker population and in old trees suitable for nest holes, as well as increasing competition from the significantly more aggressive jackdaw, to which the stock dove comes a poor second. Jackdaws take most of the vacant nest holes in and around agricultural areas, and because of the shortage of holes the weaker stock dove sometimes has to wait until the jackdaw's young have left their nest in mid summer before it can breed. As a consequence, only one clutch of eggs is laid, rather than the more usual 2–3 clutches.

In contrast to the decline in Sweden, in Britain and Ireland the species has been expanding both its range and numbers since the early 19th century, apart from a short period of decline during the early 1960s, when like many other farmland birds it was badly affected by

Dimensions

Block Nest
Box

Plank Nest
Box

12 cm

12 cm

50 cm

25 cm

25 cm

Stock Dove

113

organochlorine seed dressings. In spring the male and female start to circle around a vacant nest hole in elegant aerial play. Finally, the female lays her two white eggs directly on the nest hole floor. In nest boxes therefore, a small quantity of sawdust or decayed wood from a tree stump should be placed on the floor.

The call consists of about ten rapidly repeated koos (koo-koo-koo). Both parents incubate the eggs for about two weeks and the young remain in the nest for around three weeks. They are fed with grain seeds, green leaf parts, and some insects. Scandinavian stock doves migrate to France and Portugal in October, but those in Britain and Ireland are apparently non-migratory.

Jackdaw *(Corvus monedula)*

Plank nest box The jackdaw sometimes breeds in nest boxes and, more often than not, in colonies, so several nest boxes should be set up, preferably in wooded pasture in the vicinity of cultivated land. Excellent accommodation is afforded the jackdaw by a plank nest box with an internal depth of 35 cm, an inner floor side measurement of at least 25 cm, and an entrance hole diameter of 12 cm.

Once a pair bond has formed between one-year old jackdaws, the male and female stay together faithfully all their lives. Everyone at one time or another must have seen a pair of jackdaws huddled together on a chimney to enjoy the warmth of the smoke.

In May jackdaws begin their courting, and their fast and skilful aerial games during the spring courtship are a joy to behold. All the arts of flying are displayed here, including looping and the falling leaf, with a constant sound of 'kjaa-kjaa-kjaa' being emitted. Their aerial displays capture the attention of many an admiring onlooker and help to draw a veil of forgiveness over some of their less likeable traits such as the blocking of unguarded chimneys with their nests.

Because of the jackdaw's tendency to live in large flocks, its droppings can cause annoyance and so it is sometimes considered, along with the feral pigeon and black-headed gull, as an insanitary nuisance in built-up areas.

It will often breed in nest boxes, but is most accustomed to using church towers, holes in trees lining motorways, and chimneys. Four to seven eggs are laid in May and incubated by the female only for 18 days. The young remain in the nest for four weeks. The jackdaw lives off both plant and animal food, which it seeks out in fields and meadows at considerable distances from the nesting place. Life in the colony is

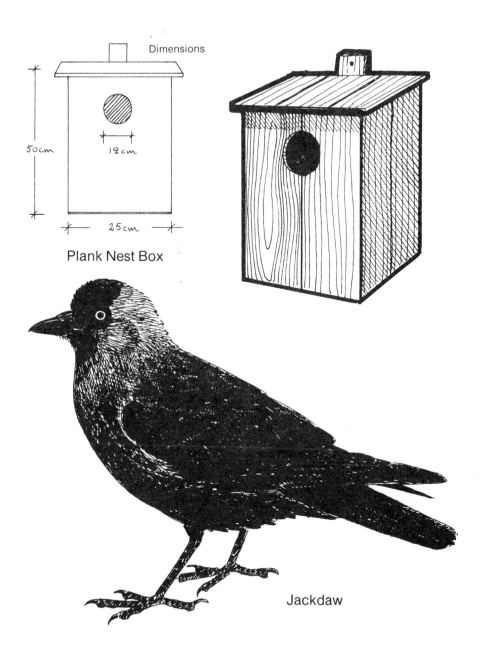

Dimensions

12 cm

50 cm

25 cm

Plank Nest Box

Jackdaw

115

deafeningly noisy during the night as well as the daytime. The nest consists of twigs and the bowl is lined with wool, thread, hair, grass, straw, and rags.

Outside the breeding period, the jackdaw will roost in or near its nest site and fly out in the late or early morning to find food with the other members of its flock on nearby farmland, although like other crows and gulls, it is increasingly turning to our food-rich waste tips for its pickings.

Kingfisher *(Alcedo atthis)* and Sand Martin *(Riparia riparia)*

There are many species which do not breed in nest boxes or artificial nests but which can be helped indirectly to find good nesting places, and these include the kingfisher and sand martin.

The kingfisher digs out its nest tunnels in river banks and occasionally in the faces of sand quarries near to water. If one excavates a part of a river bank to give it an almost vertical slope, this will ideally suit the kingfisher, which will then dig out its tunnel and nest chamber in the bank. If there are kingfishers in your area, you might consider this course of action.

The kingfisher's size is midway between those of the sparrow and starling. Its head is disproportionately large and it has a long spear-like beak. It is a dark grey-green on its upper side which shines with a shimmering green-blue, while the underneath is red-brown, the chin white, and the cheeks brown and white. The feet are small and the tail very short. It flies over the surface of the water and often sits on a small branch from which it dives into the water below the water for small fish. It is a shy bird, and often one can catch no more than a flash, as it were, of blue 'jewelry' as it speeds past. It has an exotic appearance and is a veritable pearl amongst our birds. If on a frosty, sunlit, snow-covered scene, you spy this blue 'diamond' sitting in the sunshine, it is a sight you will never forget.

In contrast the sand martin is a rather sombre pale brown bird with a pale whitish underside. In contrast to the completely feathered feet of the house martin, those of the sand martin are scaley with just a few vestigial feathers between the toes. Like the kingfisher it breeds in sand and gravel pits and in exposed sandy banks beside river bends, which must have been its natural nest site before man started excavating sand and gravel. It digs out its tunnel and nest chamber in the same way as the kingfisher and can be helped by keeping the sides of old disused gravel pits free of vegetation and cut back so that sufficient vertical face is available. Once the faces of sand pits have started to erode and collapse they soon become unsuitable and too low for the martins to feel secure. Unfortunately many sand pits are valuable as land fill sites and this destroys them permanently as nesting sites. Even if left, many owners feel constrained by current safety legislation to level off the vertical faces of disused sand quarries, which is equally disastrous for the sand martins. After having been a fairly common bird in Britain and Ireland in the 1960s, the sand martin is now at an all time low, largely it is thought for the same reasons which have affected the other birds which over-winter in the Sahel zone of Africa (see under redstart).

9   Ducks in nest boxes

Ducks can also be helped to breed through the provision of nest boxes. The nest box should be set up in a tree near to the bank of a river or stream for mergansers or goldeneye. But for mandarin ducks and mallard the boxes should be set up on trees near to still water like ponds and lakes. As an alternative to boxes on trees most surface feeding ducks like mallard will accept a basket set on poles just above the water. A decoy anchored on the pond or lake will attract ducks if they are not already used to visiting it. In Scandinavia fishing folk have always made such decoys for use in hunting, but unfortunately this fine old tradition is dying out. Many of these decoys were finely crafted by hand and painted in the traditional manner. You can make them yourself, or you can buy some excellent models made from plastic at reasonable prices in various hunting and sports shops. A decoy can be anchored in place using a piece of nylon line tied to a weight.

The mating games amongst the small flocks of ducks and mergansers occur on the water and these normally take the form of rather involved rituals. After this the female often flies along the shore or even into woodland in search of a suitable nesting hole. The nesting place can be a natural cavity in a hollow tree, a nest box, a duck basket, or a nest box, or in Scandinavia even an old black woodpecker nest hole.

As with owls, sawdust should be hard at the bottom of the nest box, so that the ducks have some soft material in which to form the nest cup. The female plucks a large amount of down from her own body to line the nest cup. If there is down around the entrance hole in a nest box or tree hollow, then one should be very careful, as this indicates that the nest is occupied and incubation is taking place. Most birds will not return to the nest once frightened from it.

Within the nest box itself, grooved rungs must be nailed to the front side under the entrance hole, otherwise the young ducks, with their webbed feet will have great difficulty getting out. Deep nest boxes without such provisions have tragically become death traps for large numbers of young ducks, which could not clamber out and which were only discovered when the boxes were cleaned out.

The young stay in the box for 1–2 days. After hatching, the female flies around the neighbourhood to check that everything is quiet and there are no predators nearby. She then lands on the ground or water below the nest box and calls eagerly to the young, who respond by jumping fearlessly out of the box. They come to no harm, even from a height of 8–10 m.

The young tip themselves out of the box by spreading out their short, small tail quills and their webbed feet, and land rigidly on their backs. Though a little shaken, they always manage to survive intact, and immediately rush to join their mothers on the water. There is no need to learn how to swim, as this is an innate skill, as also is diving. On the other hand, they do need to learn what is and what is not edible. They begin with insects on the water's surface.

If a predator approaches, the female and her young flee across the water. She will often take the young onto her back as they rapidly tire, and swim or run desperately through the water. If one approaches too closely, she will draw attention to herself by feigning injury, giving the young time to run for safety. When she sees that the danger has passed, she will immediately go to them. Even though the mother duck is always in attendance the voracious pike harvest many victims from amongst these small balls of down.

More and more people are using newly purchased boats to visit the small islets in lakes and close offshore with their children and unleashed dogs. These places are often important nesting areas for wildfowl and other waterbirds. Wild ducks brood very intensively, but if scared from their nests they seldom return. As soon as these people leave the island, crows descend for a feast. When the female duck leaves her nest in her own time to go and feed or bathe she always covers her eggs with down and nesting material, but not if she is frightened off, thus making it easier for crows to find the eggs. So if a female has unfortunately been scared away from her nest, do at least carefully cover over her eggs with some of the down from around the edge of the nest, retire quickly and leave the islet as soon as possible. If the crows do not find the eggs and the female has not been too badly scared, she will return to the nest when you have left. If you find yourself in a boat on the water, be careful not to disturb a female duck or merganser with her brood of young, as separated young can easily fall victim to trout, crows or, in the north, even ravens.

Goosander *(Mergus merganser)*

Nest boxes The goosander likes a plank nest box or a block nest box with an internal depth of 40–50 cm, and inner floor side measurement of at least 30 cm, and an entrance hole diameter of 20 cm. The box should be fixed securely, preferably with props running from the tree trunk to the box, as the goosander flies directly into its box at high speed. It should be situated near the shore line where it is clearly visible from the water, with no overhanging branches to obscure it. It is essential to place a layer of dried moss on the floor of the box, 10 cm in thickness. Where dried moss is not available, surface soil, or rotten wood can be used instead.

As early as January, the nest box should be cleared of any squirrel nests or other rubbish, as eggs may be laid in February. Some nest boxes containing old squirrel nests should be left untouched in areas where there are kestrels, so as to encourage breeding amongst these birds.

The goosander is rather long in the body. The male is white with a black back and glossy green head, while the wings are white on the inside and black outside. The female is smaller, with a brown head, white throat, a short tuft on the neck, ash grey sides and back, white underside and white specula. The goosander's beak is red and long, with serrated edges which facilitate the grasping of fish. In Britain it breeds only in Scotland and northern England, although odd pairs have also nested in Wales and Northern Ireland.

Where there is competition for a nest box between a tawny owl and a goosander, it is normally the owl which prevails, because it starts its breeding earlier. However, where there is a direct fight between the two species, it depends on the individual owl and goosander as to which emerges victorious.

The goosander returns to its breeding areas in March–April. Breeding pairs seek out hollow trees or suitable nest boxes as nesting places. The female subsequently makes several visits to the site she has chosen and lays her first ivory-yellow eggs there in the middle of April, at average intervals of 36 hours. The completed clutch usually numbers 7–16 eggs, and only one brood is raised each year. The female lines the nest cup with grey-black down plucked from her body and this is also used to cover the eggs whenever she leaves the nest. Brooding begins once all the eggs have been laid.

One can immediately tell that a female goosander is brooding in a nest box by the presence of down around the entrance hole. Young females, and even older experienced ones are sensitive to disturbance at the start of the incubation period and there is a risk that they will not return to the nest if frightened away from it. Because of this one should avoid approaching the vicinity of their nest boxes during brooding. The female leaves the box 2–3 times per day to fish and bathe, but otherwise she sits alone on the eggs for the whole 34 days incubation. The male remains in

120

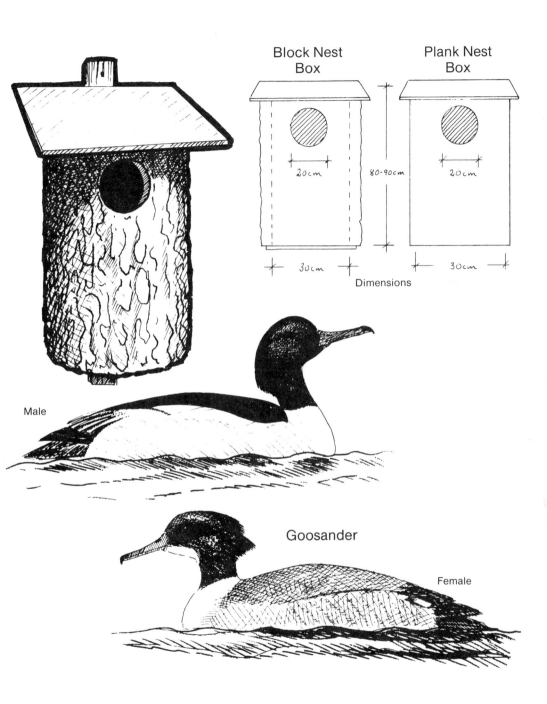

Block Nest Box

Plank Nest Box

20cm

20cm

80-90cm

30cm

30cm

Dimensions

Male

Goosander

Female

121

the neighbourhood of the breeding place until the start of the moult at the end of June, when he goes off to join other wild fowl on open waters.

The young leave the nest box a mere two days after birth. Egg shells and any unhatched eggs are left in the box, so one should clear them out after breeding. The young have acquired a relatively large fat reserve from their eggs and can manage without food for their two days in the nest. When the time has come for them to leave the nest box, the mother makes several flights of inspection in the surrounding area to check that all is quiet. She then lands on a stretch of water below the nest box and calls to her young with a harsh, jarring cry. After a few minutes scraping on the box's inner wall, the head of the first youngster appears at the entrance. Following a few seconds of deliberation, the young bird jumps fearlessly into the air, lands on the ground below or in the water, and shakes itself dry. The remaining young follow in rapid succession.

They immediately begin swimming, diving and catching insects on the water's surface, all under the mother's watchful eye. They are a dark olive-brown in colour, with white undersides and a black beak still equipped with the hard, white egg tooth with which they broke out of their eggs. For the first 2–3 weeks, they eat small crayfish and water insects, before going on to a fish diet, starting with little ones no more than 5 cm long. The youngsters grow quickly and by the end of the summer are as large as their parents, but only in their second year of their life do they reach sexual maturity.

During migration large flocks of mergansers gather together at good fishing places. I have seen flocks of up to a thousand fishing at Hjalmaren. They work collectively in order to achieve the best distribution of food, operating in a line about 300 metres long and diving every so often to locate fish. When a shoal of fish is spotted the flanking birds move inwards until the line of goosanders has become a horseshoe, then a ring, thus trapping the fish for the ensuing feast. These flocks are mostly composed of males, whose white sides shine beautifully in the November sunshine. After perhaps two such fish round-ups, the whole flock lands on an islet to rest. Such a large-scale harvesting of fish can happen when visibility in the water is good all the way to the bottom, or at least down to several metres. When visibility is clouded by mud thrown up by swirling currents, the goosanders are obliged to dive and actively seek out fish prey by winkling around under stones and in nooks and crannies. In searching for food, the bird normally swims along the surface while watching what is going on below by holding its head down so that the eyes are just under the surface. Now and then the bird will dive down to scrutinise the bottom more closely while holding itself steady against the current. The head moves in jerks, which apparently helps the bird's observation of any movement on the bottom. Moving or projecting objects, such as sticks, are routinely examined with the beak. The same food-seeking behaviour is seen in the related red-breasted merganser.

The goosander lives on whatever fish happens to be present in its area, though particular species of fish are sometimes taken in large quantities, partly because of the nature of their flight response which makes them susceptible to capture but partly also because of their common occurrence.

Kjell Sjoberg of Umae University has conducted experiments with goosanders in an artificial water current at the Holle salmon farm near Indalsalven. This bird is regarded as a predator of commercially valuable fish such as salmon and sea trout. In the artificial current, the goosander had greatest difficulty in catching the sea trout, a fish which tends to swim through those parts of rapids where the goosander finds it easiest to catch fish, namely near to the shore. Young salmon on the other hand, which the goosander found relatively easy to catch in the artificial current, normally swims through the deep turbulent water at the centre of the rapids, where goosanders have more difficulty in catching fish. The results suggest that these two species make only relatively meagre contributions to the goosander's intake of fish (Sjoberg, 1975).

The goosanders from Scandinavia move southward in front of the advancing ice in October and November, and overwinter beside ice-free coasts and canals in the Netherlands, and around Britain and Ireland, in the latter case probably joining up with the goosanders which have bred in Scotland and northern England.

Smew *(Mergus albellus)*

Nest boxes Smew normally nest in holes in trees but will readily take to nest boxes if these are available. The smew likes a block nest box with an internal depth of 50 cm, an inner floor side measurement of 20–25 cm, and an entrance hole diameter of 8.5–9 cm. Sometimes it will also breed in a smaller nest box intended for goldeneye, with an internal depth of 40 cm, an inner floor diameter of at least 25 cm, and an entrance hole diameter of 10 cm.

A layer of dry moss at least 10 cm thick at the bottom of the box is an absolute necessity. Where moss is not available, wood shavings or rotten wood may be used instead.

The smew will also accept a plank nest box with an internal depth of

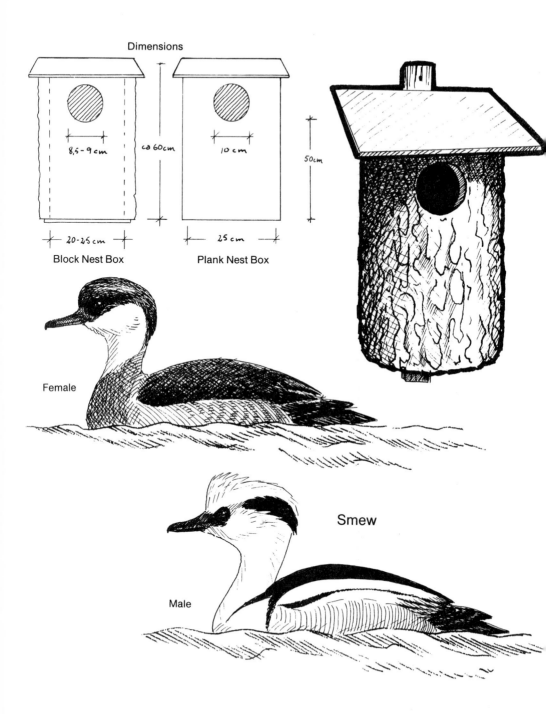

Dimensions

8,5 - 9 cm   ca 60cm   10 cm   50cm

20-25 cm   25 cm

Block Nest Box   Plank Nest Box

Female

Male

Smew

124

40 cm, and inner floor side measurement of 25 cm, an entrance hole diameter of 10 cm, and a roof of hardened board.

The smew is a rare duck in terms of its overall population; in size it is slightly larger than a teal. The male has a highly decorative black and white plumage. It is a fairly rare visitor, with a small breeding population in southern Lapland. Most of those which stop off to rest on open water in southern Sweden in the spring are en-route to breed in northern Finland and Russia.

Red-breasted Merganser *(Mergus serrator)*

Nest boxes The red-breasted merganser will breed in nest boxes set out for wild ducks. These should be placed out on the ground and a good situation is, for example, the water-facing side of a bush growing near the shore. The measurements for the box, as for an eider duck or mallard, should be 60 × 40 × 40 cm with an entrance hole of 20 × 20 cm.

The red-breasted merganser is decidedly smaller than the goosander and is similar in size to the mallard. The white markings visible under its wings during flight are similar to those of the goosander, although the dark band around the breast of the drake distinguishes it at once. The female goosander and red-breasted merganser are very similar in appearance. Both are predominantly grey with white undersides and reddish brown heads. The larger size of the goosander and white gullet separate it from the female merganser in which the white throat extends right down to the breast.

In Britain it is much more widespread as a breeding bird than the goosander occurring all the way down from the Shetlands, through Scotland and north west England into north Wales. It is also fairly widespread in the west of Ireland.

Eight to fourteen eggs are laid in May-June and the female incubates them for 28 days. In winter red-breasted mergansers move out to the coasts and spread southwards, so that large groups can be seen on the sea in estuaries.

Goldeneye *(Bucephala clangula)*

In Britain goldeneye only nest at present in a small area of the Scottish Highlands. Roy Dennis, Highland Officer for the Royal Society for the Protection of Birds, first put up about 30 boxes for goldeneye in 1960, after an earlier attempt had been made to attract them in the 1950s. However, it was not until 1970 that the first pair of goldeneye

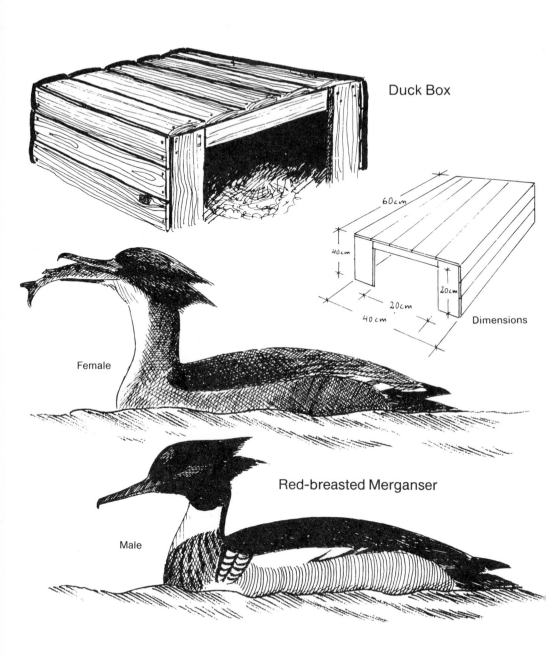

Duck Box

60cm

40cm

20cm

20cm

40cm

Dimensions

Female

Red-breasted Merganser

Male

126

successfully reared a brood in Scotland. Now over 30 pairs are nesting and as described in the introduction, much larger scale efforts are being made to encourage them.

Block nest box The simplest way to make a block nest box for the goldeneye is to use a dead tree with a rotten interior. One can easily hollow out sections of trunk using a power saw, though this is recommended only for those who are familiar with this tool which can be very dangerous in untrained hands. A simpler tool is otherwise recommended, for example, iron wedges can be used to split out the wood. The nest box should have an internal depth of 40 cm (from the centre of the roof to the floor), an internal diameter of 25 cm, and an entrance hole diameter of about 12 cm. One can also make a block nest box from fresh tree trunks. A little surface soil should be placed at the bottom of the box; this is reminiscent of what is found at the bottom of nest holes in nature. Alternatively a layer of moss around 10 cm thick can be placed on the floor of the nest box. When moss is not available, wood shavings or rotten wood can be used. The Swedish Hunting Association's game management school at Ostermalma, whose staff have many years of acquaintance with the goldeneye, say that the ducklings, which leave the nest within two days of hatching, are equipped with sharp claws with which they grasp onto crevices and surface irregularities when climbing towards the entrance hole. These boxes should be therefore made from rough sawn and never planed timber to ensure that the inner surface is rough below the entrance hole so that the young can climb out.

For those who have neither the time, opportunity, nor ability to make such a nest box, commercial models are available such as Aledals, details of which are given in Chapter 3. The total height of these boxes is 60 cm, the inner floor diameter 19 cm, the internal depth 35 cm, and the entrance hole diameter 11 cm.

Plank nest box The same measurements are also appropriate for making plank nest boxes, except that the minimum inner diameter of 25 cm, would be a minimum inner floor side measurement of 25 cm. An ordinary wooden nest box 50 cm high and 25 cm wide can be used with an entrance hole of 12 cm diameter or a square hole 12 × 12 cm sawn in the side. It should be given a roof of hardened board, which will be more durable, or alternatively the roof should be covered with roofing felt to waterproof it. The box should be dark and compact, otherwise the goldeneye will not breed in it. If rough sawn timber is not used then an alternative way of making sure that the ducklings can escape after hatching is to fix around 5–8 mm thick cross lathes as steps below the entrance hole.

The box should be set up 3–4 metres above the ground, with the entrance hole facing out over a surface of water. The cross lathes, which enable the young to clamber out through the entrance hole, are absolutely essential. The newborn birds have sharp claws, but these cannot fasten onto planed wood or smooth planks. A year or so ago, some nest boxes for goldeneye were set up alongside lakes at Bergslagen. When it came to cleaning out the nest boxes they were found to be full of dead young. None had managed to get out.

The goldeneye is not a particularly shy bird, but one cannot expect it to suddenly start breeding in areas inhabited by humans. Instead one should try to place nest boxes in quiet places so that when the family has grown up, the birds have gradually become accustomed to the presence of humans. It is essential for breeding that the nest box is firmly secured, and if necessary, extra steadiness can be achieved by fixing supports above and below the box, holding it to the tree trunk.

Crushed stubble can be used to fill the nest box which should be cleaned out annually, not later than the beginning of March and preferably in autumn. Moss should be cleared away, but nest filling should not be removed.

The male goldeneye is white, with a black back, throat and head, and distinct white cheek markings. The female has a grey back and breast with a white neckband and brown head. The characteristic white wing markings are visible during flight. The head is large and conical shaped, with a high forehead and short beak.

It belongs to the diving ducks, being the most expert diver of this family and able to go to quite significant depths to acquire the mainly animal based food which it eats.

Its most unusual characteristic is the whistling sound made during flight, which is produced by the rapid vibration of wing quills.

Goldeneye like to gather in small flocks on lakes near their breeding sites during springtime. Pair bonding can be a rather overcrowded affair in these situations, with males chasing females over the water and strutting around, bending their heads backwards almost to their tails then snapping them violently forward with a cracking noise. Sometimes they will all dive together as if in response to some silent signal.

After pairing the female will fly into woodland and search for an uninhabited hollow in a tree or a suitable nest box. In Sweden old black woodpecker holes are often used; she is sometimes accompanied by the

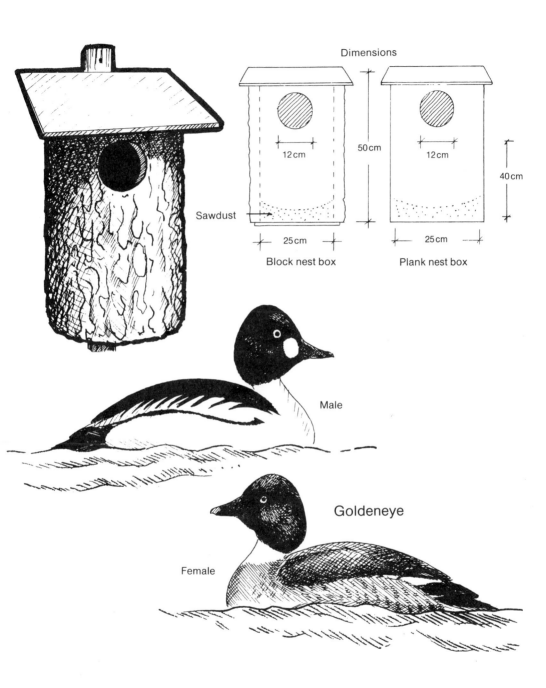

Dimensions

Sawdust

12 cm

50 cm

Block nest box

12 cm

40 cm

25 cm

Plank nest box

25 cm

Male

Female

Goldeneye

129

male. Having found accommodation, she will lay 8–12 green eggs and pluck white down from her body to line the nest at the start of incubation.

Down around the entrance hole is the most sure sign that the nest box has a duck in residence. Once the female has begun brooding, great care should be taken not to disturb her. If she is frightened from the nest, the eggs may deserted. During brooding, the male clears off with other males to spend time moulting by some inland water or out at sea.

Brooding lasts 28–30 days and on the day after hatching the female flies around the area surrounding the nest on a tour of inspection to check that all is quiet and there are no predators nearby. She then lands on the ground or water beneath the nest and calls to her young, which one by one scramble up to the entrance hole and immediately throw themselves out. If this event is filmed with a high speed camera, the young birds can be seen to tense themselves, toss themselves out backwards and, as far as is possible, to attempt to slow their fall by stretching out their webbed feet and short tail feathers. This parachute technique is surprisingly effective in enabling the young to perform their big jump safely.

As soon as they are all down the female gathers them together and draws them to the nearest body of water with her anxious calling; the distance to be travelled may sometimes be a kilometre or more. The young can swim and dive to a depth of up to 4 metres as soon as they reach the water but still need to learn what they can and cannot eat. Within a few weeks they have become self dependent and leave with their mother for larger waters.

Like red-breasted mergansers and goosanders most goldeneyes overwinter in coastal waters often moving southwards for considerable distances to do so.

Mallard *(Anas platyrhynchos)*

Nest boxes for the mallard The mallard has very catholic tastes when it comes to choosing a nesting place. A tuft of grass, the old nest of a crow, bird of prey, or magpie, a hollow tree, a duck basket or even a nest box, are all acceptable to this bird. The nest can be found on the ground, with a hard or soft foundation, in an open or a secluded situation. The nesting place is normally close to open water but is sometimes situated perhaps a kilometre away. The mallard has such a large accommodation register that advice on the provision of nesting sites is hardly necessary.

However, it is not availability of nesting places which determines the

60cm

40cm

20cm

20cm

40cm

Dimensions

Male

Mallard

Female

131

breeding rate of mallards but other factors such as access to the right sort of food, nesting places, zones of protection etc. Nevertheless, the availability of an attractive range of nesting places to choose from is still a significant factor.

It is worthwhile creating facilities around waters suitable for ducks, which will help stimulate breeding in as many pairs as possible.

Willow duck basket The platted Dutch duck basket made from willow has proved to be very acceptable as a nest site for mallards. It should be set up alongside water at a height of 0.5 to 1 metre and bordering on an area of reeds or other vegetation.

Duck baskets can also be set up in natural forks in for example, willow bushes, or on a sawn-off pole (8–10 cm thick) firmly driven into the bed of an area of water and having a natural fork or a couple of sawn off branches between which the basket can be secured. In water courses where mink are found, the basket should be set up on an iron pipe, for example, a galvanised water pipe, which will prevent the mink from plundering the nest. Mink can also be kept away using smooth posts fitted with impassable collars or other devices which stop animals from climbing up. Duck baskets should be set up so that they are either horizontal or leaning slightly backwards. If it lies forwards there is a danger of the eggs rolling out into the water. The baskets should be 'serviced' after hatching, with new nesting material being provided to replace the old nest ball, which will have become flattened out and almost pulverised. A neat bundle of straw and moss-rich surface soil should be rolled over with the hand until it forms a nest bowl in the innermost part of the basket.

Nowadays, duck baskets are also made with a landing platform and an elongated tunnel leading to the nest bowl. At one time it was noticed that certain females found the landing platform too short and tended to fall off, but if the platform was expanded it became too easy for jackdaws to plunder the nest. The elongated tunnel solved this problem. If a couple of spruce twigs are threaded through the roof of the basket, this will also prevent jackdaws landing on the basket and disturbing the female during breeding.

The basket should be about 70 cm long with an entrance hole diameter of 20 cm. They are produced in Sweden by Birger and Gunne Johansson at Asljunga, and can be bought directly from them or through the Game Management Association.

Duck box Mallard will also use plank nest boxes provided they are placed in well-covered positions under bushes. Several times I have had mallards breed in these boxes. They can be placed on the shorelines of lakes, archipelago inlets or reservoirs. The box should be 60 cm long, 40 cm wide, with a 20 cm square entrance hole. It is placed bottom-side up with a stone placed on top to prevent any predators from overturning it.

Plank or block nest box In exceptional cases, mallard will breed in nest boxes, principally those intended for goldeneye, so special boxes need not be made for these birds. However, if you do want to have a go, the dimensions are the same as those for the goldeneye box, ie an internal depth of 35 cm, an inner floor side measurement of 25 cm, and an entrance hole diameter of 12 cm (or an equivalent square hole). Crushed rotten wood, leaf mould, sawdust or grass should be placed in the bottom. These boxes should be placed at a height of 3–4 metres.

All the criteria which have been described for mallard nests are particularly suited to artificial waters which thankfully are increasing all the time. This is almost entirely the work of hunting interests and provide wild life conservation of the highest standard. Those who can, should also attempt to create such pools and wet areas, because this type of habitat has almost more than any other been destroyed by intensive land use practices. Farmers have often been held to blame for much of the habitat destruction which has gone on especially since 1945, but they are far from being alone. Some of the worst ecological disasters perpetrated on wetlands have been the work of the water authorities and internal drainage boards.

The mallard is a surface-feeding duck, which means that it searches for plant and animal food by up-ending itself in the water and paddling with its feet. It is the most common and well known of the ducks, and is what the man in the street is referring to when he talks about ducks. It is seen in all types of water, including large and small lakes, ponds, streams, rivers and artificial watercourses which can be on flat countryside, or in the uplands. The male is called a drake and has a beautiful shiny metallic blue speculum with a rainbow-like sheen. The female or duck is grey-brown. The mallard's call is the well-known quack attributed to all ducks by children.

The female normally has white down, but in spring this becomes grey-black. She plucks this down from herself and lays it around her 6–12 eggs. If the down was white the nest would become clearly visible on the ground, so the mallard has evolved in this respect, and the nest is well camouflaged.

The eggs are generally laid in April and incubated for 27–28 days. The first clutch is often plundered because at that stage the surrounding vegetation has not grown tall enough to hide the nest from view. When this happens the female usually lays a replacement clutch. As soon as the young are hatched and dried out they follow their mother to the water where they start to feed on water insects and small pieces of vegetation.

Eider *(Somateria mollissima)*

Duck boxes for eiders Near to my research area there is an islet called Stora Granholmen which is uninhabited and rarely visited by holidaymakers. There are other islets in the vicinity where eider ducks are frightened off their nests by human visitors, and in such situations, the ducks fail to cover over the eggs with their famous eider down, as they normally would do when leaving their nests, for example, to dive for sea mussels. So the eggs lie there, a shining open invitation to watchful crows, and marauding gulls, which plunder the nest as soon as the people have left the islet and before the ducks have had time to return. Unattended eider nests are thus often plundered en masse, especially the earliest clutches of eggs. Those ducks which lay a replacement clutch of eggs usually build a new nest in a more secluded spot. Simply because disturbance of this nature, during springtime in the eiders' breeding period, was so infrequent on Stora Granholmen, I asked the owner for permission to carry out some research there and this was willingly given.

The first five duck boxes were set out in 1969 and five more were added in 1974; all of which are still in use. The boxes measure 60 × 40 × 40 cm with a 20 cm square entrance hole. They are laid upside down with a stone placed on top and dried straw inside to stimulate breeding.

Breeding of eider and mallard ducks in these boxes has occurred as follows:

Year	Boxes available	Eider	Mallard
1969	5	–	–
1970	5	–	–
1971	5	1	–
1972	5	–	–
1973	5	1	–
1974	10	2	1
1975	10	2	1
1976	10	3	1
1977	10	2	–

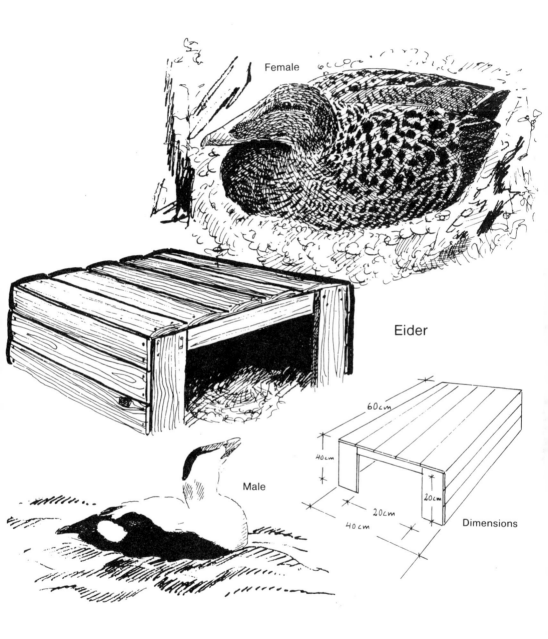

Female

Eider

Male

60cm

40cm

20cm

40cm

20cm

Dimensions

135

To start with, the usual observations were made on the islet during the breeding season, but it soon became clear that despite great care being taken, the observer himself can have certain negative effects on breeding. The crows soon notice that the ducks are disturbed and before long have plundered the nest, so since 1973 observations of breeding have been limited until after the female and her young have left the nest. At this stage, fragmented eggshells, whole egg membranes, and intact eider down in the nest are used to determine whether breeding has been successful.

If the eggs are whole but holed or broken in two with the contents removed and scattered around, then it is extremely likely that the nest has been plundered by crows or gulls. In field observations with binoculars, all cases of nest plundering were carried out by crows, and none by gulls.

When the ducks use these boxes breeding has almost always been successful, though in one case in 1976 a nest was plundered, and it is suspected that the duck was attacked by a mink. Some maintain that these duck boxes can be veritable traps if there are mink on the islet, which one surely cannot disagree with. The fact is that during one year, five adult ducks were found dead not far from their plundered nests with teeth marks in their throats, so the finger of suspicion falls heavily on the mink. In one of these cases, the incident took place during breeding under a duck box, while the other four happened in open nests.

In many cases the ducks have laid a new clutch of eggs after plundering by crows and have usually ensured that it is better hidden than the first. The second clutches are therefore not plundered to the same extent as the first. Observations have shown that when ducks are attacked by crows while brooding, they will lash out angrily and refuse to budge, at which point the crow quickly desists. In no cases have crows been seen to force ducks from their boxes. So despite all the problems, the ducks do at least have this behavioural aspect to promote breeding success.

To obtain a little information on how effective crows are at plundering nests, I painted ten sets of hens' eggs the same grey-green colour as eider eggs during the spring of 1977; these were noticeably smaller but otherwise similar to the real thing. I placed three of these under an empty duck box and the others in two open eider nests recently plundered by crows. I laid a little eider down around to simulate a normal nest which had not been covered over. I had no sooner rowed from the island than I saw the crows close in. On the following day I found that the eggs had been removed from the open nests, with broken egg shells lying 4–50 metres from the nests. The eggs under the duck box were completely intact and had not been disturbed. This shows that even if a duck has been frightened off and not managed to cover her eggs before leaving, there is a very good chance that they will still be there when she returns, provided they are under a duck box.

The eider is our largest diving duck. The male has a magnificent spring plumage, with a black crown, light green neck, white back, and black sides and abdomen. The female is speckled with a grey-brown colour. The flight is heavy, with slow wing beats.

The eider's spring song is not as well known to most people in Sweden as that of the long tailed duck. Nevertheless it is the highlight of bird activity here in the spring, with the 'auu-aaaau-aaaau' sound being amplified as it echoes between the islets of the inner archipelago. The male first throws his neck back then forwards with great violence while uttering a powerful 'aau-aaaau'. Any female that ventures near will be chased across the water. The male normally disappears out to sea after breeding, while the female builds her nest, but in recent years, more and more males have taken to staying around longer during spring.

The female makes her nest in a crevice or between stones on a skerry or islet. She returns regularly every year to breed in the same area. Females which have just reached sexual maturity make their first nest an open one, and it is often plundered by crows, which are a great scourge of eiders and other shorebirds. About 50% of the nests in my research area were plundered, while other researchers have found a 43% plunder rate. Even mature birds often have their clutch of eggs plundered, but with better concealment, because of the growth of vegetation as the spring progresses, the replacement clutches are rarely touched. But generally, as ducks get older they seem to either learn to conceal their nests better from predators or maybe to get higher in the order of priority for the better nest sites.

The female lays 2–6 green-grey eggs and surrounds them with quantities of the prized down plucked from her breast. This down was formerly collected from eider nests in the springtime and used in bed covers and pillows, being much prized as a marvellous insulator. The eggs are laid in the last week of April or first week of May, and are incubated by the female for 26–28 days. If she is frightened while brooding, she will spray a green, foul-smelling liquid over the eggs, before leaving the nest. Unfortunately, the smell does not deter crows from plundering the eggs, as like other birds, their sense of smell is poor. But if any of this liquid gets on your clothes, they will need to be washed to remove the smell. Normally, the female does not leave the eggs, except for short periods when she bathes, drinks, or dives for the staple diet of sea mussels (an eider can dive 10–12 metres).

The young leave the nest immediately, following their mother onto the water. They appear like small brown balls as they dive delicately into oncoming breakers and fly up like corks on the other side. Research carried out on the east coast of Sweden has shown that the plundering of nests by crows is extensive except where eiders are breeding amongst colonies of terns, where the crows have no chance of success against the white defensive wall of sharp beaks. Eiders breed very successfully in such situations, while on other islets, 40–50% of eggs are plundered each year. Gulls, mink and the cold all take their toll on the young eiders. Things have gone very badly on the four islets which I have been observing for some years. In 1975, the black-headed gull colony disappeared and almost all the eider nests were plundered. Only 13 young survived to adulthood. But in 1976, 13 pairs of terns began breeding on the islet and round about 60 young eiders reached maturity.

The eider overwinters on the southern Baltic as well as on the shores of the North Sea and right along the south coast of England. In Britain it breeds all around the Scottish coast, and as far south as the Farne Islands on the east coast and the Mull of Galloway on the west coast; it also breeds all around the coast of Northern Ireland.

10 Owls and other birds of prey in nest boxes

Owls willingly breed in nest boxes, and the best way to encourage them to breed is to locate the areas where they are calling during the long mid-winter nights when they are pairing up, and set up nest boxes there.

The breeding of some species of owls in Scandinavia fluctuates greatly with the availability of mice and voles, which for some of the sub-Arctic and grassland species constitute virtually 100% of the diet. This phenomenon is also seen with the short-eared owl in Britain. In the years or areas where there are high populations of small mammals, especially of the short-tailed vole *(Microtus agrestis)* the owls lay more eggs than normal (as many as ten). Outside of these years, there is less food available and the owls' numbers decline, and the clutch size falls to only perhaps 2–4 eggs, or may not occur at all.

Both owls and diurnal birds of prey (eagles, falcons, harriers, buzzards, hawks, ospreys, kites) as a rule commence incubation as soon as the first egg appears. Because of this the hatching dates of the eggs are staggered, which means that the young in the nest are of different sizes. In those years when the food supply is good, the young fare well and may all grow and fledge successfully, but in less bountiful years it often happens that the older and stronger young eat their younger, weaker siblings. Such cannibalism seems gruesome, but when food is so scarce that the parents cannot feed all the young, this ensures that at least the first hatched and largest survive. Owls generally sleep during the daytime up against the trunk of a thick fir tree, or in a hollow where small birds cannot see them. Fieldfares, which nest in small colonies, have been known to attack owls by defecating on them, in an effort to protect their nest and young. The resulting very sticky and exhausted owls have only managed to survive thanks to kind human beings who have taken them in hand and cleaned them. Less extreme mobbing by small birds is common, and one of the easiest ways to see owls during the daytime is to listen out for the alarm calls of blackbirds, and other small birds, as they mob them.

Owls start looking for a suitable tree hole or nest box early in spring. Once they find one, the female sleeps in it while the male sleeps on a branch in a neighbouring tree. Owls do not build a proper nest as such, but the female simply lays her eggs on the decayed wood and soil in the bottom of the hollow. After a few seasons' use by owls suitable hollows are well lined with their pellets and remains of prey.

In years when there is a high small mammal population a store of dead voles and mice is often laid down in the nest before the young hatch.

The young make a vigorous snapping noise with their beaks whenever they hear their parents, while the parents snap their beaks anxiously when disturbed by anything.

The young stay with their parents for a couple of months until they are ready to fly. Northern European owl populations are migratory, while those further south are resident in their breeding areas throughout the year.

Block nest boxes for owls The following table compiled by Arthur Liedgren of Dakka gives the appropriate measurements for block nest boxes (hollowed-out sections of tree trunks). He set up a total of 500 owl nest boxes and observed the breeding birds for many years.

Boxes made for owls should be camouflaged on the outside with waste wood from saw mills with the bark still on it. A layer of dry moss at least 10 cm thick must be placed at the bottom of the box, or if moss is not available, sawdust, wood shavings, leaf mould, or decayed wood can be used instead. The Ural owl likes to have a thin floor in its nest box, covered with a layer of moss and soft pine branches, which should be renewed every year. The box should not be set up near water as the young leave the nest before they are entirely ready to fly and might run the risk of drowning.

Nest box measurements for owl species

Species	Internal depth	Inner floor measurement*	Entrance hole diameter
Hawk Owl	40 cm	25 cm	10–11 cm
Tengmalm's Owl	35 cm	20 cm	9–11 cm (oval)
Pygmy Owl	40 cm	16 cm	6 cm
Ural Owl	60–70 cm	30 cm	20 cm
Tawny Owl	50 cm	35 cm	18 cm
Barn Owl	60-70 cm	40 cm	17 × 15 cm (in a corner)

*minimum width or diameter

140

Tawny Owl (Strix aluco)

Plank nest boxes The tawny owl likes a plank nest box with an internal depth of 50 cm, an inner floor side measurement of 35 cm, and an entrance hole diameter of 18 cm. Unless rough sawn wood is used, a stepped series of rungs should be nailed on the inside of the box below the entrance hole to enable the young to get out of the box. It should be situated, for example, in an tree within a glade, at a height of 3–5 metres. Sawdust or wood cuttings should be put in the bottom of the box. It should be quite near to open ground where there will be a good supply of mice and voles.

Trivsel-Bo nest box The tawny owl will also readily breed in this sort of box, which has a height of 62 cm, an internal floor measuring 20 × 22 cm, an entrance hole diameter of 11.5 cm, and rungs under the entrance hole. A little sawdust or wood shavings should be placed at the bottom of the box.

Block nest box Tawny owls also breed in block nest boxes, which should be made to the dimensions given in the table above. A commercial model of this type of box for tawny owls is sold by Aledals (see Chapter 3).

The tawny owl is grey-brown in colour, with a large head and large black eyes surrounged by grey circles. The sexes are similar. Their hooting goes on all year round, although they tend to be quieter after May–July.

By March, the female has already normally selected a nesting place, which can be a hollow tree or nest box. In Britain the first clutches are laid by early March. The eggs are pure white when first laid but quickly become soiled in the nest. Usually there are 2–4 eggs, but in good years as many as eight may be laid.

The eggs appear at a rate of one every other day, and brooding begins as soon as the first egg appears. Hatching starts 36 days later, the young being blind when first hatched. Just before this happens, the parent lays up a store of field mice and the occasional young bird.

The eggs hatch at two-day intervals, and the mother remains in the nest for 14 days after the completion of hatching. The male arrives now and again with food, which the female tears apart and distributes amongst the young. When the chicks are 10–12 days old they are being fed about once every hour, through the hours of darkness. However, although the tawny owl tends to be strictly nocturnal unless disturbed during the day, in central Sweden the mid-summer days are so long that it is forced to start its hunting in the gloaming at around 10pm.

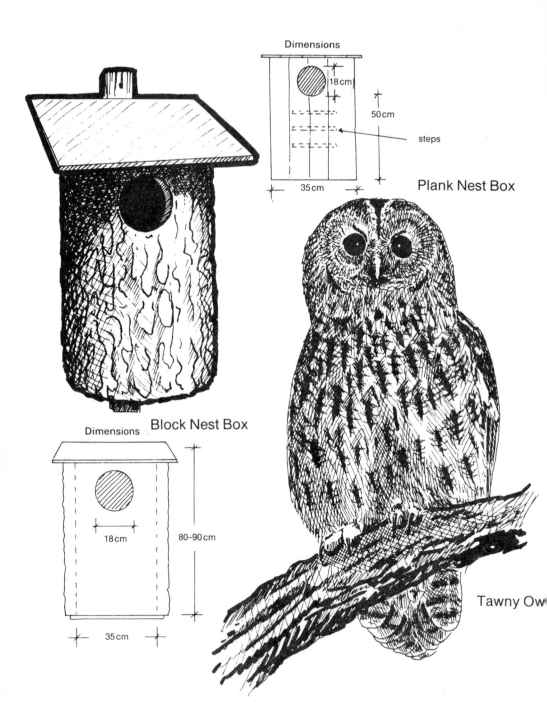

Dimensions

18 cm

50 cm

steps

35 cm

Plank Nest Box

Block Nest Box

Dimensions

18 cm

80–90 cm

35 cm

Tawny Owl

142

At first the prey is mostly field mice, as the young cannot eat anything larger; though tawny owls also prey on small birds. Later on, the young get larger prey such as water voles and small rabbits, which the mother tears apart with her beak and stuffs in tiny pieces down her chicks' throats.

The adult bird lands about 10 metres from the nest box before flying into it, while the young squeak and click their beaks in answer to their parents' calls of encouragement. The owlets leave the nest 38–40 days after hatching, though they are not completely ready to fly at this stage.

The tawny owl is a non-migratory bird which remains in its territory all year round.

During the light evenings of midsummer one can often hear these birds screeching and hooting from copses, groves, and parks. The young remain in the home territory for about three weeks and are fed by their parents, becoming independent by the middle to end of August.

They start by hunting just insects, but need to collect at least 60 grams of food each day (an adult tawny owl can eat up to 170 grams per day). This is difficult for first-year birds and 47–77% die before the end of their first winter.

Care should be taken when observing breeding in tawny owls. You probably will not hear the female come swooping down on you as you stand on your ladder, just before you fall off and injure yourself. She always goes for the head, a fact which the large scars on many bird watchers remind us of, though sadly some people have paid for their curiosity with the loss of an eye.

In the past in Sweden one would sometimes come across a dead tawny owl with its head clipped off, which was a clear sign that the eagle owl (*Bubo bubo*) had been around. But this bird is now so rare that the tawny owl is seldom preyed on in this way.

Little Owl *(Athene noctua)*

The little owl is not easy to persuade to go into a nesting box, but it will use either a wooden box made from planks or a block box cut from a solid piece of trunk, with an internal diameter or side of 16–18 cm. The box should be rather deep, so that it gives the illusion of a hollow tree. The entrance hole should be 7 cm in diameter or square.

A clay drain pipe seems to be even better than a wooden box, so long as it has approximately the same dimensions as shown in the diagram. Four holes should be bored through the bottom of the pipe, through which steel wire is stretched in the shape of a cross. The bottom of the

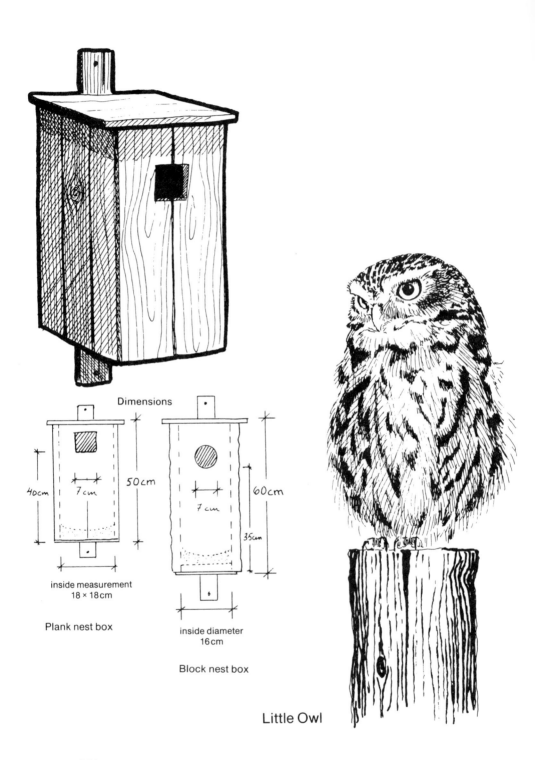

Dimensions

40cm 7cm 50cm

inside measurement
18 × 18cm

Plank nest box

7 cm 60cm

35cm

inside diameter
16cm

Block nest box

Little Owl

144

pipe can then be sealed off by pouring in about 4–5 cm of concrete, which will be strengthened and held in place by the wire. A lid can be made with a piece of tile or thick wood, and a suitable hole chiselled in the top rim of the pipe will act as the entrance.

A little sawdust or even better some owl pellets can be spread in the bottom of the box, to help the little owl feel at home.

Boxes for little owls do not have to be hung very high. They can be hung on fence posts around fields, or in large gardens opening onto cultivated land where the owl can find food.

The little owl is a small greyish brown bird only slightly larger than a blackbird. It has sulphur yellow eyes and a very short tail. Its call is a sharp miaow-like kiau as well as a very characteristic uuut....uuut....uuut, repeated with about 4 seconds between the cries in the mating season.

In the past the little owl was very common, but in recent years its numbers have decreased perhaps because many of its hedgerow nesting trees, such as the old pollarded willows and poplars in Denmark, and, as already mentioned, the hedgerow elms in Britain have been felled. The little owl likes to nest in natural holes but it can also breed in lofts, under roofing and in holes in walls and drystone dykes. It also uses rabbit burrows for nesting, and in Britain its habit of inspecting burrows and tunnels leads to the death of many little owls which are caught in spring traps set by keepers in such places, with the intention of trapping rats, stoats and weasels.

The little owl is distributed throughout the Continent as far north as Denmark, but in Britain it occurs as far north as the Scottish border with only a few scattered pairs up the east coast of Scotland. In Wales it is only thinly scattered in most of the upland areas and it is absent in Ireland. In Britain it is not native, its presence resulting from a series of late Victorian introductions in Yorkshire, Norfolk, Northamptonshire, Essex, Hertfordshire, Kent and Sussex.

There can be no doubt that a widespread distribution of nesting boxes for this particular bird will help to increase the population. As a species it has been very much restricted in its choice of nest sites, following the loss of so many elms killed by Dutch elm disease. This hedgerow tree which was often hollow was one of its favourite sites.

In May the little owl lays 4–7 round white eggs. As with the other owl species no attempt at nest building is made and these eggs are laid straight onto the floor of the nest cavity. Incubation is by the female alone and takes 26–29 days. When the young hatch the male feeds them at first, the female remaining in the nest to brood the young.

After about 26 days the young leave the nest but are still dependent upon their parents. Even so many are lost at this time and the little owl, like many other species of owl has a very high rate of mortality in its first year of life.

Their food consists mainly of earthworms and insects; but mice and small birds are also taken.

The little owl is sedentary and on the Continent it suffers badly during severe winters.

Pygmy Owl *(Glaucidium passerinum)*

Nest boxes for the pygmy owl The pygmy owl population can sometimes reach 'epidemic' proportions, on which occasion nest boxes are very much in demand. Stores of dead mice and small birds are laid up in the boxes, but sometimes the winter is so mild that the food is spoiled and these small bullfinch sized owls starve to death. I have found such food pantries in starling nest boxes with an internal depth of 30 cm, floor diameter of 17 cm, and entrance hole diameter of 5 cm. Once, even a tit type nest box was used, with its internal depth of 19 cm, floor diameter of 15 cm, and entrance hole diameter of only 3.5 cm. The pygmy owl has been known to use nest boxes with entrance hole diameters of 3.4 cm and nest boxes with oval entrance holes measuring 2.8 × 2.7 cm or 2.9 × 3.2 cm. Old woodpecker holes are often used as nest sites by pygmy owls. In the north of Sweden the holes made by three-toed woodpeckers are invariably used in the following year by pygmy owls.

Plank nest boxes Pygmy owls have bred in normal timber nest boxes or plank nest boxes, with an internal depth of 40 cm, inner floor side measurement of 18 cm, and entrance hole diameter of 6 cm. Dried grass should be laid in the bottom of the box.

Block nest boxes Pygmy owls will also breed in block nest boxes. The dimensions should be about the same as those for the starling boxes with an entrance hole diameter of 5.8 cm. A 10 cm thick layer of dry moss should be laid on the bottom, or if no moss is available, wood shavings or decayed wood can be used.

In Norway Geir Sonerud maintains that pygmy owls can only be persuaded to breed in nest boxes if the right type of box is used and if it is correctly situated. He has used block nest boxes. These need to be placed in old dense pine forests. The box which he has found to be most favoured is 60 cm high, 36 cm deep from the lower part of the entrance hole to the floor, has a floor diameter of 16 cm and an entrance hole

146

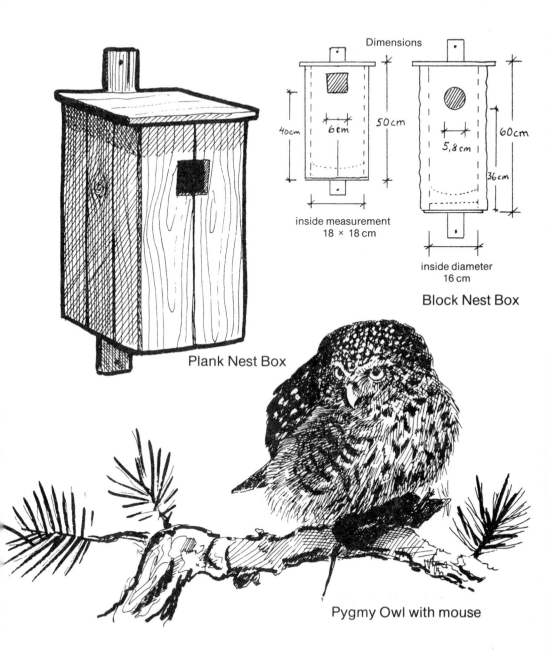

Plank Nest Box

Dimensions

40cm
6cm
50cm

inside measurement
18 × 18 cm

5,8 cm
60cm
36cm

inside diameter
16 cm

Block Nest Box

Pygmy Owl with mouse

diameter of 5.8 cm. A 5 cm layer of wood shavings should be placed on the floor and the box should be set at a height of 5 cm.

The pygmy owl is truly a dwarf amongst owls; this neat little grey-brown bird is no bigger than a bullfinch.

In February–March it starts its spring whistling which is high-pitched and clear, very similar to the bullfinch's mating call. It is a daytime owl which is constantly on the go in the morning, and also early in the evening. The nest is normally built in an old great spotted woodpecker hole, sometimes even in goldeneye nest boxes, and very occasionally in starling nest boxes. The 3–8 eggs are rounded and white.

The male feeds the female while she is brooding, initally calling to her in the evening around 8pm. She flies out to him and accepts the morsel he has caught, usually a mouse and normally returns to the nest box to eat while brooding. When the young hatch they are fed from between 8pm and 11pm each evening until between 4am and 7am the next morning. The female spends a lot of time with the young in the nest. If the male does not arrive with food within a certain period of time, she will fly out and try to make a quick kill herself, which is normally a small bird.

When the female is out hunting, small birds let out an anxious warning cry. Despite the fact that they are potential victims, they approach her as she sits on a branch and emit a stream of verbal abuse. When they approach too closely, she snorts as if sneezing. After a while she becomes visibly irritated by the company, at which point she blows air out through her beak and flaps her small tail in a circular motion.

If looking for an old woodpecker hole inhabited by pygmy owls, it is useful to imitate the owl's call. The female will often look out of the hole curiously, and on seeing it is you, rather than a male owl, will snap her beak in disapproval; this behaviour is generally seen in owls when upset.

Pellets are normally found below the nest hole, as the female removes them from the nest as soon as she or the young bring them up. They consist mostly of hair and bones from mice, but also feathers from small birds such as great tits, young starlings, blackbirds, and goldcrests. Even the remains of great spotted woodpecker can sometimes be found.

When the pygmy owl is angry it blows, giving a good imitation of a panting dog. The head turns in all directions, sometimes stiffening and fixing a penetrating black and yellow gaze on whoever has dared to disturb the peace. This aggressive little look can be quite intimidating.

Its whistling is remarkably similar to the bullfinch's mating call. I once witnessed an amazing meeting between pygmy owls and bullfinches, in which a male bullfinch with two females answered a pygmy owl's mating call, and a duet between the two parties soon started. The bullfinches flew much closer to the owl, believing that they were communicating with 'relatives'. Eventually they caught sight of the owl, and became confused by the disparity between what they saw and what they heard. They still considered it was one of their kin calling, and despite their bewilderment they approached nearer and nearer. The pygmy owl sometimes eats bullfinches, but in this case it stood there amazed by the close presence of these unperturbed birds. Finally, one bullfinch came too close and the owl flew towards it snorting, hissing and letting out a loud, sharp shriek of anger; nevertheless, it did not try to kill the bird. The owl, whose young had only recently flown from the nest, became very worried about the apparently fearless bullfinches which she had seen. After a little while longer she feigned a couple of attacks on the bullfinches, which soon snapped out of their trance and disappeared.

The female incubates the eggs for 28 days. The young remain in the nest box for about 25 days, and fly out immediately after midsummer. Once the young have left the nest, both parents call incessantly to them in order to keep them together.

Research has shown that the pygmy owl takes about 2–3 mice and 1–3 small birds (daily) during the winter, whereas in summer the diet is predominantly one of mice.

In winter it may occasionally visit bird tables to catch small birds, like all birds of prey. It plays a necessary role in maintaining the balance of nature, always going for those birds which for one reason or another are slightly disadvantaged because they are sick or injured. Thanks to the pygmy owl and sparrowhawk, salmonella and other diseases in birds are kept in check.

Thanks also to recent mild winters, their numbers have increased in central Sweden, and some have laid up food stores in nest boxes in my research area. Analysis of nine pellets from these nest boxes revealed that they contained feathers, bone fragments, and the gizzard and stomach contents of a small passerine, probably a yellowhammer. They also contained hair, bones, and teeth from at least two wood mice (*Apodemus sylvaticus*), a short-tailed vole, a pygmy shrew (*Sorex minutus*), and one small unidentified rodent.

Barn Owl *(Tyto alba)*

Box style nest box The barn owl likes a nest box with an internal depth of 60–70 cm, an internal floor side measurement of 40 cm, and an entrance hole in one corner measuring 17 × 15 cm. The box should be placed fairly

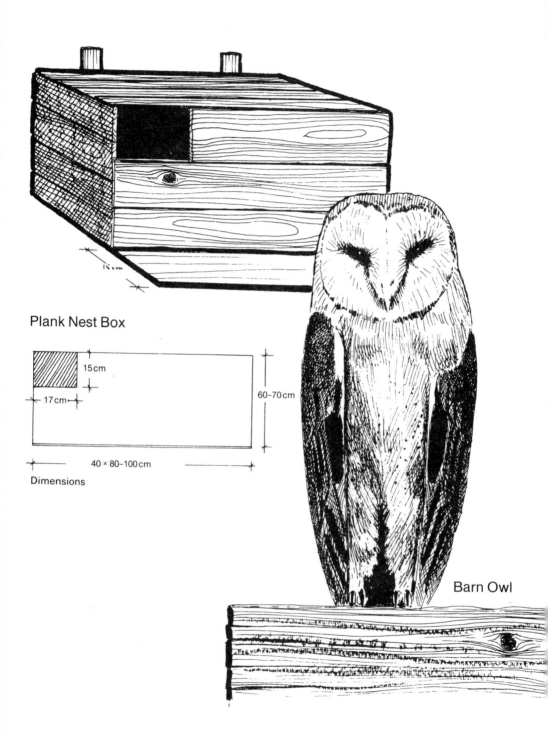

Plank Nest Box

15 cm

17 cm

60–70 cm

40 × 80–100 cm

Dimensions

Barn Owl

150

high up on a gable end inside a barn. It has sometimes been shown to be a good idea to have two boxes, the barn owl using each in turn for its first and second broods. There are three advantages in having nest boxes within the barn:

1. The owls and their young are protected from wind and weather during the breeding period.

2. The small rodents which inhabit the barn provide the owls with an indoor food source. This is particularly important in winter and during long periods of bad weather.

3. The boxes are not noticeable from the outside, which is very useful when it comes to avoiding curious visitors and possible egg collectors.

The pellets should be cleared out of the boxes at least every other year, otherwise the box will become too heavy.

The barn owl is a very light-coloured bird with long wings. Sharply delineated seven facial circles give its face a heart shaped appearance. The markings are very fine, with yellow, grey, and red-brown colours, and pearl-like spots all over the back. Its call is a very nightjar-like 'errrrr'. It often lays up large stores of voles and mice. The barn owl remains resident within its breeding territory throughout the year.

Nest boxes are very readily accepted by barn owls, and are guaranteed to give better breeding results than nests built on small beams or projections. In the past when unthreshed cereals were stored in barns to await the annual visit of the threshing circus, few barns were built without owl holes in the gable ends and nesting trays placed high up on the rafters. Unfortunately these are almost always forgotten in these days of asbestos built barns and grain silos. However, the barn owl remains a popular bird among farmers and many are happy to co-operate with ornithologists and allow boxes or nesting trays to be put up in their buildings if asked.

The barn owl lays 4–6 white eggs over a 25 day period. The young leave the nest after about 40 days, though they do not become independent until late autumn.

As with all other owls, barn owls get rid of the indigestible parts of their prey by sicking up pellets containing remains of hair and bones. These pellets are surprisingly large considering the bird's size. They appear polished, almost as if covered with a thin, transparent plastic skin.

Tengmalm's Owl *(Aegolius funereus)*

Plank nest boxes Tengmalm's owl likes a plank nest box with an internal depth of 35 cm, an inner floor side measurement of 20–25 cm, and an

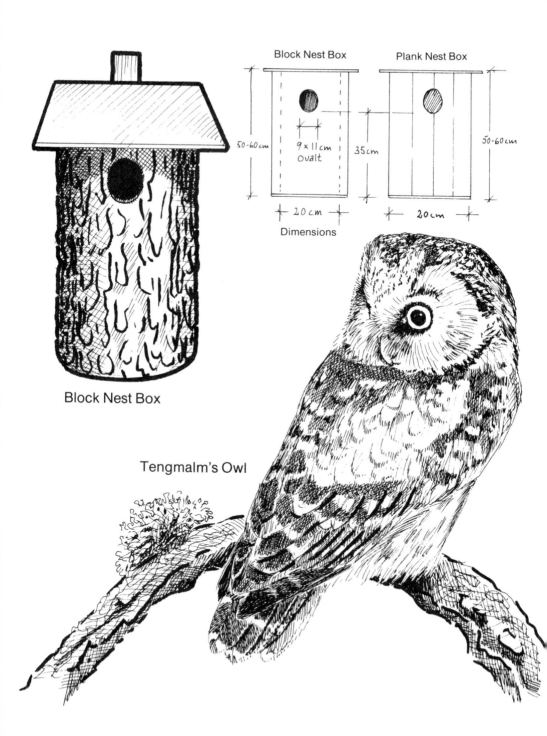

Block Nest Box

Block Nest Box

Plank Nest Box

50-60 cm

9 x 11 cm
Ovalt

35 cm

50-60 cm

20 cm

20 cm

Dimensions

Block Nest Box

Tengmalm's Owl

152

oval entrance hole 9–11 cm in diameter. Dried grass should be placed in the bottom. The box should be set up near the edge of a bog or other open area within a forest, at a height of 3–4 metres and with the entrance hole facing the bog. There should be open grassland or arable land not too far from the box, where the owls can hunt for voles and mice.

Block nest box Tengmalm's owl is particularly fond of block nest boxes made from sections of tree trunk. These should have an internal depth of 35 cm, a floor diameter of at least 20 cm, and an entrance hole diameter of 9–10 cm. A 10 cm-thick layer of dry moss should be placed on the bottom, though where moss is not available, wood shavings, sawdust, leaf mould, or decayed wood can be used instead. As mentioned earlier for those who have not the time, opportunity or skill to make a nest box, Aledals block nest boxes can be bought (see Chapter 3). The box should have a total height of 60 cm, a floor diameter of 19 cm, an internal depth of 35 cm and an entrance hole diameter of 11 cm.

Up until about 20 years ago, the Tengmalm's owl was only found north of Dalalven, but since then it has spread southwards so that now it is quite common in the forests of central Sweden.

Apart from the pygmy owl it is our smallest owl, with an enormous head and long tail. Its plumage is brown-grey with drop-like white spots (hence the Swedish name 'pearl owl'). It will often be seen sticking its head out of the nest hole (frequently an old woodpecker nest) as you pass by during the day, but once she has drawn her head back inside, it is impossible to get her to show herself again, her curiosity having been satisfied.

The spring call consists of 3–7 small notes 'po-po-po-po-po-po-po' which is repeated after an interval of 1–3 seconds and can go on for hours and be heard over a wide area. The Tengmalm's owl also tends only to breed in those years when there is a plentiful supply of food. It often goes on trips, and a whole series of examples have been caught and ringed at our bird observatories along the east coast.

The female lays 4–8 eggs, and sometimes ten. Incubation lasts for 20 days and the young leave the nest after 30 days by which time they are a dark brown colour.

It is not at all afraid around its nesting place and will arrive with voles or mice and eat them in front of you as long as you do not move. At the slightest sound she will turn her head right round and stare at you with her sulphur-yellow eyes. This particular owl has increasingly started to breed in nest boxes set up for goldeneye.

Hawk Owl *(Surnia ulula)*

Plank nest boxes The hawk owl prefers a plank nest box with an internal depth of 40 cm, an inner floor side measurement of 25 cm, and an entrance hole diameter of 12 cm. It should be placed at a height of 3–4 metres. The brooding female likes to have a small vertical chink or fissure under the entrance hole through which she can keep an eye open for possible enemies; she becomes uneasy if she cannot view what is going on outside. The chink should not go all the way up to the entrance hole, otherwise the bird's feet may catch in it as it passes through the hole. This slot should measure 15 cm by 1.5 cm.

Block nest box The hawk owl will also breed in a hollowed out section of tree trunk. This should have an internal depth of 40 cm, an inner floor side measurement of at least 25 cm, and an entrance hole diameter of 10–11 cm. A 10 cm-thick layer of dry moss should be laid in the bottom of the box, though if moss is not available, wood shavings or decayed wood can be used.

The hawk owl looks like a sparrowhawk in the way it flies with a vigorous wing action and a long tail trailing behind. It is the large head which gives away its identity as an owl. It seems to show great delight in winging its way to the top of a bare tree and there waggling its tail about. The hawk-like cross-bands on its underside distinguish it from other owls. Hawk owls are found in Lapland.

The female's call when the young are nearby is a screeching, merlin-like 'kui-kui-kui-kui-kui', though this is not uttered as rapidly by the owl as it is by the merlin. If you look upwards when you hear this call you may catch sight of the owl in the process of diving steeply towards your head, and this is often followed by your hat flying off your head and your neck being gashed. Unfortunately, the male may join in the attack, at which stage it is advisable to beat a hasty retreat. This sort of incident usually happens only within the breeding territory.

The hawk owl is a distinctive day-time bird. It most often breeds in those years when there is a plentiful supply of prey, and in between these times it wanders around the countryside. Sometimes in late autumn or winter, it makes appearances in both southern and central sweden. At such times, this hawk-like owl perched in the tops of trees is identifiable by its bright black and white plumage and the hawk-like cross-bands. It is a very beautiful owl, with fine markings. Its spring call is a lively 'ho-ho-ho-ho'. Normally it lives in tree stumps and bare pine trees, but also in nest boxes put up for goldeneye.

154

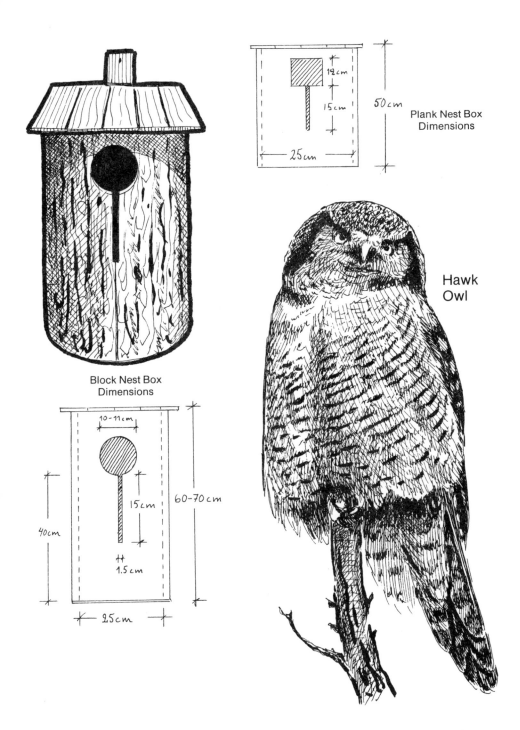

Plank Nest Box
Dimensions

12cm

15cm

50cm

25cm

Block Nest Box
Dimensions

10-11cm

15cm

1.5cm

60-70cm

40cm

25cm

Hawk
Owl

155

Three to nine eggs are laid and incubation lasts for 28 days. The young, which are fed entirely on voles and mice, leave the nest after 32 days.

Ural Owl *(Strix uralensis)*

Nest boxes for the Ural owl This owl needs broken hollow trees, so-called 'chimneys', for breeding purposes, the female laying her eggs in the uppermost cavity in the tree. In these days of intensive forestry, many of their natural nesting places are disappearing. At the same time, paradoxically, there is an increase in the number of forest clearings, which make ideal hunting grounds for this owl, living as it does primarily on voles.

The Ural owl's dilemma can be helped by the setting up of nest boxes. It is a bird of conifer forests in Scandinavia and Northern Europe, and can be found wherever good nesting places are available. Nest boxes should be set up in autumn or winter, so that it is not disturbed during its breeding season.

Wooden nest boxes In order to simulate a hollow tree, one can saw off the top of a tree and fix up a wooden nest box on the stump at a height of about 4 metres, using steel wire. The box can also be set up on the trunks of pine or fir trees. The best places are in forests on the edge of clearings and swamps deep within undisturbed areas.

The box's internal depth should be 60–70 cm and the inner floor side measurement 30 cm, while in each side a spy-hole hole should be drilled 40 cm up from the floor. The roof should be made from hardwood. The floor should be covered to a depth of 5 cm with decayed wood and the box is placed in an open, but secluded spot. An alternative type of nest box is recommended by Nils Pers, who has many years of experience in the field with Ural owls, and considers that the boxes should have complete roofs so that early breeding is not spoiled by snow falls. These boxes have an internal depth of 70 cm, an inner floor side measurement of 40 cm, and an entrance hole measuring 20 cm vertically by 40 cm horizontally (the full width of the box).

Block nest boxes The Ural owl also breeds in block nest boxes, which should have an internal depth of 70 cm, and a floor diameter of 30 cm. For breeding to occur, the floor should be covered with a layer of dry moss and soft fresh pine twigs, which should be renewed every year.

The Ural owl looks like the tawny owl but has entirely dark eyes and a

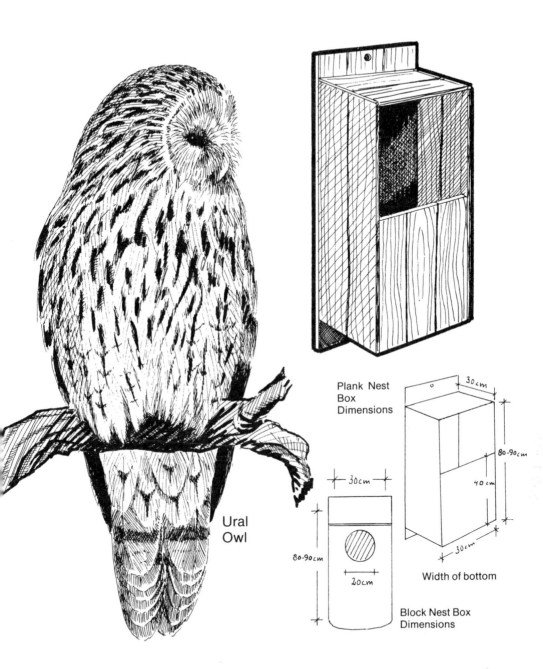

Ural
Owl

Plank Nest
Box
Dimensions

30cm

80-90cm

40 cm

30cm

Width of bottom

30cm

80-90cm

20cm

Block Nest Box
Dimensions

157

light, striped plumage. On bright spring nights it can be seen flying out buzzard-like over open territory in Norrland, hunting for voles. In areas rich in voles, it sometimes just sits on vantage points and watches for its prey.

The male's 'vo-ho-vo-ho-vo-ho' call can be heard on spring nights; it is dull and like that of an eagle owl, but with a different accent. Each call is separated by a pause of about three seconds. It also produces a dog-like 'vo-vo-vo-vo-vo-vo', which is more familiar.

The Ural owl breeds in tall old pine trees, often in old woods where trees have been broken in storms. This sort of habitat is becoming scarcer every year because of rationalized forestry, and nest boxes need to be set up to a greater extent than they are at present.

The Ural owl is a non-migratory bird and stays in the same territory all year round. Breeding often coincides with those years when there is a plentiful supply of voles, which is normally every fourth year. In the intervening periods it makes do with shrews, squirrels, and small birds. The female lays 3–4 eggs which are incubated for 28 days. The young, which are fed entirely on voles, leave the nest after 32 days.

Kestrel *(Falco tinnunculus)*

Plank nest boxes In Holland, kestrels often breed in nest boxes intended for ducks, set up on poles amongst reeds. This type of nest box has also been successfully used for kestrels in young forestry plantations in southern Scotland. In Norrland, they have been known to breed in old black woodpecker nests and even in goldeneye nest boxes.

The kestrel prefers a nest box from which the female can observe the surrounding area and check that all is quiet. Those artificial nest boxes in which kestrels have bred have often been almost filled with old squirrel nests. Kestrels normally breed in disused crows' nests or on rocky ledges.

The nest box should have an internal depth of 40 cm, an inner floor side measurement of at least 35 cm, an entrance hole of 12 cm square, and should be set up in a tree on the edge of the wood or forest. In areas where there is any disturbance at all, the box should be set up at a height of 4–5 m on a tree. As much as anything this height is required to keep the nest free from human disturbance. In isolated areas, for example on the Dutch polders or in forestry plantations, they will happily nest in boxes set on poles only 2 m above ground level. Twigs and dry moss should be laid on the floor of the box, almost up to the level of the entrance hole.

The kestrel has a brick-red back and a speckled breast. The male has a

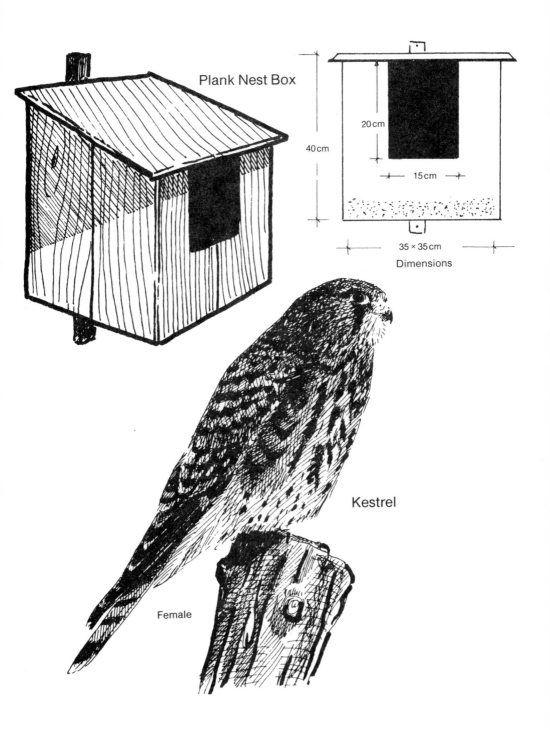

Plank Nest Box

40 cm

20 cm

15 cm

35 × 35 cm

Dimensions

Kestrel

Female

159

grey head and tail, while the female is light brown with darker brown barring across its upperparts; the paler underparts are speckled like those of the male. In both sexes the tail has a wide dark subterminal and a thin white terminal band.

Four to six eggs are laid. These are coloured brick-red with rich dark tan flecks, and are incubated by the female for 29 days, with the male occasionally taking a turn. The young are virtually ready to fly by midsummer.

The kestrel can often be seen hovering with its head held motionless and its wings quivering rapidly, as it surveys the ground below. When some small mammal, beetle, or even grasshopper is seen it may either turn and dive headlong in true falcon style, or it may lose height in a series of sudden side slips before pouncing, feet first on its prey. It inhabits open countryside and is often seen hovering over fields, meadows, and motorway verges where it adds interest to many a long journey.

Smaller prey is eaten where it is caught, whereas items such as mice or voles are first taken to a nearby vantage point, such as a post. Though voles and mice are the principal prey, beetles, grasshoppers, lizards, earthworms and the occasional skylark chick are all included in the diet.

Merlin *(Falco columbarius)*

Nest boxes for merlins Although in many of the Northern European countries where it breeds the merlin is associated either with disused crows' nests, or ledges in small gullies or with ground nests among heather, in Finland merlin nests are found relatively frequently in old woodpecker holes. Quite a few successful breedings have also occurred in goldeneye nest boxes. These have an internal depth of 40 cm, an inner floor side measurement of at least 25 cm, and an entrance hole diameter of 10 cm. The floor should be liberally covered in old dry moss all the way up to the entrance hole.

It seems to be a matter of learned preference as to which type of nest site the merlin takes up, and the family habit of breeding in boxes is starting to become more and more frequent. Goldeneye nest boxes should be set up to an ever greater extent not only alongside water but also in forests where merlins can make use of them.

The merlin is little bigger than the fieldfare. They breed throughout Northern Europe and Scandinavia, the uplands of Britain and in Ireland, as well as in Iceland, where they are a common sight sitting on roadside telegraph poles.

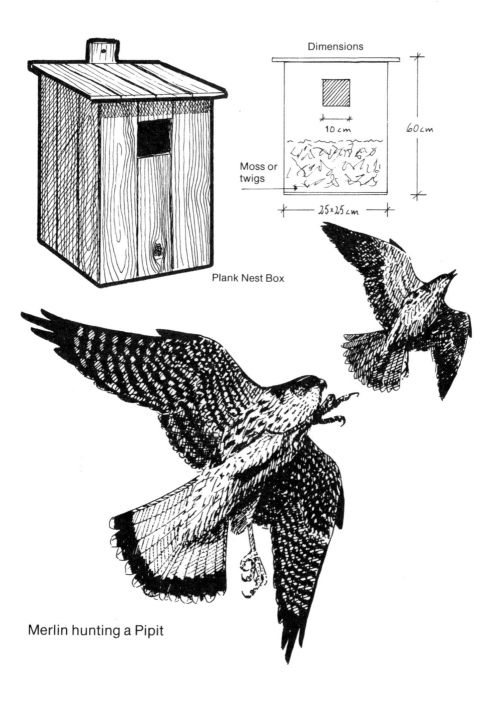

Dimensions

10 cm

60 cm

Moss or twigs

25×25 cm

Plank Nest Box

Merlin hunting a Pipit

The 4–5 reddish brown-flecked eggs are laid at the start of June and incubated for a month, mostly by the female. The merlin's diet consists mainly of small birds, especially the meadow pipit, insects, and lemmings. In winter most of the population moves southwards to Western Europe and North Africa. At this time the sight of a merlin flashing low over a sea wall makes a red letter day for bird watchers looking for waders around estuaries.

Project Merlin Over most of its range the merlin population has been falling badly for reasons which are not entirely clear. In Sweden numbers have fallen approximately 50% since the 1940s and reports of even further declines in numbers led the Swedish Nature Conservancy Association to initiate 'Project Merlin' in 1975 before the situation became critical for the species. It was decided to make a relatively limited effort early on to avoid having to resort to expensive and difficult last-minute measures. The preliminary plan included literature searching; the collecting together of population figures from Ottenby and Falsterbo; the ringing of as many chicks as possible; the analysis of environmental toxins in unhatched eggs and dead young; research into food eaten during breeding seasons; and reproductive studies. The work has been led by Bergt Olsson of the Zoological Institute in Gothenburg. Similar work has been carried out in Britain and as noted in the introduction special efforts are being made in some areas to provide artificial nest sites for merlins so as to give those which are present the maximum possible chance to breed successfully.

11 Artificial nests for birds of prey

All birds of prey have experienced falls in population, principally because of habitat changes, persecution by man and environmental toxins. Unfortunately, even today there are still cases where these birds are illegally shot, trapped and poisoned, despite the fact that they have been protected by law for many years. Those people responsible retain the prejudiced attitude that birds of prey compete for the same small game which they themselves preserve for shooting. This ignorant and out-dated attitude does a great deal of harm to shooting interests as well as to conservation of the species themselves. Public attitudes are likely to line up against field sports as long as this kind of behaviour continues. This is a great pity, when as noted earlier the activities of sportsmen in creating game covers are very beneficial in terms of conservation, because these covers often form the only scrub and woodland habitat in arable areas, and provide a living space for many other wild plants and creatures.

Research has shown many times that, although these birds of prey do take some game, the effect on the game population is negligible in terms of the numbers present and which will eventually be available for the guns.

Many of our large birds, especially those birds of prey whose populations are threatened, breed in stick nests in trees. Many of these nests which may be used year after year are destroyed during felling or are blown down in autumn and winter storms. Moreover, rationalized forestry has meant that fewer and fewer suitable nesting trees are available. Sometimes nests can be located on very exposed ledges on crags. In both these types of site, one can attempt to set up artificial nest platforms in suitable sheltered spots and those nests which have become tattered can be repaired. Sometimes branches can be sawn off to create the right setting for a nest or nest platform, and old dry branches can be laid on the platform in the shape of a nest base to stimulate breeding.

There have been several successful attempts to create artificial nest sites for large birds of prey in Sweden, and as mentioned in the

Introduction, this has also been done recently in Scotland where sites for ospreys have been set up. Artificial osprey platforms have also been used very successfully on the eastern seaboard of North America.

To be acceptable to large birds of prey these platforms must be placed in sheltered spots near to good hunting territory. Once the place has been chosen, building material should be selected from amongst the brushwood in the surrounding area. The height of the platform above the ground is partly dependent on the height of the tree and partly on the length of your ladder. On lofty trunks, the nest can be fixed directly to the tree trunk, underneath healthy branches so that some shelter is provided. The base of the brushwood nest is made from chicken wire folded double and fastened to the upper side of a wooden frame. Fresh twigs are platted into the chicken wire, forming the base. A simple nest cup is then constructed in the centre of the platform of branches and twigs using grass and moss. The platform can also be placed on a network of healthy branches within the chosen tree, without recourse to any artificial base. The golden eagle, great grey owl, rough-legged buzzard, buzzard and osprey have all bred in this type of nest.

Consideration of the needs, and provision of help for, our hard-pressed birds of prey and owls should form part of normal forestry planning and work schedules before, during and after felling and replanting activities. From experience, we know that areas with lots of nests are inhabited more frequently and by many more species than areas with few nests. So, with the help of artificial nests for birds of prey, it should be possible to induce breeding in goshawks, buzzards, rough-legged buzzards, and great grey owls within forest areas.

Forestry should spare nesting trees. In Sweden regulations contained in the forestry conservation laws of 1979 stipulate how felling operations should proceed. Nesting trees used by threatened or rare species of birds, or trees or other vegetation which protect their nesting places, must be spared. Similar protection is now provided in Britain and Northern Ireland by the 'Wildlife and Countryside Act', although in practice this is ineffective in the absence of careful forward conservation planning by the foresters. In some areas such as the New Forest this planning has been in effect since the 1970s, and plans are checked each year to ensure that felling is not carried out in known bird of prey nesting areas during the breeding season. Similar initiatives could easily be applied elsewhere at little additional cost, and with great benefits for the survival of these exciting birds.

In Sweden, according to the recommendations concerning felling operations in the vicinity of nesting sites of rare birds of prey, felling

164

should not be carried out within 200 metres of nesting trees, and not within 1000 metres of nests occupied during the specified breeding seasons.

In order that these regulations become more than mere bits of paper, everyone involved in forestry work must be aware of the restrictions which they impose.

Osprey *(Pandion haliaetus)*

Ospreys most often breed in trees and always in the uppermost part. They can be helped by construction of artificial nest bases in some of the largest pine trees in their areas. One can also saw the top off such a tree and make a platform there from branches. An alternative nest platform for ospreys can be made by setting four large poles onto the bed of the lake, leaning them against each other, and driving them down into the mud as far as they will go. A wood platform finished off with an artificial nest made from branch wood can then be built in the cradle formed by the poles at a height of about 4 m above the water surface. This work should best be carried out in winter, when in Sweden there is the added advantage that the water is frozen over making access much easier. Other nesting sites which the osprey uses in Europe and also on Sweden's western coast include lighthouses, power line supports, and air defence warning towers. Such an array of nest sites is also used by the North American ospreys. In Scotland, where there are still only around 35 to 40 pairs, which are still subjected to some persecution by egg thieves, the ospreys all nest in trees.

The situation is rather better in Sweden where around 2000 pairs of ospreys breed at present, and the population does not appear to be threatened, even though breeding results are not entirely good. There is, nevertheless, every reason to carefully follow the progress of this bird, especially as many birds die or become sterile through eating fish contaminated with environmental toxins.

The osprey can often be seen hovering over water before dropping steeply from a great height for fish. Its nest is usually formed with a large untidy pile of brushwood at the top of a tree, from where it can be seen for a considerable distance. Despite this, it is amazing how often holiday makers stop for a rest directly under the nest despite the large quantities of foul-smelling fish remains deposited there.

Many young die from sunstroke after being deprived of their mother's shading wings when she is frightened from the nest by such intrusions.

The tree should
be cut here

Support here

Osprey

166

Platform for Osprey and White Tailed Sea Eagle

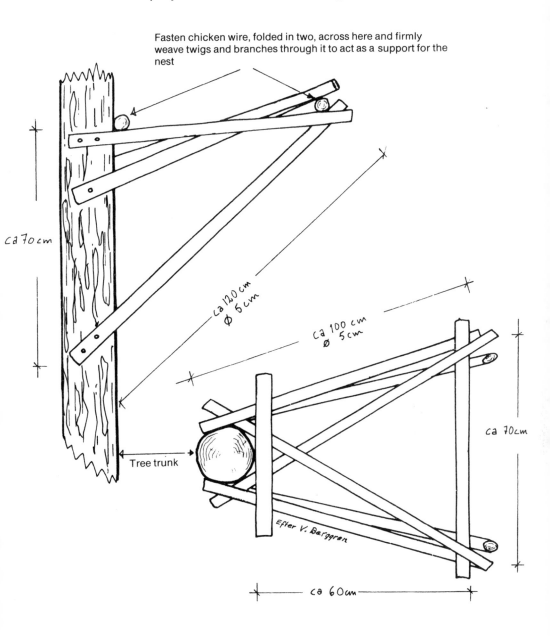

Fasten chicken wire, folded in two, across here and firmly weave twigs and branches through it to act as a support for the nest

ca 70 cm

ca 120 cm
Ø 5 cm

ca 100 cm
Ø 5 cm

ca 70 cm

Tree trunk

Efter V. Berggren

ca 60 cm

These nests are also susceptible to disturbance from motor boats and canoeists.

The growth of outdoor activities by people on the large inland lakes where Sweden's densest populations of ospreys live has subjected this bird to serious disturbance during breeding seasons. In Britain conscious disturbance of rare birds such as the osprey is an offence under the 'Wildlife and Countryside Act', although in practice this legislation is often worthless in acting as a deterrent because there is seldom anyone around in remote areas to enforce it. Much more is to be gained through the goodwill of the general public towards wildlife.

The nest is used year after year, though like other birds of prey the osprey has several nests which it can alternate between.

The 2–4 eggs are incubated for 35 days, mostly by the female. The young are ready to fly after about eight weeks.

Golden Eagle *(Aquila chrysaetos)*

The golden eagle is found throughout the mountainous areas of Europe from the Mediterranean to the Arctic. In Sweden its distribution is limited to mountain and forest areas from northern Dalarna to northern Lappland; there are about 800 pairs. In Britain the Scottish Highlands is its stronghold with around 400 breeding pairs. It just maintains a toehold in England with a solitary pair being fairly well established in the Lake District.

Like other birds of prey, this eagle kills its prey with its talons before taking it back up to its nest, being able to lift as much as 3–4 kilos. Young golden eagles fly south to central and southern Sweden for the winter. They are poor hunters and often take cats or even fish left on the ice by anglers. In Scotland golden eagles are resident in their breeding territories throughout the year, although young birds, recognisable by the white roundels on their wings, can sometimes be seen wandering outside the breeding areas especially in winter.

During the breeding season, golden eagles take mountain hares, occasionally foxes, and game birds, and also, to a much greater extent than is generally thought, small birds down to the size of pipits as well as small rodents. In winter they become very dependent upon carrion, and on sheep-walks in Scotland they may feed extensively on the sheep carcases which are usually abundant.

In Sweden the brushwood nests are built in trees, although in Scotland nests on ledges on crags are more the rule and tree nests are infrequent. Display and nest building usually begins in February long before the winter snows have seriously begun to recede on the high ground. Between one and three eggs are laid at three to four day intervals. These have a white ground colour and are often beautifully marked with dark red brown blotching. Incubation is by the female only and lasts for 40–45 days. The young are ready to fly after about ten weeks but stay with their parents, receiving food from them for a further six weeks.

Great Grey Owl *(Strix nebulosa)*

The great grey or Lapland owl is almost as large as the eagle owl and breeds far up in the north in those years when voles are plentiful. It has an enormous head and a rather long tail, while the fluffed out plumage makes the bird look even larger than it actually is. The colour is lichen grey and the face large with concentric rings, reminiscent of a harvest spider's web, with small yellow ringed eyes (12.5 mm in diameter compared with the 17 mm of the tawny owl) at the centre of these facial discs.

It breeds quite frequently in old goshawk and steppe buzzard nests and sometimes in nest boxes set up for Ural owls. Two to six eggs are laid normally, though this number can reach nine in years when for example the lemming population is high, even though the great grey owl lives only on voles and mice.

According to Juhani Vuorinen, in Finland the great grey owl often breeds on nest trays measuring 70 × 70 cm, with a surrounding 10 cm high edging. These trays should be lined with decayed straw stubble or sawdust. The tray should be fixed to the trunk of an old bare pine, at a height of 3–4 m above the ground.

Steppe Buzzard *(Buteo buteo vulpinus)* and Buzzard *(Buteo buteo)*

The steppe buzzard or northern buzzard is the Eurasian race of the buzzard. The steppe buzzard is rust-red in colour though like the nominate race is very variable and can be confused with the long-legged buzzard. Its most distinctive feature is its tail which is a warm orange red colour. It tends to seek out scrubby, boggy spruce forests and is shyer and quieter in its nest than the more southerly buzzard, though it does show the same exclusive dietary preference for mice and voles.

Two to five eggs are laid and incubated by both parents for about 30 days. The young leave the nest after eight weeks but are still dependent on their parents for a further eight weeks. The steppe buzzard

Great Grey Owl

Nest Box
for Great
Grey Owl

170

population is dwindling somewhat, and measures should be taken to halt this.

Rough-Legged Buzzard *(Buteo lagopus)*

The rough-legged buzzard is a medium-size bird of prey found in mountainous areas, but sometimes overwintering in central and southern Sweden or even further south in Europe, with some turning up in most autumns in the eastern counties of Britain. It differs from the buzzard in its characteristic flight which is to execute only 2–3 wing beats between each glide. Also by comparison with common buzzards, rough-legged buzzards are invariably very pale in appearance when seen from below. The undersides of the wing are white with just a dark mark on the carpal joint. The tail is pale whitish with a broad dark terminal band. The young birds have yellow-white heads in the autumn. The diet consists exclusively of voles and mice.

The nest is made from sticks and built on cliff ledges or in trees. Two to five eggs are laid and incubated for 31 days, mostly by the female.

Goshawk *(Accipiter gentilis)*

The number of goshawks in Sweden fell sharply between 1950 and 1960 because of mercury poisoning. This had been used as a seed dressing by farmers and reached the goshawks through the food chain. Pigeons and other birds ate mercury treated seed and were in turn eaten by goshawks, which consequently became sterile and in the worst cases died.

Since a ban on mercury seed treatments in 1966, the goshawk population has recovered though because it is a difficult species to produce statistics on, it is difficult to be certain how many breeding pairs there are in Sweden. At present there are still large areas where there are virtually no breeding goshawks. It is widespread in the rest of Europe, though nowhere common. In Britain after disappearing as a breeding species after much persecution in the 19th century it is now re-established in small numbers. These pairs, which are thought to have derived partly from falconers' escapees, are breeding in the large blocks of conifer forest largely planted in Britain since 1945.

They feed on birds of the crow family, gulls, squirrels, small rodents, pigeons, certain forest birds, and sometimes even small birds. In Sweden their most controversial habit, however, has been that of preying on pheasants at their feeding places in winter. The problem is not made any easier by large numbers of Finnish goshawks coming to overwinter, mostly in Malardalen, where they take a share of the pheasants. Those who are involved in pheasant breeding really ought to expect a certain amount of wastage to occur, including that taken by goshawks.

Much research has been carried out into goshawks, and with varying results. A study by Revingehed in Skane (Goransson, 1975) showed that goshawks took 0–8% of pheasant stocks in normal winters, though in one particular year when the pheasants were suffering from tuberculosis, 25% was taken. This shows how goshawks, like other birds of prey, in the 'first' instance take sick birds which are falling behind the main group and are already doomed. A later, more comprehensive survey which was carried out in the Malardel area under the direction of the Swedish Hunting Association indicated that goshawks did not particularly select sick or otherwise less able victims amongst the pheasants. I think that an increased goshawk population will help to keep down the rather dense populations of gulls and crows. Studies of goshawk nests have revealed that kills include considerable numbers of these birds, principally jackdaws, jays, and black-headed gulls.

During the long breeding period, the smaller male does the hunting, leaving the food near the nest at points where it is collected by the female which carries it to the nest, before tearing it apart and distributing it to the young. Breeding often take place in large old coniferous forests, though also in mixed and deciduous forests in which case it is still usually a long way from pheasant breeding areas. Crows, gulls, and squirrels form the bulk of the prey at this time, along with smaller numbers of pigeons, mostly wood pigeons, small rodents and small birds.

Goshawks build a stick nest, usually hidden well within a forest. Three to four eggs are laid and incubated for 35–38 days, mostly by the female. The young leave the nest after about 35 days, and move into the canopy near the nest where the female continues to feed them for some weeks.

In Sweden rationalization of the forest industry has made it increasingly difficult for the goshawk to find old forests to breed in. As yet, the effect of this on the species as a whole is uncertain. In Britain the expansion of commercial forestry has had the opposite effect, making it possible for the species to become established as a breeding bird once again.

White-tailed Eagle *(Haliaeetus albicilla)*

In Iceland and Norway the white-tailed eagle often nests on small offshore islets in fjords, or on crags facing the sea. However, in Sweden they often use a tree with a height of about 3–4 metres, often in a three or

172

four branched fork. The nest must be positioned so that it permits free flying access both inwards and outwards, and at the same time is not openly exposed. Despite the fact that these nests grow rather large over the years, it is surprising how often they remain entirely hidden.

Unfortunately, tree tops are in very short supply and the white-tailed eagle does not have an easy task in finding suitable nesting places. A survey in Aland showed that only one out of 1450 available trees was suitable as a nesting tree for the white-tailed eagle (Kulves, 1973). If certain branches are removed from the tops of trees then a suitable fork can be created in which a nest can be placed. Some old branches can be laid in the fork to create an artificial nest base, which the white-tailed eagle will normally accept.

In 1964, the Swedish Nature Conservancy Association began annual inventories of the white-tailed eagle, and reports came in of a drastic deterioration in breeding results. In 1971, the Association started 'Project White-tailed Eagle', to investigate the causes of this worsening situation and to take the necessary measures to save the species. The study encompassed population surveys, location of breeding areas, and winter feeding with toxin-free meat. There are also plans for captive breeding of these eagles for replenishment of wild populations.

At the moment, the species is mostly distributed in two areas: about 60 pairs on the shore of the Baltic Sea and about 40 in the interior of Lapland. Of the 60 east coast pairs, 36 pairs were checked in 1977, and only seven were found to have bred successfully, raising nine young. Of the 40 Lapland pairs, 16 were examined and found to have produced six young. White-tailed eagles are still persecuted in some areas despite having been a protected species since the 1940s.

It is especially in the coastal eagles that high levels of environmental toxins have been found and where breeding results are poor, though in recent years these results have improved. There is therefore a degree of optimism over the bird's future.

One to four eggs (usually two) are laid in February–April and incubated for about 40 days, principally by the female. The young remain in the nest for around 12 weeks and are ready to fly by July, but stay with their parents and receive food from them for a further six weeks.

These birds need to have a number of large, sheltered and protected archipelago areas with wooded islets where it can breed in peace and quiet. They are highly sensitive to disturbance, especially at the start of the breeding season, when the eggs can be quickly destroyed by the low temperature.

Peregrine Falcon *(Falco peregrinus)*

Research in Sweden has shown that the large majority of peregrine falcons nest on the ledges of steep cliffs. Their nests are often clearly visible and their whereabouts known to all and sundry. Because this bird is so rare its eggs are prime targets for thieves, so it can help if the nests are kept under close observation. Moreover, environmental toxins have greatly depleted the falcon's ranks, and for this reason the policy of captive breeding and releasing into the wild has been adopted, and with some success.

Around 4% of Swedish peregines breed in trees, mostly in osprey nests, but also in white-tailed eagle, crow, and raven nests. The main areas where this occurs are Norrbotten, Uppland, and Malardalen. Research carried out by Bengt Fahlgren in the 1940s and 1950s around Malaren showed that increased pressure from human disturbance on mountain slopes was causing the falcons to breed with ever increasing frequency in osprey nests. Artificial nests intended for ospreys and other large birds of prey may therefore, inadvertently encourage the peregrine to breed.

The species is rapidly dying out in Sweden, with only about 10 pairs left in the late 1970s. Surveys carried out by the Swedish Nature Conservancy Association in the mid 1960s showed that the population was in the process of rapid diminution.

Environmental toxins are the major threat in Sweden, but egg collectors and nest-plundering falconers are also putting the tiny population in jeopardy. The sport of falconry has become a fashionable trend in West Germany and England, and has always been important in the Arab states. Because the peregrine is in such high demand as one of the finest falconry species, and at the same time has become a rare species in world terms, the black market price for the young birds has reached astronomical proportions. This has naturally attracted large numbers of unscrupulous international adventurers who see this as a wonderful opportunity to make a lot of money with little effort. Hence, nests are guarded night and day during the breeding season not only in Sweden but all over the world.

In Britain, especially in Scotland, the situation for the peregrine is now much healthier with the population gradually regaining its pre-1939 level. It is still a rare and beautiful bird and it is doubly sad that keepers on many of the red grouse moors in eastern Scotland continue to destroy nests and breeding adults.

Peregrine falcons will take whatever medium to small bird species are available to them. However, their favourite prey is feral pigeons and these seem to be taken even in areas where there are apparently plenty of wood pigeons available. They are however, catholic in their selection and jackdaw, black-headed gull, woodcock, manx shearwater, cuckoo, starling, thrushes, meadow pipit, bullfinch, and a host of other species have all been recorded as prey in the eyries of peregrines. In southern Sweden, the peregrine lives mostly on pigeons, black-headed gulls, starlings, and thrushes, whereas black-headed gulls form the bulk of the diet in northern Sweden. Ducks make up about 10% of kills.

The peregrine lays 2–4 rich red brown eggs between mid-March and mid-April in Britain, the date very much depending upon the weather. In Sweden laying takes place in April or May. The eggs are incubated by both parents though mainly by the female for about 29 days. For at least two weeks after hatching the young are brooded by the female, especially if the weather is wet or cold, while the male does the hunting. In spite of this close attention a late fall of snow at hatching time or a cold wet spring, such as 1986, can be disastrous with few chicks surviving to the flying stage. The young are ready to fly after four to five weeks, but remain with their parents for at least another six weeks after leaving the nest.

During the time that peregrines are in occupation of their breeding crag they are unfortunately extremely obvious. At the approach of anyone both birds will leave their vantage points and start to circle overhead calling with a loud cry of 'kak kak kak kak kak . . .', which they keep up until the intruder departs. When they are in the air together like this the larger female is easy to distinguish from her mate in voice as well as size. Often the voice of the female is so deep that she sounds like a mallard.

Peregrines are found all over Europe if not as a breeding bird then as a winter visitor. Those from the north and east of Europe are much more migratory than those found in the south and west, such as in Britain, where they tend simply to disperse somewhat outside the breeding season. Most of the Swedish falcons overwinter on England's south coast, as well as in Germany and France.

12 Nesting platforms for the White Stork *(Ciconia ciconia)*

Storks can often be helped by the provision of a suitable nesting platform set up on the roof of the house. In those parts of Europe where storks nest they are often considered a symbol of good luck and many villagers put up nesting platforms to encourage them to nest on the roofs of their houses. The construction shown in the diagram is particularly suitable as a nesting platform. The laths resting on the roof should be secured to the rafters of the house (these rafters or roof riders are the two crossed laths used on thatched roofs on the Continent to hold the straw down along the roof ridge) using wire or galvanised bolts. (This construction is used on thatched roofs, whereas the diagram shows tiles. On a tiled roof, a pole is nomally put through the roof-ridge and that is then secured to the rafters as described – Ed.) Instead of the 'bed' of slats shown in the diagram, a cart-wheel can be used, as shown, which should be at least 125 cm in diameter. Thin willow twigs can be woven between the vertical pegs and it would certainly be an advantage to build up part of the nest so that the stork can finish it quickly on arrival. Very often the young storks from a newly built nest are never fledged. This is because the actual building of the nest takes so long that the storks are late in starting egg laying and the young have insufficient time to grow and learn to fly before the adults begin to migrate southwards.

The stork is very well known by every European child, at least from pictures if not from seeing the real thing. But now a days it has become an increasingly rare sight, and even in villages where there were good numbers nesting even as recently as the mid seventies there are now very few. This is most likely the result of drainage in its European nesting areas combined with the continued use of insecticides which have long since been banned in Europe but not in its African wintering quarters.

If we wish to preserve this popular bird we must do our best to help it, both by constructing new nest sites, by repairing old nests and even by considering artificial feeding while the young are in the nest, using fishmongers' waste etc spread in its feeding areas. Moreover, storks should be protected from too much disturbance by tourists, birdwatchers and photographers.

Rooftop nesting platform for Stork (after E. Schüz)

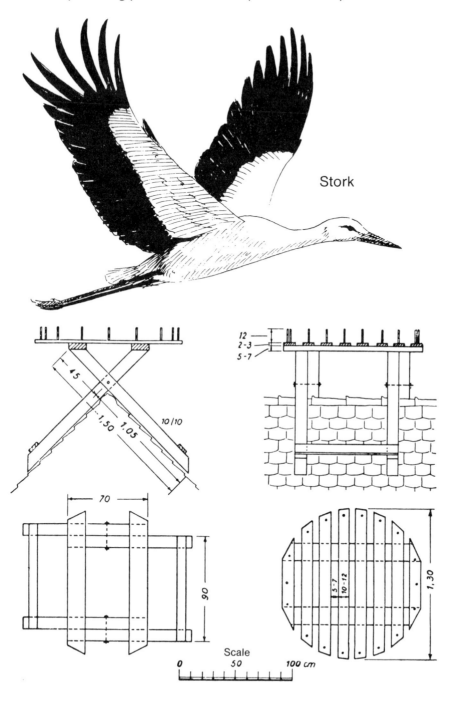

Stork

Scale
0   50   100 cm

At the end of April or beginning of May the female stork lays 3–5 white eggs, which are incubated by both parents. During every meeting or change-over at the nest the storks carry out an elaborate and delightful bill rubbing and clattering ceremony which fills the street below with sound like a slow drum roll. The incubation, which starts as soon as the first or second egg has been laid, takes 29–30 days and the young then remain in the nest for a further 53–55 days. During this period they are fed by both parents and this continues for about a fortnight after they have flown the nest.

In crowded stork colonies, which sadly are increasingly infrequent, polygamy is not unusual.

Their diet is catholic. They will eat earthworms, beetles, and other insects, but larger animals such as mice, frogs, grass snakes, lizards and fish are all eaten just as readily.

The stork leaves Europe at the end of August or in September and most of them winter in East and Southern Africa, from where they return in April.

13   Gulls and Terns in nesting colonies

Gulls

One can encourage colonies of black-headed gulls on lakes or larger ponds by setting up suitably large wooden boxes on poles or iron piping by the side of rushes. Common gulls also occasionally breed on theses raised trays, although in Britain these are very much a Scottish breeding species.

Terns

Common and black terns will nest on lakes and ponds if platforms are provided for them. In Britain floating rafts have often been used for common terns in bird reserves, with some success. Raised trays are much less well known but have considerable advantages, especially since escaped mink have become well established and such a devastating pest to water birds.

These platforms are also prized as resting and preening places by wild ducks.

Both gulls and terns are effective deterrents against the egg-plundering of crows, so that ducks and other water birds such as waders are more successful when they nest in close proximity to these colonies.

Black-headed Gull *(Larus ridibundus)*

Breeding box The black-headed gull breeds readily in a wooden box measuring 50 × 50 cm with a 10 cm edging on all four sides. Hammer into the lake bed some wooden stakes or galvanised iron piping, preferably on the outside edge of a reedbed in a pond or lake, and nail the box on top of these. Remember when driving in the stake to allow for high water in the winter and spring. The top of the pole should lie at least 1 m above the surface of the water when the water is at its normal height, and one has to be particularly careful on coastal sites where there are large tidal variations in the water level.

The bird, which has a dark brown hood, makes its presence known

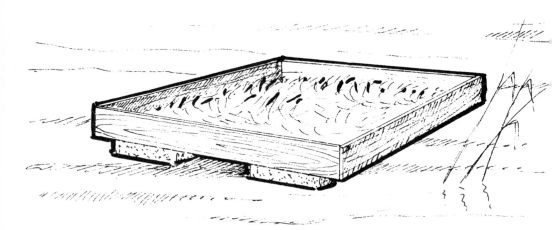

Box for Black-headed Gulls

Black-headed Gull

180

with a loud screaming call, from the time of its arrival on the breeding sites in spring until its dispersal in autumn. In Britain and Ireland the black-headed gull is not a true migrant, simply dispersing from its breeding areas in the winter. On the Continent however, especially around the Baltic, it is a summer visitor and in the autumn most of these birds migrate to Western Europe and Britain. Thus rather like the starling those birds which throng our parks and rubbish tips, or follow the plough on farms in winter are just as likely to have been raised on the shoreline of the eastern Baltic as in local colonies. In the winter the brown hood disappears to be replaced by a white head, marked only by a distinctive black spot behind each eye. The black-headed gull can easily be distinguished from the much less common little gull. In the little gull the chocolate brown hood extends down onto the neck, and in flight the underside of the little gull's wings are dark grey in contrast to the pale underwings of the black-headed gull.

Like other gulls it lays 2–3 eggs in April or May. These are often beautifully marked with dark brown or olive splodges on a pale brown eggshell. Incubation is by both birds and takes 21–27 days. The young are able to swim and walk soon after hatching and usually leave the nest within a few days and hide under tussocks of grass nearby until they are able to fly after about five weeks.

Black-headed gulls are truly catholic in their diet and will consume anything remotely resembling food, from rubbish tip scraps to earthworms thrown up by the plough.

Common Tern *(Sterna hirundo)*

The common tern is the most abundant of the terns. It is a slender bird, with long pointed wings and a forked tail. It is a light ash grey above with a black cap and pure white underparts. It has a red beak tipped with black, and orange-red feet. It has a loud screaming call, and flies into the wind with a skipping motion when it is fishing, which it does by diving headlong into the water from up to 10 m above, to seize small fish in its beak.

Rafts One can construct nesting rafts to encourage breeding by terns. Chicken wire is stretched over a simple wooden frame measuring 75 × 75 cm, and on top of this is placed a 2–3 cm layer of plant remains from the lake or pond bottom. The ability of the wooden frame to float can be enhanced by wrapping the wire around a slab of expanded

Raft for Common Tern

Black Tern

Common Tern

polystyrene. To avoid these rafts all floating into the shoreline in the breeze a simple anchor should be attached using some nylon line and a brick.

Black Tern *(Chlidonias niger)*

In areas within its breeding range, which includes most of Northern Europe except for Britain, Ireland and Scandinavia, the black tern can also be induced to breed on rafts similar to those described for the common tern. However, this is much more difficult to achieve and your best chance of success will be if the rafts are placed a long way out on a pond or lake. It also helps if the rafts are surrounded by lots of lily pads, which will help to protect it against buffeting by waves.

In spring and early summer the black tern has a black body with light blue-grey wings, but as they moult out of breeding plumage the underside becomes white while the back remains dark grey. The wings are shorter and broader than those of the common tern.

The black tern flies low over the surface of ponds, grassy swamps, lily covered water and meadows in search of insects which it catches in mid-air. Its flight is steady like that of a gull, but there will be a sudden jerk towards any passing insect. It also gathers insects from the water surface rather than performing the high dives characteristic of the other terns. Its call is sharp and nasal.

Pieces of boggy vegetation are used to construct the nest. It lays three eggs, usually in May and these are incubated by both parents for 14 days. Unlike most other terns the young remain in the nest and are able to fly after three weeks.

Like the other terns it is only a summer visitor to Europe and winters in tropical Africa.

14   Other inhabitants of nest boxes

Bats

Bats like living in nest boxes. It is not only birds which suffer from the shortage of accommodation. Bats have been, if anything, hit harder. During winter they hang in a state of torpor in a hollow tree or some other frost-free place, often in the company of others to help stay warm. Their temperature can sink so low that heart activity and body metabolism are reduced to a minimum. You can set up nest boxes to help this excellent little fly and midge catcher. To do this you can either use an ordinary bird box which should be placed upside down so that the bats can hang from what used to be the floor; or you can construct a box specifically for bats. These bat boxes do not have the conventional round entrance hole in the front, but instead have a narrow 1.5 cm wide slot running across the floor at the back of the box. Bats enter by landing on the tree, or backboard, below the box and then squeeze up through the slot before hanging themselves upside down from the roof or sides of the box. Boxes which are intended for bats should be constructed from rough sawn wood so that the bats find it easy to hang onto.

If a bird box is used then a starling sized model is the one to choose. However deliberately you set out to provide either bird or bat boxes the accommodation will be used by the other creature. Every year, small bats come to stay in my 'All-year' box for tits and flycatchers; this is hung right way up and the bats use the part between the roof and entrance hole. Equally if you put up the boxes designed specifically for bats, you will invariably have blue tits nesting in one or two.

Bats' droppings are small, dark, and have the odour of musk. In summer the females form nursery colonies, sometimes in large numbers. In areas where arable farming predominates bats have declined in numbers quite dramatically during the last 25 years. Presumably this has been caused by a combination of habitat loss and the use of agricultural chemicals and other toxins in the countryside. However, in areas where farming is less intensive such as Ireland and Scotland very large colonies can still be found, sometimes running into hundreds in these summer nursery colonies. The height above the ground at which bats fly, and the

184

habitat in which they hunt varies with the species. Some of the larger bats such as the noctule will occasionally hunt in large groups 20 to 30 metres above the ground in open areas, while Daubenton's bat specialises in hunting only over water and the delicate long-eared bat likes to fly around the woodland canopy, often settling to take moths off leaves.

It is possible to observe them during the day by carefully removing the front of the nest box ('All-year' type). They sleep heavily while hanging from the roof of the box but should not be disturbed, not least because they have a fine set of tiny but very sharp teeth and know how to use them.

In most Northern European countries, where conservation is considerably more advanced than in some of the less civilised southern parts, bats are fully protected by law. In Britain they should not be disturbed and no action may be taken to destroy a bat colony while it is in residence. This it not as inconvenient as it sounds because different roosts are usually used in summer to breed from those used for hibernating in during the winter. Thus if your house needs reroofing or you really do want to shut them out, it is only a matter of patience and time before this can be done without harm to the bats. Local bat conservation groups have now been set up throughout Britain, and these people, who can be contacted through the nearest Nature Conservancy Council office or through the county naturalists' trust, will always be willing to come and help and advise people who discover that they are sharing their house with bats.

Bats are renowned for their large ears and acute sense of hearing. During flight they send out high-frequency sound waves, outside the range of human perception, which bounce off surrounding objects and are picked up again by the bats. This 'radar system' enables them to avoid colliding with obstacles in the dark.

Hornets

Wasp nests often appear in nest boxes during middle to late summer, particularly in tit or starling boxes. At the beginning of June 1976, a female hornet began building in one of my block nest boxes made from alder. To start with her presence was not very noticeable. The hornet begins to establish its nest in August, when the caterpillar population has reached its maximum size. This is the only time that this has happened in the 29-year history of my nest box study, and it happened to coincide with a very warm summer. However, hornets often make their nests in old green woodpecker nests and in hollow trees.

During the summer worker hornets prey upon insects which cause damage to forests and problems for the forest industry. Notorious insect pests such as the large white butterfly (which, along with the small white, is the cabbage white to gardeners) and its larvae, often turn up in the hornet's nursery, a fact which people who rush to exterminate hornet nests on discovery overlook. In fact hornets are usually fairly peaceful insects unless their nest is disturbed, or one is accidentally sat on during cool autumn days when like wasps they become rather groggy.

Male hornets, and some females, are born in large cells which are built in autumn. By the end of September they are sexually mature and fly from the nest to mate. Soon after mating the males die, but the young fertilised females search out suitable places in which to overwinter, with the spermatazoa held in a small container above their oviducts. In April or May, depending upon how far north in Europe they are, they re-emerge to seek out suitable nest sites and build a new nest before laying the first batch of eggs to restart the colony. Like wild bees, hornets are also experiencing difficulties in finding places in which to nest. Bees, of course, fulfil a great service in pollinating fruit trees and berry bushes, but the wild variety is becoming increasingly rare.

Block nest boxes are clearly the most popular with these insects. We should not begrudge them what they richly deserve, so let us make a point of leaving their nests in peace.

Bumble Bees

In today's rationalised and cultivated landscape, with the minimum of verges left on roadsides and clinically clipped lawns, even bees have problems finding mouse holes or other suitable accommodation for their nests. Most bumble bees nest in holes in the ground, but they will also nest in the disused remains of birds' nests left in boxes which have not been cleaned out. This point should be kept in mind when cleaning out nest boxes after breeding. If bees do occupy the nest box then one should wait until after they have finished before cleaning out the box.

One can even make a bumble bee box from wood, measuring 20 × 20 × 20 cm and containing dried peat or grass. The bee box should be set out early in spring when the queen bees are in search of suitable nesting holes. If the box is placed above ground it will be occupied by *Bombus hypnorum* or *Bombus lapidarius*, but if it is buried beneath the soil with an entrance up to the surface, many different species of bee will be attracted to it. The entrance to the nest should be sited alongside a farm lane, a forest ride, a woodside verge, or a mound of stones.

15   Environment and Feeding

Planting a garden for birds

In addition to the hole nesting species of birds which build their nests in nest boxes or natural holes, many species of small passerines build nests in the open amongst vegetation. These include birds of the crow family, sparrows, thrushes, and warblers. In order to provide for these species at least one small corner should be left undisturbed to encourage some of these birds to breed. Small alterations in your gardening schedule will make a big difference to the suitabilty of your garden for birds. If bushes are pruned during the autumn, they will grow thicker in early summer, and these should form part of a protective thicket of grass and bushes, which provides not only cover but also the berries needed as food for the approaching winter. Similarly, if hedge trimming is carried out in the autumn instead of the spring you will avoid exposing nests in the middle of the breeding period.

No birds, whether they are nest box users or not, thrive in bare, open areas, so one of the reasons for birds not nesting in your garden may be that it is too prim and proper.

If you are planting up your garden the inclusion of a few evergreen bushes will make a great difference to its suitability for birds. As well as providing sites for early nesters such as the song thrush and blackbird, some of the evergreens which carry berries such as holly and cotoneaster, also provide a source of food.

As well as hollies, several other shrubs are also well worth including for their value as berry bearers. Room should be made if possible for the inclusion of hawthorn, rowan, and blackberry. Thorny bushes such as hawthorn and blackberry give good protection against the enemies of small birds as well as providing an excellent source of vitamins in their berries during autumn and even for part of the winter. Vitamin-rich berries and fruit are also available from crab-apple trees, elder and wild cherry. We often plant hedges around our gardens without considering which type of hedge could be both attractive and good for birds. As well as those already mentioned privet, hornbeam and beech can also be used to serve both purposes. The production of berries is not the only criterion for deciding whether or not the plant will be a useful food source. In fact birds clearly do not like some berries. Snowberries, most cotoneasters, except the small berried 'horizontalis' varieties, and berberis berries are all usually ignored until the birds are in really dire straits in cold weather. Because of this they may actually be considered a good back up for hard weather. The birds themselves cannot realise that it might be useful to keep some berries in reserve, and an example of this is the speed at which the rowan berries are eaten as soon as they ripen in the autumn.

If your garden does not already contain a good thick shrubbery, then it is quite simple to set one up. The bushes should be planted fairly close together, so that they form a dense thicket when they mature. This can be performed with small spruce, pruning the tops to cause a sideways bushy growth, or almost any other shrubs provided that a good proportion of evergreens is included. As well as providing a daytime retreat for birds evergreen shrubberies also make popular roosting sites, where small birds can sleep safely hidden from owls and other predators.

There are also good climbing plants which provide birds with both food and nesting places, such as honeysuckle. Other climbers such as Virginia creeper, which gives a glorious blaze of red as its leaves change colour in the autumn, ivy, and *Clematis montana*, are all favourites as nest sites for birds like the spotted flycatcher, pied and grey wagtails.

Thus it is relatively simple to carry out environment protection in your own garden plot, and the results are usually amazingly good. Besides the joy of flowering bushes in the spring, brilliantly coloured berries in late summer, and the pale leaves of autumn, the abundance of birds will certainly impress you. With the right mixture of plants and cover, many small birds visit your garden to seek shelter, food, and nesting sites.

Bird Baths

Having access to water can present a considerable problem to birds both in the summer and winter. This is especially true in coastal areas, where rain water evaporates rapidly on rock faces and small pools dry out in the usually dry early summers; the sea water of course is undrinkable. A bird bath provides water for both drinking and bathing in.

Birds like to bath and preen daily. This is vital in terms of keeping their plumage in good condition, which is a prerequisite for efficient flight and ultimately their survival. While they have young in the nest the feathers of the adult birds are especially prone to wear and tear, particularly those of the hole nesting species which may be pushing themselves in and out of confined spaces all day long. Research has shown that during the growth period of the young, the female pied flycatcher loses a full 3 grams in weight, and the male almost 1 gram. They often like to take a break from their labours to bathe and preen and oil their plumage. The latter is done by rubbing oil from the preen gland just above the tail onto the beak, and then transferring it to their feathers. Preening also serves the important function of getting rid of the insect parasites that all birds are infested with. Initially the young produce excreta contained in small membranous sacks. As the young grow, the parents are less and less able to cope with the increasing amount of droppings and so the nest often becomes heavily soiled. The parents themselves also become quite dirty after several feeding sessions and thus need to bathe often.

The lack of a bird bath containing water could be the underlying cause of birds ignoring your nest boxes. You can either make one yourself using concrete and a mould, or buy one made from plastic, concrete or metal. If you do make one, make sure its maximum depth does not exceed 5 cm.

Bird baths are often placed on the ground or even sunk into the soil, and flowers, ferns, and other plants set around it. Such a bath, however, may prove to be a death trap to small birds, which can easily be caught unawares by stalking cats. It is best to fix the bath on a pole, or a galvanised water pipe from a scrap merchant would be suitable. The pipe, which should be about 2 metres long and 5 cm in diameter, is inserted to a depth of 30 cm into the soil so that it stands firmly. A round piece of wood is filed down so that it fits the pipe precisely and a hole is drilled in the bottom of a plastic water bath which is then fastened to the wood using screws, with washers and possibly bits of rubber from old wellington boots to seal the point of attachment. A neater job of the seal can be made by buying a tube of silicon sealant. This is available in DIY hardware shops for use in plumbing, or alternatively can be bought at aquarists shops. Fish keepers use it to make and seal leaks in glass aquaria. The piping may then be painted. In climates which are rather milder than in Northern Europe and Scandinavia, water should also be provided in winter. Providing that it is not actually freezing, birds will bathe in the coldest of weather, and of course they need to drink just as much in winter as in summer.

Remember that on warm days, the water in bird baths will evaporate very quickly, so if you are going off on holiday, ask whoever has volunteered to water your house plants also to put some in the bird bath.

It is really wonderful to have your morning or afternoon coffee to the accompaniment of the cheerful chirping and splashing of birds as they have their baths.

'Abandoned' fledglings

Every summer millions of young birds leave the relative safety of their nests and begin their free flying lives with a few precarious days, during which they learn to become competent fliers. Many species leave the nest shortly after hatching and long before they have developed the feathers which will enable them to fly. These are the 'nidifugous' or precocial nestlings of species such as game birds, waders or ducks, which are covered with often cryptically coloured down and are able to run or in the case of young waterfowl, swim within a few hours of hatching. Other birds are born naked and sometimes blind and are totally dependent upon parental care often until some time after they have left the nest and learned to fly. These are termed 'nidicolous' or altricial nestlings. Both groups are represented among the nest box users described in this book: all of the ducks discussed being 'nidifugous', and all the remaining species being 'nidicolous'. Thus goldeneye ducklings which leap from their tree bound nest boxes to start swimming on nearby lochs, goosander ducklings which venture into fast flowing rivers and eider ducklings which leave their offshore islets, all within hours of hatching, typify 'nidifugous' chicks: while the blind, naked and helpless nestlings of tits and flycatchers, as well as the down covered, but equally helpless kestrel chicks in their nest boxes, all exemplify 'nidicolous' nestlings.

It is not uncommon to find young birds during the spring and summer which are alone and apparently abandoned. They rarely are. In the case of 'nidifugous' chicks, the young bird should always be left alone unless it is in immediate and obvious danger. In such cases the minimum necessary to remove it from the danger should be done. That is, for example, if a duckling or wader chick has wandered onto a road, then remove it to the neighbouring field, but no more. Having placed it out of danger you should leave the area and allow its parents to return. Even if you cannot see them, they will invariably be watching their young and you from a safe distance.

The same rule applies to 'nidicolous' nestlings, unless they have clearly left the protection of the nest too early, or have been frightened into leaving by some interference by a predator or unthinking person. You should not, therefore, look inside nest boxes or open nests when the young are well feathered and near to flight readiness. In nest boxes, they are normally seen crammed up against the entrance hole, begging for food. If they are startled when almost fully grown they will fly off in all directions into the surrounding terrain on their small wing stumps. If you inadvertently cause such an incident, it is best to quickly and carefully gather together all the tiny escapees and place them gently back in their nest or nest box, otherwise they will fall easy victim to cats and other predators. Once they are back inside the nest or nest box, cover them over for a few minutes with a handkerchief, or even your hand so that they are in darkness. Most wild creatures will calm down if they are gently covered in this way, and after a few minutes you should be able to slowly withdraw the cover and retreat, leaving the young safely settled in their nest, ready to make a natural departure when they are fully ready.

Amongst birds of prey, especially owls, the young always leave the nest before they are ready to fly. Remember that these birds have in no way been abandoned and that their parents are close by. So do not disturb them, and leave the vicinity as quickly and carefully as you can.

If your children should come home with an abandoned young bird, then try as speedily as possible to return it to the place where it was found. If necessary, you can deposit the young bird, like a foundling, in another nest of the same species provided the young are about the same size. There are no problems with adoption among birds as there often are among mammals, and such implants are normally adopted straight away, though the situation should be observed a short while later to check that the ploy has worked.

If you have to return a young bird to the place where it was found, place it at such a height that cats cannot reach it. All young birds continue to be fed by their parents for a certain period after leaving the nest, and for this to happen the young bird must be able to manage a loud and vigorous call to let the parents know of its whereabouts. You can check that this happens using a pair of binoculars.

Any young bird which you return to its nest or near to where it was found will have virtually as good a chance of survival as other nestlings which have not had the misfortune to be discovered by humans. Should you try to care for it in your own home, you can be 99% certain that it will die an unpleasant death and at the same time you will be subjected to a great deal of inconvenience and mess. It is very difficult to rear a young bird. Usually we give it the wrong food and too much of it, and the fact that the bird is accepting and swallowing the food does not necessarily mean that it is faring well and that it will survive. Young birds will open their beaks and swallow whenever there is food to be had, but only their parents provide the correct food. Moreover, it is the bird which opens its beak and cries the most which is most in need of food. These actions trigger the feeding instinct in the parents, so that each young bird is fed regularly and is safe from starvation. Humans do not make successful surrogate parents for young birds.

If despite everything, you do attempt to care for an abandoned bird, remember that swallows and flycatchers eat midges and flies, while tits feed on caterpillers. Most pet shops stock meal worms, which you can feed to young birds as a substitute for insects and caterpillars, and they can also be given boiled egg, minced beef, apple, and cheese, with of course fresh water all the time. Usually in such cases, people tend to feed these young birds to death, causing them to suffer so much that death must come almost as a relief. Moreover, the bird may have sustained internal injuries on falling from the nest or may be suffering from some illness. If either of these possibilities is suspected it is kindest to have the bird destroyed as humanely as possible, by a veterinary surgeon if you are in any doubt how to do this. Those birds which do survive, generally become tame and unable to return successfully to the wild. Their would-be rescuers frequently tire of them when once they become adults and are no longer the cute little chicks they used to be. I can fully understand someone taking pity on a small, lonely, helpless, and charming young bird, but feelings should not be allowed to overcome reason, neither should you let your children's whims and pleas be the deciding factor in such an important question. To treat young birds in this way is very inhumane and not at all helpful. Birds fare best in the wild, where they can fly in the company of other birds and live a free life.

Winter feeding

In gardens The best way to help birds over the hard winter is to give them protein-rich foods. Hemp seed and sunflower seed are excellent for this purpose and eagerly consumed by all tits, nuthatches, tree sparrows, and house sparrows.

It is best to use a bird food dispenser made from plastic which can be hung up or set on a perch. They are easy to keep clean and significantly reduce the risk of those diseases which have claimed may victims in recent winters, such as salmonella and bird pox.

Tits are also fond of coconut halves and of peanuts contained in plastic-net or wire-net holders. Plastic net bags are, however, are more often that not ripped apart by squirrels and jackdaws, which gobble up the contents in no time. This can be prevented by fastening plastic covered chicken wire around the bag, the same sort of wire one uses in the garden to support climbing plants. In Northern and Eastern Europe and Scandinavia, where the winters are much more severe than in Western Europe, wire basket nut containers and squirrel guards made from uncoated chicken wire must be avoided. Birds have exposed skin between the horny toe pads on their feet and this can become frozen fast onto the bare metal wire in severe cold.

Tallow is also a fine food for birds, though this can sometimes become a source of infection in mild weather, and I personally prefer to avoid using it, especially for tits.

In woods Many small birds such as the coal tit and treecreeper tend to stay away from our gardens and remain out in the woods throughout the winter. Not many people think of setting food out in the woods for birds, but provided that this is done at regular intervals throughout the winter it can be an enormous help for these shyer birds. The coal tit is fond of tallow and coconut halves, and once again plastic chicken wire should be used to protect the food from squirrels and large birds such as magpies and jackdaws. One can also fasten an half-kilo packet of coconut fat to a tree trunk; this is very popular with tits.

For the treecreeper one can lay out strips of tallow or lard measuring 20 mm by 2 mm at the foot of a large tree where they will not be covered with snow. In areas where there are pygmy owls sugar lump-sized pieces of raw meat can be scattered around in their hunting places and the areas left undisturbed. This is especially useful in severe winters, but is should be remembered that once this feeding has been started it is essential that it be continued until the warm weather of spring has clearly come to stay.

Insulated nest boxes for winter roosting Just as important as birds being able to find food to enable them to survive the cold of winter, is the presence of insulated accommodation in which they can roost. Hence, well insulated nest boxes should be set up near to feeding places. I have carried out tests to establish the insulating properties of nest boxes. These clearly showed that nest boxes made from wood-cement board, wood, or expanded polyethylene gave good protection against severe winter cold. It is not sufficient that construction is draught free and provided with a layer of insulating cotton on the floor. The material of the walls must also have good insulating qualities if the birds are to cope with changes in temperature without becoming over-stressed. Tits can freeze to death on cold winter nights if they seek shelter in the wrong type of nest box.

The nest boxes I tested were kept for 30 minutes in
1. A fridge at +5°C.
2. An ice-box at −23°C.
3. 50 cm from a heat lamp, giving a maximum temperature of +42°C.

Nest box model	Treatment °C		
	+5	−23	+42
	Temperature in nest box after 30 minutes		
Birch block (wood)	+14	+9	+23
'All-year' nest box (wood-cement board)	+14	+6	+23
Expanded polyethylene	+17	+5	+26
Trivsel-Bo (Wood and masonite)	+12	+5	+28
Wood with roof and floor of sheet metal and internal floor of insulating board	+9	0	+24
Timbered with small wooden laths	+12	+2	+28
High-density polyethylene	+9	−23	+32

The insulating ability of the nest box can also have some effect on breeding results. Certain plastic nest boxes and sheet metal boxes can afford such poor insulation that birds which shelter overnight in them during cold winters freeze to death. In addition, abnormal amounts of condensation can build up inside the box, creating a damp nest and causing the young to die. A poorly insulated box can be dangerous for young birds if it is exposed to excessive intense sunlight at the warmest times of the day, the heat causing the mucous membranes of newly born birds to dry up.

One cannot, however, assume that poor breeding results are due to unsuitable nest box construction, as these results under normal circumstances vary from one year to the next, especially amongst tits. Cold springtimes can result in many unhatched eggs, which the parents have been unable to keep warm, or dead young because of a shortage of insects. Environmental toxins have a considerable negative effect on breeding results.

Cement piping – nest box As described in Chapter 6 cement piping can be used to provide nest sites for wheatears. These can also make quick and simple nest boxes for tits or nuthatches. They should be stood on one end and buried in the ground in a suitable spot. A hole measuring about 5 × 5 cm can be knocked in it near the top, and a slab or flat stone used as a roof. Ideally if the pipe is set at ground level, which is perfect for coal tits, some twigs should be stuffed into the bottom of the pipe to keep the nest, when it is built, clear of the damp ground. Alternatively, provided that both ends are securely sealed, these quick and easy pipe 'boxes' can be tied up on garden walls or on tree trunks, using wire to hold them in place. If you do use wire to tie a box to a tree, remember to loosen it off and retie it every autumn, otherwise the wire will gradually cut into the tree as it grows, either killing it eventually or making a weak point at which it may snap off during a wind.

Cement piping–seed dispenser In winter, cement pipes can be made into seed dispensers. This can be done by using a hammer to chip out a small (5 cm wide and 2 cm high) hole in the rim on which the pipe which is to be stood, and then standing it on end on a stone slab or flat piece of ground, filled with seed and with a stone cover on the top end. The disadvantage of placing this on the ground is that it will quickly attract mice, and these will consume as much, or more, seed than the birds for whom it is intended. Placing the home-made dispenser up on a window ledge should overcome this problem.

Plastic buckets as seed dispensers A 12–15 litre plastic bucket with a lid can be converted into an excellent dispenser by drilling a few holes into the bottom of the bucket and fixing a plastic or metal lid (this should have a small edging all the way round and be slightly larger than the base of the bucket) onto the base of the bucket, with screws, nuts and washers, so that it is suspended a few centimetres below the bottom of the bucket. With a lid or cover placed over it, the bucket filled with seed can then be hung on a suitable branch. The advantage of such a large dispenser is that it will not require refilling for several weeks, which, especially if you are feeding the birds in woods away from your immediate garden, could be an advantage.

Mix 50 kg oats with 25 kg hemp seed and 25 kg sunflower seed, and this will give you enough of a suitable mixture to last the whole winter. A single bucketful will last about 2 weeks. This type of dispenser is ideal for use near a holiday cottage, where it is not possible to replenish food everyday. Remember that once you start to feed birds in a particular spot, you should continue to do so. Once birds locate a source of food, then it is of great importance to them that it continues into the start of spring. People often forget that although things may be critical for birds during snow and ice in mid-winter, it is usually the late winter which is a threshold period for small birds, and many can die at this time.

Hygiene at feeding sites

Salmonella Since the winter of 1968–69, Sweden's bird communities have been ravaged by *Salmonella typhimurium*. Salmonella has also become more common during mild winters elsewhere in Europe. The presence of these bacteria among small bird populations is probably nothing new, but as we have become increasingly conservation conscious since the 1960s, and more people have started to feed birds in their gardens, the risk of the spread of the disease has increased. At feeding stations such as bird tables food is unnaturally concentrated in a manner which does not occur in the wild. Birds usually defecate as they feed and the droppings of diseased birds contain the bacteria. Where food is thinly scattered, as would be the case in natural situations, these droppings probably seldom fall where another bird will be feeding. However, where food is continually being replenished at exactly the same spot this is extremely likely. There is particular risk of a localized outbreak of disease during mild weather in the February–March period. Avoid putting food out for birds on tables where birds have left their excrement, or if you do use a bird table clean it frequently using boiling water. Where possible use instead a bird seed dispenser made from plastic which is easy to clean, and hang it up or place it on a pole so that the birds' droppings will fall to the ground, thus reducing the risk of disease spreading. Clean out the dispenser several times each winter. Avoid using tallow or any other food which can easily become infected during mild weather; although tallow should still be made available for the great spotted woodpecker. Care can be taken to avoid infection, including changing the tallow daily in mild weather. If despite all precautions dead birds are found near the food table and salmonella is suspected, feeding should be stopped immediately. In such a case, the birds will look for feeding places elsewhere and it is probable that this particular outbreak will die out. It is simply a matter of choosing the lesser of two evils, as salmonella takes a heavy toll of tree sparrows, greenfinches, house sparrows, bullfinches and yellowhammers.

If you see a bird sitting and panting, then do put it out of its misery. Salmonella often produces a neurosis of the throat, causing the bird to slowly suffocate, and once a bird has reached this stage of the illness it cannot survive.

Should you find dead birds in circumstances which lead you to suspect salmonella then bury them so that no dogs or other animals can come into contact with them and spread the disease. Also see to it that your children are kept away from sick birds.

Bird Pox Since the end of the 1950s, bird pox has become rife amongst tits feeding at bird tables during winter, especially great tits. This viral disease attacks in particular the epidermal cells, giving rise to wart-like growths of various sizes. These warts appear principally on the unfeathered parts of the body such as the root of the beak, between the horny toe pads on the feet, and on areas of the skin above the eyes, and can become very large, giving rise to 'baldness', deformities, and other problems.

This disease has been observed in a large number of bird species, being relatively common amongst pigeons and partridges, while great tits and chaffinches appear to include chronic carriers amongst their numbers. Winters, especially mild ones, are when the disease hits hardest, with communal feeding at bird tables magnifying the risk of infection through contact between diseased and uninfected birds, and droppings and food. Similar precautions to those recommended above will help reduce the risks.

Bird pox is not normally fatal, but during severe winters may place the birds infected at a disadvantage so that they succumb to other factors more quickly than uninfected birds.

16   The enemies of nest box birds

Hole nesting birds and those using nest boxes are afforded significantly more protection than those in open nests. Tit nest boxes are sometimes plundered by weasels, but generally they provide a very safe nesting environment. As discussed in Chapter 9 the eiders which nested in the duck boxes which I put down on the islet of Stora Granholma were virtually 100% safe from egg predation by crows.

Nevertheless, nest box birds do have some enemies which can interfere with breeding. The most common are:
1. Humans
2. Squirrels
3. Magpies
4. Jays

Humans Small boys are of course always curious, and if nest boxes are within easy reach then their contents run the risk of being vandalised. This should be regarded as the fault of whoever put the boxes up as much as of the youth whose mindlessness destroyed the nest. By the very act of putting up a nest box you are encouraging birds to nest in something that is very obvious; and while the nest will be much safer from natural predation, a box offers little protection from human interference. Therefore, unless you are putting nest boxes up in the relative safety of your own garden, rule number one should be to use a short ladder when siting boxes. Their destruction soon loses its appeal for youths if an awkward shin up a bare trunk to reach each one is involved.

Education is always better than prohibition, and a good way to nip the problem in the bud is to involve young people in making and putting up nest boxes themselves. Various forms of group activities and youth clubs are often excellent places for meeting young people. The toughest and liveliest of them can show a sudden keenness for carpentry when they find that they are losing the undivided attention of their audience to the pleasure of hammer and nails. Such 'leaders' will immediately want to re-establish their position as 'cock of the roost' and knuckle down enthusiastically to carpentry. They get a real thrill out of the nest boxes they have made themselves. The course leader should always issue a word of praise, even if the box is such that any self-respecting bird would turn its beak up at it. They get still more satisfaction and pleasure if they set up their own boxes and observe any subsequent breeding. In this way one can teach many of these 'disruptive' youngsters to show an interest in and concern for wildlife.

But there is another group who constitute a danger to nest box birds, and these are inexperienced, enthusiastic ornithologists who are not fully acquainted with the habits of the various species. Sometimes they disturb birds at the most crucial of periods, immediately before and after laying. Such unfortunate happenings are of course unintentional and the people concerned quickly and regretfully realize their mistakes. One can certainly learn from mistakes, but for the sake of the birds, a more well-informed approach to bird watching would be desirable.

Squirrels Squirrels often build their dreys in owl nest boxes, as well as in more natural sites such as in forks or hollows in trees. Their diet during the autumn and winter includes pine and spruce seeds. One often comes across cone scales and shelled cones on tree stumps in forests. Conifers produce different numbers of cones from one year to the next, and in those years when there is a bumper crop there tends to be a higher population of squirrels.

Squirrels produce several litters each year, and the female becomes very thin during those periods when she is carrying young (Hammarsten, Pehrson, Sefve, 1954). At such times she and her offspring eat enormous quantities of food, including eggs and young birds in nest boxes.

Birds will attack squirrels with considerable violence, and the pied flycatcher in particular is regarded with great caution. If a squirrel approaches a pied flycatcher's nest, the flycatcher will fly directly at the squirrel, swooping at its head, until it scampers up into the top of the tree to avoid the harassment.

What can one do to protect birds from squirrels? Fixing sheet metal around the entrance hole is one way, though the metal must be fitted very closely with no loose ends on which the birds' feet may get caught. 'All-year' nest boxes of wood-cement board or of certain expanded polyethylenes with thick walls are also excellent and protect against gnawing predators. Also note that a perch should never be fitted to the outside of a nest box as this is a great help to squirrels, cats, magpies and jays in plundering nests.

The pine marten and the goshawk are the squirrel's natural enemies,

199

but are often shot for the purported reason that they are depriving hunters of small game. This disturbance in the balance of nature means that hunting is necessary to keep the squirrel population under control. Mankind's intervention in the natural world is seldom of a beneficial nature, and I think all individuals should have in mind the need to maintain a natural environmental balance in the most practicable way.

The complications of spring cleaning When nest boxes are cleaned out early in spring, before the end of February, they may be found to contain nesting material introduced by squirrels or possibly an owl's winter pantry of dead mice. All of this must be removed if breeding is to occur in the boxes.

One is quite justified in removing half-made squirrel dreys especially if these belong to the grey squirrel (*Sciurus carolinensis*). This animal is a serious pest in broadleaved woodlands where it damages the trees by stripping bark, often killing the tree above the point of attack. It is also a significant predator of small birds' nests. A more sympathetic attitude should be extended to the native European red squirrel (*Sciurus vulgaris*). Although this also sometimes causes damage it is now much less common in many parts of its range where it has been replaced by its grey cousin, and in many countries, including Britain, it is now a protected animal.

If the drey is completed and one suspects it may contain young squirrels, then things are not quite so straightforward. If the drey is that of a grey squirrel then the best approach from a practical conservation standpoint is to destroy the drey and young in a humane manner. If the drey is that of the red squirrel then it should be left intact and unharmed.

If there are kestrels in the area, they can be encouraged to use the nest box by leaving old squirrel dreys in nest boxes.

Magpies The magpie is particulary noted for raiding and taking the eggs and young of other birds. It is particularly good at cleaning out starling nest boxes, to which it is attracted by the loud cries of the young starlings every time one of the parents arrive to feed them. This behaviour by magpies is distressing to human observers, although in practical terms it probably makes little long term difference to the population of the predated species. The magpie lays 5–11 eggs in April–May, with the female brooding for 17–18 days, and the young flying from the nest after 24–27 days. The magpie's breeding season coincides with those of many of the smaller passerines, so the young of these other species naturally become a major part of the diet of the young magpies. However, although starling broods do suffer somewhat, most nest boxes afford good protection against the unwelcome attention of magpies.

The 'Trivsel-Bo' nest box will give the starling protection against magpies, with its tapering roof overlapping the sides. I once had the opportunity of watching a magpie trying to take eggs from an occupied starling's nest. The parents resisted violently and five other starlings joined in the mobbing of the magpie which was successfully repulsed. In recent years, game-keeping associations in Sweden have called for the shooting of crows and magpies during springtime, with a bounty on those killed. But this has been happening so late in spring that there has been a considerable risk of killing birds which already have dependent young in the nest. In both Sweden and Denmark corvids may only be shot at the nest during the breeding season, the purpose behind this being to ensure that the nest is also destroyed so that the young are not left to suffer unnecessarily. In Britain carrion and hooded crows, rooks, jackdaws, jays and magpies may all be shot at any time of the year, but only by authorised persons. In practice an authorised person is anyone who has the right to shoot on the land in question. However, this may change because recent regulations introduced by the EEC include the protection of all the corvid species. This regulation is due to be introduced in West Germany in 1988, and may eventually be implemented by all the member states. The destruction of corvids is so strongly accepted by the shooting fraternity and also by many conservationists as being a necessary and correct thing to do that this will inevitably cause much heart searching. In practice such a change will probably make little difference to corvid populations. They may increase locally as they have done recently in the eastern counties of England as the intensity of gamekeeping has declined; but overall any major change is unlikely. It is well established by ecologists that the numbers shot reflect rather than control the population size.

If you think a pair of nesting magpies in your garden would constitute a nuisance, then place an empty bottle in the nest, though only before eggs or young have made their appearance. The birds will be unable to remove the bottle and will look for another place in which to nest.

However, not all of the activities of crows are without their uses. Several birds of prey often breed in old crow nests. Methods of creating artificial versions of such nests are described in Chapter 11, but crows themselves provide many times the number of nests that any amount of well intentioned effort by conservationists can ever hope to achieve. Some birds of prey are almost wholly dependent on old crow nests as nesting sites. These include the red-footed falcon which nests in eastern

Europe in small colonies situated in rookeries. In England the hobby, a small falcon which specialises in feeding on swallows, martins, swifts and large insects like dragonflies, breeds almost exclusively in disused carrion crows' nests. Thus all of these animals have a purpose and interaction and it is only man's perception and interference which upsets the balance. So try to understand rather than interfere if magpies or crows predate the nests in your garden.

Jays The jay is a known predator of the nests of small birds, particularly tits, which use nest boxes with entrance hole diameters exceeding 3.5 cm. The jay lays 5–7 eggs in May and broods for 17 days. The young hatch out in June, when nature seems to be just one big nursery, and consume huge amounts of food at a time when virtually all parent birds are scouring the area to get food for their own nestlings. Almost all the open nests of small birds in the vicinity of jay nests will be raided. Because the jay has a relatively slender build and a thin beak, it is difficult to prevent it from raiding nest boxes which have an entrance hole with a diameter greater than 3.5 cm. Smaller varieties of the Trivsel-Bo nest box, for pied flycatchers and tits, have the advantage of a protective overlapping roof. This is a design feature which you can build into the boxes you build yourself if jays start to become a problem. The roof does not need to be pointed as in the Trivsel-Bo; it is the overlap and the lack of a perch at the entrance hole which are important. These features prevent jays from being able to perch and reach into the box to withdraw the nestlings. In nature the goshawk maintains a check on all the corvids, while the smaller sparrowhawk also takes jays. While a goshawk will undoubtedly take pheasant poults, a crow or jay which discovers a pheasant nest will continue to return to it until it has consumed all the eggs. Thus on balance the goshawk probably contributes more than it takes and by persecuting this beautiful bird of prey, the keeper is making his own task harder.

17   Conclusion

This book was written after 30 years of running my own nest box scheme in Sweden. Inevitably much of what is written is based upon my Swedish experience, but birds do not have the language problems of humans and you should find that the hints and suggestions contained in this English edition will be just as applicable elsewhere in Europe. Some of the northern forest species included, such as the three-toed woodpecker, pygmy owl, Ural and great grey owl are very unlikely to occur elsewhere; but for ornithologists their retention in this edition should add interest and wet appetites for what is to be seen on a birding trip to Scandinavia.

Every year large numbers of birds breed in nest boxes, showing how profitable and rewarding the setting up of these boxes can be. Above all it can be seen as a task of caring for both wildlife and the environment.

In Sweden in 1886 the society 'Smafoglarnes vanner' (Friends of Small Birds) was formed through the initiative of A. W. Malm. In an address given immediately afterwards, Professor Malm said, amongst other things, 'Small birds are far more important for our country than all the meat and all the feathers which so-called game provides us with, because small birds contribute in a very considerable degree to the preservation of our forests and the filling of our barns'.

Even though it is more than one hundred years since these words of wisdom were uttered, they are still as relevant today as ever. There is every reason in these days of spraying and hormones to consider Professor Malm's words.

Land owners should be setting up nest boxes, including large boxes for owls, to a far greater extent than they are at present. If there are suitable trees and areas alongside farm tracks and woodland rides, then these in particular should be used as sites for nest boxes because access to them is greatly facilitated; making cleaning and maintenance of the boxes much easier. Sometimes individuals and organisations mass produce nest boxes and set them up, which is a great thing in itself; but the question of cleaning the boxes tends to be forgotten during construction, so that when this becomes essential as inevitably it will, the only way that this can be performed is literally by tearing them apart.

After a few years, these boxes will be crammed full of nesting material and effectively unusable.

In Sweden, where woodland ownerships are less clearly defined than in other European countries, because they are simply part of a large continuous area of forest, a small number of the woodlot owners actually mark out their boundaries by placing nest boxes at set distances apart, thus simultaneously fulfilling practical and aesthetic functions. This practice provides a clear boundary mark which lasts for many years as well as helping the forest birds with their accommodation problems, so that they in turn can help the landowner and his forest by consuming large numbers of insect pests.

The majority of us have only the relatively small garden areas around our houses in which to put up our nest boxes: but do not be deterred by the apparently limited scope that this may offer. Even a small garden should have room for one or two tit boxes, a spotted flycatcher or wagtail box in among the creeper growing up the wall of the house, and some house martin, swift and starling boxes under the eaves. If you are slightly more ambitious, then why not add an owl box to the gable end or on the tree in the garden if you are lucky enough to have one high enough. There are plenty of owls even in cities, and their lack of suitable nest sites is inevitably greater than for those out in the countryside. As well as benefitting the birds which use your boxes, you are guaranteed a great deal of satisfaction and enjoyment.

The pied flycatcher, for example, would not be so common as it now is in Sweden, had it not been provided with nest boxes.

As well as putting up the usual tit type boxes with which success is most often assured, do try some of the specialised boxes for species such as owls, stock doves, and treecreepers. These types of birds are often more restricted by a lack of nest sites than those which use tit and starling type boxes.

If you decide to send off and buy a nest box by post, then find out not only the price of the box but also the postage cost, as it is not uncommon for people paying cash on delivery to find that the postage and packing is costing them more than the box itself.

The outsides of nest boxes should be treated with Cuprinol or creosote, whereas the inside should not be touched, and insecticides, of course, should not be used in the box to kill off vermin.

A further reason for setting up nest boxes is the fact that breeding is often much more successful in boxes than in natural nesting holes. Research has shown that nest predation, is very common in these natural nesting sites, but fairly infrequent in nest boxes.

204

Setting up nest boxes for all birds which are accustomed to using them will prove both entertaining and rewarding. Birds are a delight to both the ears and the eyes.

18   Tables of Dimensions

Standard measurements for plank nest boxes

The text of this book quotes box measurements for various species, based on the field experiences of myself and others. The most important thing of all is that lots of boxes are set up, irrespective of which species they are intended for. The following measurements may be used as a basis for 'mass-producing' boxes. They have been adapted to suit all those birds which breed in nest boxes. Building nest boxes is easiest when using 2–2.5 cm thick softwood planks for the floor, front and sides while, although it is slightly more difficult to work with, hardwood should be used for the roof.

If for any reason you are unwilling or unable to build and set up more than a few nest boxes and wish to attract a particular species to them, you can of course study the data more carefully for your intended bird species. Using these measurements will slightly increase your chances of enticing the birds you have in mind, but there is certainly no guarantee that you will get what you are looking for. Every nest box set up is effectively an invitation to all birds (please note that the sections on treecreepers, wheatears, house martins, woodpeckers, wagtails, robins and spotted flycatchers contain information on the specialist nest boxes required for these species).

Species	Nestbox internal depth or height of side (cm)	Inside floor dimensions (cm)	Entrance hole diameter or side (cm)
Group 1 Pied Flycatcher, Tree Sparrow, Blue Tit, Marsh Tit, Crested Tit, Coal Tit	19	7.5 × 12.5	3.2
Group 2 Redstart	10	10 × 15	5.0
Group 3 Great Tit, House Sparrow, Great Spotted Woodpecker Three-toed Woodpecker	20 25 25	10 × 15	3.5 4.5 6.0
Group 4 Swift, Starling, Nuthatch, Wryneck	25–30	12.5 × 17.5	5.0
Group 5 Pygmy Owl Black Woodpecker, Tengmalm's Owl	40 40 35	15 × 20 10.0 10	6.0
Group 6 Jackdaw, Stock Dove, Mallard, Kestrel, Hawk Owl, Smew, Merlin, Goldeneye	35–40	20 × 25	12
Group 7 Tawny Owl	50	20 × 28	15
Group 8 Ural Owl, Barn Owl, Goosander	60–70 40–50	20 × 25	30 20 20
Group 9 Mallard, Red-breasted Merganser, Eider (duck box)	60	40 × 40	20

Summary of nest box measurements for all species

Species	Nest box's internal depth (cm)	Inner floor size (cm)	Entrance hole diameter (cm)	Height above ground (m)	Aspect	Nest box type
Pied						
Flycatcher	19	12	3.2	2–3	S,E	Plank box
Great Tit	20	15	3.5–4	2.5–3	S,E,W	Plank box
Blue Tit	18	11	2.8	2–3	S,E	Block box
Marsh Tit	19	12	3.1	2–3	S,E	Plank box
Marsh Tit	19	10	3	2–3	S,E	Block box
Crested Tit	19	12	3.2	2–3	S	Plank box
Coal Tit	20	12	3–3.5	1–2	S,E,W	Plank box
Coal Tit	18	12	3.5	1–2	S,E,W	Block box
Nuthatch	22	15	5	2–3	S,E,W	Plank box
Nuthatch	23	11.5	5	2–3	S,E,W	Block box
Treecreeper	14	15	10 × 2	0.75–1	S,E	Plank box
Treecreeper	18	12	10 × 3.7	1–3	S,E	Block box
Rock Pipit	10	50 × 17	6			Pipit box on ground
Pied/Grey						
Wagtail	17	20	8	1–3		Open-fronted
Dipper	13	20	7	2–3		Plank box
Wren	3	15	12 × 10	1–2		Wren box
Starling	30	17	5	3–5	S	Plank box
Spotted						
Flycatcher	10	15	1.5		S	Open-fronted
Robin	12	15	8 × 6	0.5–1		Open-fronted
Redstart	10	15	5	2–3	S	Plank box
Blackbird	15	25 × 30	10 × 30	1–2		Plank box
Tree Sparrow	19	14	3.5	2–3	S	Plank box
House						
Sparrow	20	15	3.5	2–3	S,W,E	Plank box
House						
Martin	17	16	5	2–4	S	Artificial nest
Swift	30	15	7.5 × 15	2–4		Box under eaves
Swift	28	20	5	2–4		Gable end box
Swift	30	20	5	2–4		Plank box
Swift	30	20–25	5	2–4		Block box
Wheatear	100	–	12–14			Underground pipe
Wryneck	25	17	5	2–3	S	Plank box
Green						
Woodpecker	40	15	6	3–4	S	Plank box
Black						
Woodpecker	40	20	10	3–5	S	Plank box

Species	Nest box's internal depth (cm)	Inner floor size (cm)	Entrance hole diameter (cm)	Height above ground (m)	Aspect	Nest box type
Great Spotted Woodpecker	25	12	6	2–4	S	Plank box
Three-toed Woodpecker	25	12–14	4.5	0.6–2.5		Block box
Hoopoe	30	15.5	6.5	1.5+		Plank or block box
Stock Dove	35	25	12	2–4		Plank or block box
Jackdaw	35	25	12	2–4		Plank box
Goosander	40–50	30	20	3–5		Plank or block box
Smew	40	25	10	2–4		Plank box
Smew	50	20–25	8.5–9	2–4		Block box
Red-breasted Merganser	60	40	20 × 20			Plank duck box on ground
Goldeneye	35	25	12	3–4		Plank box
Goldeneye	40	25	12	3–4		Block box
Mallard	60	40	20 × 20			Plank duck box on ground
Mallard	70	–	20	0.5–1		Willow duck basket over water
Eider	60	40	20 × 20			Plank duck box on ground
Tawny Owl	50	35	18	3–5		Plank box
Little Owl	40	16–18	7	1+		Plank or block box
Pygmy Owl	40	18	6	3–4		Plank box
Pygmy Owl	36	16	5.8	3–4		Block box
Barn Owl	60–70	40	17 × 15	5		Plank box
Tengmalm's Owl	35	20–25	9 × 11 oval	3–4		Plank box
Tengmalm's Owl	35	20	9 × 10 oval	3–4		Block box
Hawk Owl	40	25	12 × 12	3–4		Plank box
Hawk Owl	40	25	10–11	3–4		Block box
Ural Owl	60–70	30	30 × 30	6–7		Plank box
Ural Owl	70	30	20	5		Block box
Kestrel	40	35	12	4–5		Plank box
Merlin	40	25	10	3–4		Plank box

Comments

The nest boxes for the birds listed in groups 1 to 3 should be placed at a height of 2–3 m above the ground (NB that for the coal tit should be only 1–2 m from the ground). Nest boxes in the remaining groups should be at a height of 3–5 m (height is given from the lower part of the entrance hole to the ground). The entrance hole should face southwards or eastwards.

Nest boxes for owls, ducks, and mergansers should have grooved steps fitted inside, beneath the entrance hole, to enable the young to leave the nest box after they have hatched.

The roofs of all nest boxes should project a little over the sides of the box as well as over the entrance hole. In all other respects, a nest box's design and placing should be as recommended for the particular species.

Boxes for owls, ducks, and mergansers should be set up a short way from water. Owls often use these boxes and as the owlets tend to leave the nest and move onto nearby branches before they can fly properly, they could possibly drown if water is too close. The boxes should be anchored firmly to the supporting tree with cross bars, because ducks and mergansers fly directly into them using the front of the box to stop themselves, so the structure has to bear a great deal of stress.

The Tengmalm's owl likes its box to be situated on the edge of a peat-moss, bog, or other place in a forest. This is a case of the siting being of much greater importance than the type of nest box.

On the other hand both nest box type and situation need to fulfil very strict criteria in order to be successful in attracting the pygmy owl to breed. The box should be of the block type, set up in a dense old spruce forest. The merlin and kestrel like a shallow nest box, preferably filled with moss or twigs almost up to the entrance hole or provided with a chink-like spy hole (as with the hawk owl), through which the female can keep an eye out for enemies, thus avoiding being caught unawares during the time they are sitting on their eggs. The chink should not extend all the way up to the entrance hole, otherwise the bird may be in danger of getting its foot caught in it.

The Ural owl's nest box looks like a chimney with a hardwood roof and the floor should always be covered with a layer of dried moss or soft fresh pine twigs.

Old dry grass straw should be laid in both duck baskets and duck boxes. A 10 cm thick layer of dried moss or top soil should be laid in boxes for owls, swifts, stock doves, jackdaws and some ducks and mergansers. If this material is not available, wood shavings or decayed wood can be used instead.

References

Goransson, Gorgen. 1975. Duvhokens (Accipiter gentilis) betydelse for vinterdodligheten hos fasaner (Phasianus colchicus). Anser 1, 11–22.

Hammarsten, O. D., Pehrson, T. and Sefve, I. 1954. Ekorren. Biologi 2 for 4 och 5-arig realskola utgiven ar 1954. 92–95.

Kluijver, H.N. 1951. The population ecology of the Great Tit (Parus major L.) Ardea, 39 (1–3), 1–135.

Kulves, Haken. 1973. Havsornens ekologi pa Aland. Alands landskapsstyrelse, Mariehamn.

Lack, David. 1966. Population studies of Birds. Clarendon Press, Oxford.

Sjoberg, Kjell. 1975. Bytesval och predationseffektivitet hos skrakar i laboratorieforsok. Fauna and Flora 6, 241–246.